PRAISE FOR *VISITORS*

This is an inspired piece of personal journalism that takes us to Eastern Europe where we follow the social and political adventures, over a period of twenty-five years, of one of the great feminists of the Second Wave. As Ann Snitow discovers the historic antagonism to women's rights that marks the region, she also experiences the remarkably courageous women who are spending their lives fighting it. Richly informed, emotionally centered, beautiful written, *Visitors* is a book to be read by all who crave a deeper understanding of the times in which we live.
—**Vivian Gornick**, author, *Fierce Attachments*

The vivacious, incomparably honest, wise, perceptive, humorous and truth-telling voice of Ann Snitow makes *Visitors* a joy to read from start to finish. It may be the best book ever about the romance of political organizing, in all its triumphs, reversals, conundrums and disappointments.
—**Phillip Lopate,** author, *Art of the Personal Essay*

Ann Snitow's extraordinary gifts for friendship and organizing spill off the pages of this illuminating memoir, which lights up a formerly obscure but important aspect of our history. The lucky reader gets to follow Ann and her new friends as they create a broad, potent network of feminist activists practically from scratch in the ruins of Soviet communism.
—**Alix Kates Shulman**, author, *Memoirs of an Ex-Prom Queen*

With eloquence and insight, Snitow provides an impassioned account of her movement's struggles and accomplishments.
—*Publisher's Weekly*

A profound, wise, and very funny book that should inspire anyone building international movements today. Again and again Ann Snitow faces the contradictions of international feminist collaboration—over money, ideology, unshared histories—and insists on only one thing: that together we find a way forward. I've learned from this book not just the nuances of a dramatic chapter in feminist history, but a productive perspective of gleeful uncertainty.
—**Sarah Leonard**, Contributing Editor, *The Nation*

I loved traveling via this book with the vivid, vital Ann Snitow as this questioning American feminist activist connects in East Central Europe with rebel women, straight and queer, each surprising the other, each learning from and inspiring the other's—and our—resistance to men's privilege and rule.

—**Jonathan Ned Katz**, author, *The Invention of Heterosexuality*

This book is a delight—an exhilarating tale of travel, politics, and friendship, a personal and intellectual essay as well as feminist adventure story. Deeply aware of the pitfalls of the role of benevolent Westerner offering help to the backward East, Ann Snitow nonetheless did come, again and again. In *Visitors* we read how Ann—from whom I have learned so much—learned from us. This memoir brings the complexity of these exchanges to life.

—**Agnieszka Graff**, Polish feminist scholar and activist

Visitors is a joyous, invaluable reminder of the many gifts Ann Snitow brought to her classroom and to feminist discourse. Open, questioning, driven by Snitow's own curiosity and fascination, it offers a rich portrait of what it is to be a hungry feminist thinker. Exploring parts of the globe and politics she doesn't already know well, Snitow shows that feminism is always in motion. She wants to learn more about how movements grow, wonder at their fragility and their strengths, and get to know the people who drive and shape them. This memoir reminds us that the fights are ongoing, that they began long before we got here and will continue long after we've departed.

—**Rebecca Traister**, author, *Good and Mad: The Revolutionary Power of Women's Anger*

In this stunning work—part memoir, part activist manual—Ann Snitow chronicles her twenty-five years on the frontlines of international feminism in post-communist Eastern Europe. I know of no book like *Visitors*, one that is both theoretically knowing and rooted in the realities of broad-based feminist activism. An essential book for these polarized times, it offers a master class in how to advance feminism as a "zone of fascination" that can reach across the barriers of difference.

—**Alice Echols**, author, *Daring to be Bad*

VISITORS

Beata Kozak, Sławka Walzcewska, Małgorzata Tarasiewicz, and
Ann Snitow, in Krakow, July 2008. Photo credit: Roma Cieśla

VISITORS

An American Feminist
in East Central Europe

ANN SNITOW

New Village Press • New York

Closing poem, "Try to Praise the Mutilated World"
© 2002 Adam Zagajewski, by permission of Adam Zagajewski

Published in the United States by New Village Press
bookorders@newvillagepress.net
www.newvillagepress.org
New Village Press is a public-benefit, nonprofit publisher
Distributed by NYU Press

Paperback ISBN: 978-1-61332-130-0
Hardcover ISBN: 978-1-61332-131-7
EBook ISBN: 978-1-61332-132-4
EBook Institutional ISBN: 978-1-61332-133-1
Publication Date: March 2020
First Edition

Library of Congress Cataloging-in-Publication Data
Names: Snitow, Ann Barr, 1943–2019 author.
Title: Visitors : an American feminist in East Central Europe / Ann Snitow.
Description: First edition. | New York : New Village Press, 2020. |
  Includes index. | Summary: "Visitors tells the story of feminist
  activist Ann Snitow's work as an organizer in East Central Europe after
  the fall of the Berlin Wall in 1989. Over a period of 25 years, Snitow
  captures the changes and struggles in the new political landscape of
  post-communism as they unfold, and presents insight into the origins and
  development of the multi-faceted internationalist feminism that is
  evolving today."— Provided by publisher.
Identifiers: LCCN 2019058731 (print) | LCCN 2019058732 (ebook) | ISBN
  9781613321300 (paperback) | ISBN 9781613321317 (hardcover) | ISBN
  9781613321324 (ebook) | ISBN 9781613321331
Subjects: LCSH: Feminism—Europe, Eastern—History—20th century. |
  Feminism—Europe, Eastern—History—21st century. | Europe,
  Eastern—Politics and government—1989–2016
Classification: LCC HQ1590.7 .S65 2020 (print) | LCC HQ1590.7 (ebook) |
  DDC 305.420947—dc23
LC record available at https://lccn.loc.gov/2019058731
LC ebook record available at https://lccn.loc.gov/2019058732

Frontispiece photo by Roma Cieśla, Krakow, July 2008. Left to right: Beata Kozak,
Sławka Walczewska, Małgorzata Tarasiewicz, Ann Snitow.
Front cover author photo by Marzena Ples, Krakow, September 2018.
Front cover design: Chris Nguyen
Interior design and composition: Leigh McLellan Design

—With love—

To the extraordinary feminists I have met
in our struggle for justice and pleasure East and West

CONTENTS

FOREWORD

A COUPLE OF YEARS ago, Ann Snitow was strolling toward home down a street in lower Manhattan when she saw ahead an emergency: screaming sirens, flashing lights, police barricades blocking crosswalks, the sky billowing with smoke. She realized that not only was there a fire in her neighborhood; the building engulfed was her own. Reduced to uninhabitability was the fifth-floor SoHo loft she'd occupied for decades, since long before the neighborhood morphed from counterculture squat to couture-and-cupcake showcase, a home that had served as incubator for some unquantifiable but essential part of the conversations that had nurtured radical feminism and radical New York. Ann's loft doubled as a progressive Mission Control, in which, on almost any evening (when Ann was not at a protest march or an organizing meeting), she could be found strategizing, brainstorming, and fundraising at her long wooden kitchen table, surrounded by all manner of activists and artists, refuseniks and renegades, while simultaneously fielding calls from her ever-ringing phone.

Another cataclysm brought Ann to the revelations contained in this book: the fall of communism in Eastern and Central

Europe at the end of the eighties. Her response was true to her nature. When she saw the smoke on Spring Street in February of 2017, she didn't pause. She ran *toward*. Confronted with the news of the Soviet Bloc's collapse, she wasn't content to read about it in the *New York Times*. In March of 1991, she boarded a plane to Croatia.

Ann didn't have a long intimacy with the region, though her forebears were from there. But she understood the ways that hegemonic systems are linked, the ways that changes in economic and political regimes inevitably affect the social regime ruling women's lives. What would it mean for women in the Eastern Bloc nations, tossed overnight from state socialism's freedoms and constraints into the new and very different freedoms and constraints of the global marketplace? One government structure had imploded, and another had yet to gel. Might a new vision of feminism emerge from this molten moment? And could it mobilize in time? Already, the signs were ominous. The new Polish government's first action: drafting legislation to restrict abortion.

The woman who boarded that plane in 1991 was a battle-tested veteran of American feminism's ebbs and surges. She'd been a crucial figure in feminism's early seventies revival—a founding member of the New York Radical Feminists and a denizen of one of the longest-running consciousness-raising groups (and, in 1998, an early and key preserver of that political moment's history as coeditor of *The Feminist Memoir Project*); a regular commentator on WBAI's *Womankind*, the first American radio show dedicated to feminism; a voice of reason and subtlety in feminism's thorny "sex wars" over pornography; a pioneer of both women's and gender studies; a fount of innovative feminist thought as a literature professor at The New School and a long-time cultural seminar leader at the New York Institute for the Humanities; and grassroots mobilizer extraordinaire on countless fronts in the fight against the Reagan-era (and, later, Bush-era) backlash. She knew all the trip wires and trapdoors that can, and have, ensnared the American Women's Movement. And learned how to skirt them.

Ann had long been that rare species in the ecology of Western feminism: a believer who questioned everything she believed, an advocate whose commitment was built not on ideological certitudes but on the complexities generated by doubt. Her feminist writings read like two really smart people talking at once, a brilliant internal debate where the contentions of one self were ever being challenged by the other. This set her apart from so much of ideological feminism, and drew so many feminists, young and old, to gather around her and rely on her counsel. As a feminist who emerged in the era of *The Dialectic of Sex* (and knew Shulamith Firestone well), Ann was the true dialectician, dedicated to exploring contradictions and the possibilities (and impossibilities) of reconciling them. She was always open to changing her mind, always the questioner, never the polemicist. That capacious point of view is summed up nicely in the title of the 2015 collection of her self-inspecting, ruminative dispatches from the front, composed over four decades: *The Feminism of Uncertainty.* She was, as one reviewer of the book noted, "the Heisenberg of Feminism."

Ann's talent for embracing any and all contradictions, her ability to live with—no, exult in!—the perplexities of the divided mind, the lack of easy resolution, was intimately connected to her ability to span fault lines. She was the rare Second Waver who managed to forge ties across the DMZ of the generational divide and to transcend the virtue smackdown that can sometimes make contemporary feminism feel like a grievance-match mosh pit. Over the years, her big-souled openness and delighted response to doubt and disagreement allowed her to find common ground with everyone from queer-theory-heads to incarcerated men (whom she exposed to feminism by screening Hollywood films). I once went with her straight from a poststructuralist, acronym-heavy academic seminar on EU neoliberalism to a Slutwalk march (where she wore candy-striped stockings and brandished a goofily hand-lettered sign); she reveled in both incarnations. Her approach to gender equality was playful, protean, kinetic. It was always rushing *toward*. "I would get bored if I didn't keep moving," she told Sarah Leonard in the *Nation* in 2016. "I thought feminism had enormous capacity to turn into something boring."

If anyone had something to offer the nascent revival of Eastern European feminism in the moment after the Berlin Wall fell, and offer it with joie de vivre, that person was Ann.

Ann, being Ann, found herself full of uncertainties, even forebodings, as she flew toward Croatia that first time in 1991. It didn't help that her chatty seatmates, likewise seeking opportunities in the newly transformed region, were . . . a missionary and a salesman. She was already leery of the dangers of her enterprise, what she calls "the bad American habit of invasion." How to be an emissary of the American Women's Movement without becoming its proselytizer and marketeer? "After all those years in anti-imperialist struggles, the idea of 'Western help' sounded sinister to us," she writes in *Visitors*, "completely contaminated."

Ann was coming at the behest of the region's feminists. As a founding member of the Network of East-West Women, recently launched to link women's rights advocates on both sides of the Atlantic Ocean, she had been invited to witness and support the stirrings of the homegrown movements in Eastern and Central Europe. A few weeks before she left for Dubrovnik, she confided her "invasion" worries to Slavenka Drakulić, the Yugoslavian writer. Drakulić responded with a mordant Eastern

European stare and answer: "Don't worry. Just help us Eastern feminists meet. We promise not to listen to you." A contradictory response custom-made for the author of *The Feminism of Uncertainty*. "This is just the sort of invitation I seem unable to resist," Ann writes. In the guise of gentle envoy, a minister without portfolio or preconceptions, she embarked on a quarter-century adventure.

Now it's our adventure. *Visitors* is an uncommon ground-level memoir of what it's like to be part of the daily life of an embryonic political movement, to be embedded in the teeming lived experience of what Ann calls "the tragicomedy of activism." It is the most intimate of political chronicles, a wry, lyrical, and moving account from a perpetually conflicted feminist organizer who has catapulted herself onto strange and shifting ground. Through her bemused eyes, we are ushered into the quotidian world of women engaged in "let-it-be organizing," groping their way out of intense isolation (Ann received two letters insisting, "I am the only feminist in Romania") and toward new possibilities.

Arriving in the region with the meager funds she'd been able to glean from the shallow pockets of feminists and activist friends (she had packets of hundred-dollar bills hidden in her clothes), Ann helped convene the Network's first session in Dubrovnik. She went on to teach feminism in a radical summer school and aid in the organizing of a bare-bones feminist infrastructure that included a hotline and a gender studies library in three tiny donated rooms, and an alcove with a telephone, a precious commodity in Poland at the time. Of course, it didn't work. In *Visitors*, Ann describes a photograph taken of her and her Polish compatriots in their pint-size office, in which she's modeling the phone on her head like a hat, "since it doesn't have any other practical use." The women called their headquarters the *magiel*, the wringer. It had formerly been a laundry where washerwomen labored.

Ann appreciates the vivid and telling moment, and *Visitors* is populated with affecting vignettes of women trying, against all odds, to discover each other and the larger world of feminism. One woman pursues her lone advocacy from her cramped bedsit, an attic room in what was once the "spinster woman's home." Another woman, desperate for feminist literature, writes a letter to the American feminist writer Kate Millett, addressing the envelope simply (and wrongly), "Radcliffe College." (She gets an answer!)

Ann would, for more than two decades, serve as an ambassador for American feminism to Eastern and Central European women. In a way, this was simply a continuation of her domestic calling: She was already an ambassador for what feminism could be to American feminists. Since I first met Ann in 2009, I witnessed her remarkable ability to persuade others that feminism's success doesn't depend on the correct ideological stance, the finely tuned position statement, the foolproof political strategy—or at least not on those alone. It turns as much, she would argue, on the tender mercies of meeting people where they are, on perceiving and empathizing with women (and men) who may be in a very different place, on having the ability, as Ann states toward the end of *Visitors* (invoking Adam Zagajewski's poem), "to love the mutilated world."

Ann's talent for seeing the world from alien vantage points would stand her in good stead in her travels in Eastern and Central Europe. From the start, she recognized that she'd gone through the feminist looking glass, passing into a realm where many Western polarities were reversed. It was a topsy-turvy terrain where public life was suspect and politics something to "refuse"; where the family circle was perceived as the one safe space for free and radical thought; where liberation meant shopping malls and aisles stocked with laundry soap and tampons; where she was counseled to avoid the very term *organize* because it would be seen as "depressing"; where a female writer told Ann that she was declaring her independence by writing for *Czech Playboy* (because for once she was earning more than her husband).

As it happened, the world that Ann found herself in was less antipode to her homeland than prophecy. The Eastern feminists she worked and played with turned out to be the pioneers, the first to experience a fury of ethnic and sexual hatreds that would eventually combust across the continent—and, soon thereafter, the US. *Visitors* reads as unnerving prequel, a premonitory road map to how we came to this catastrophic moment in world politics. And, crucially, how attacks on feminism served as a polemical crank to churn political outrage and drive the electorate to the right throughout the Eastern Bloc. "Who could believe without laughing that the churches in several countries were mounting well-organized campaigns called such names as 'STOP Gender,'" Ann writes, and notes that in Poland the word *gender* is verboten in government policy proposals. "Gender is not to be a part of politics; it is natural. We were living in the absurd, and having one another's sardonic company was everything."

To the Eastern feminists, the return of the absurd came as no shock. They were schooled in dark histories and understood that the transition to a liberal democracy would be highly fragile, subject to whiplash, vulnerable at all times to strongman rule. Primed to expect the worst, they recognized the signs of trouble long before the 2015 election of the right-wing Law and Justice Party that stunned their American counterparts. "This nationalism and xenophobia, this misogyny, this authoritarian streak," Ann writes, "here was the world they knew, and no one should be surprised. Trauma there well might be, but it was of long standing. Panic was a waste of breath; now was the time to buckle down, carry on."

In our current season of political revanche, when national-ism, xenophobia, and misogyny are hallmarks of American do-mestic politics, the story of the beloved community built by the Network of East-West Women offers a model for feminist resis-tance. The experience that Ann records in *Visitors* is a primer on how to survive, even flourish, in the bleakest of times, and how to find joy and celebration in struggle. She poignantly recalls one notable outbreak of that joy, at a gathering in Krakow on the eve of right-wing electoral victory, where veterans of the movement, East and West, marked their progress with a brightly painted mural adorned with strips of paper ribbon denoting milestones in the long quest for women's equality, reaching back to when Polish women won the vote in 1918. The result, Ann writes, was a "fluttering wall [that] spoke of how activism keeps moving, imagining a future. And we were so many—awed by our very selves." As her Polish colleague Sławka Walczewskas said of their mural, "It's a feminist river of changes."

Visitors itself is that river, and we are wading in its midst with an author who is adept at riding the cross-currents, whose embrace of uncertainty allows her to lose her footing knowing she will find it again, whose resilience and ebullience buoy her sister travelers, even the ones who feel they are drowning in the enormity of the task. "Outrage alone can't sustain itself," Ann writes. But feminism will carry on. The course of the river runs toward.

—Susan Faludi
Northampton, MA
July 2019

INTRODUCTION

IN NOVEMBER OF 1969, my friend Cellestine Ware took me to what turned out to be the founding meeting of New York Radical Feminists. She had been nagging me since I had returned from three years in graduate school at the University of London: "Something extraordinary is happening here, something thrilling." As is my habit, I was busy. First she invited me to a meeting of the already well-established feminist group Redstockings. I was busy. Then she invited me to a meeting of what I think must have been the early group The Feminists. Still busy. Then it was already November, and I finally said yes. Just dumb luck.

There, sitting on the floor of Anne Koedt's apartment at 10 Carmine Street in Greenwich Village were Anne herself, already author of "The Myth of the Vaginal Orgasm," quiet, blond, and dignified, and Shulamith Firestone, soon to produce for a waiting world the startling utopian text, *The Dialectic of Sex: The Case for Feminist Revolution*. Shulie didn't so much have eyes as two dark, burning coals. Never have I encountered such intensity. The brilliance of the company fused into one galvanizing moment.

Alas, I don't remember a single thing that anyone said that first night, but this is beside the point. Every word was etched in light and illuminated a path that, as it has turned and twisted, I have followed my whole life.

Without knowing what this meant, I had dropped into the volcano that was the new feminism. We were typical, I guess, of what was happening all over the country. Celly was the only woman of color in that room. She and I were just a shade older than the rest; I was born in 1943, while Shulie and the others were canonical baby boomers, born after 1945; we shared that time after the war when so much seemed possible. The careening growth of the postwar years was fostering rising expectations. The brilliance and daring of the Civil Rights Movement showed the way, and other movements joined in the expansion of hope.

The revival of feminism in the US offered a zone of invention. When we started, the books we needed to read were out of print— and most had yet to be written, and are still being written now. Any historical record of women's past resistance to prejudice, insult, and invisibility was absent from public memory. Women's suffering—of violence, of humiliation—was unremarked and unremarkable. An aspiring woman's ambitions were laughable. Congress was virtually an all-male space, and so was the newspaper, the doctor's office, the union, and the Left, where I had always had a home; leaders were almost always—and expected to be—male, including those in radical movements. The first job was to denaturalize this enveloping reality, to bring it back into history—and into struggle.

Many have recorded what that time felt like: a love affair, a revelation, a little click of the lens that refocused everything. So now I was a feminist for life. But what would this mean?

From 1969 onward, I have worked steadily as a feminist activist. Those first years, the early seventies, are a blur. Teaching full-time at one university or another, I went to hundreds of meetings—quite literally—and made easily a hundred radio broadcasts on producer Nanette Rainone's *Womankind*, the first show about feminism in America, on the independent New York radio station WBAI. (That early work is now digitized and archived at the Sallie Bingham Center for Women's History and Culture at Duke University.) We marched; we demanded abortions—and unions; we wanted equality and something beyond equality: basic structural change. We wrote, sometimes restoring lost genres or inventing new ones. We disagreed; we reshuffled the meaning of what we were doing. The original group, New York Radical Feminists, whose meeting I had attended that enchanted evening in 1969—Shulie had named us the Stanton-Anthony Brigade—lasted only a year, a bright candle soon out. But in 1974, I joined yet another intense consciousness-raising group, which met once a week for fifteen years. We have notes somewhere; we have tapes. What's in there, I wonder? The forging of a sensibility that has had as much impact on daily and political life as any social movement in American history.

We were W.I.T.C.H. (Women's International Terrorist Conspiracy from Hell). We were the New York Abortion Project. We were No More Nice Girls (from the 1977 loss of Medicaid abortion onward), including, one time, a street full of pregnant Ronald Reagans. Some of us were the Feminist Anti-Censorship Taskforce (F.A.C.T.), disagreeing about pornography in the feminist sex wars. (The text for our side was *Caught Looking: Feminism, Pornography, and Censorship.*) We crafted women's studies programs that morphed into gender studies, including more and more of the changeable and queer. At the New York

Institute for the Humanities, I ran a seminar called Sex, Gender, and Consumer Culture for twelve years (1982–1994), and from that community poured many books. Christine Stansell, Sharon Thompson, and I edited the anthology *Powers of Desire: The Politics of Sexuality* (1983). Trying to hang on to this careening history, this fast unfolding of the new feminisms, Rachel Blau DuPlessis and I edited *The Feminist Memoir Project: Voices from Women's Liberation* (1998), and I have collected my essays culled from all these years in *The Feminism of Uncertainty: A Gender Diary* (2015). In 2002, at a moment of despair about the coming war in Iraq, some of us became Take Back the Future, both to perform street actions and to hearten each other for the long anti-war struggles that lay ahead.

I am deeply proud of us modern feminists, now in our several generations. We made life freer for many women who have not even a scintilla of love for this thing, "feminism"—nor perhaps for that scary thing, freedom itself. What do feminists want, after all? Who can sum up such a self-contradictory, diverse set of phenomena as "a movement"? No leader can claim legitimacy. No theory can establish boundaries. No gatekeeper can push anyone out. Once feminism proposed gender as a question, not a given, no one has been able to shove it back into the realm of the unspoken and unconscious.

It's hardly surprising that this kinetic feminism has aroused a storm of resistance. Backlash against our first furor in the 1970s was immediate, and by the 1980s it was clear that feminism was not going to sweep all before it by the force of either its logic or our passion. And besides all kinds of pressures from outside, feminism, like all growing movements, fractured along many fault lines. Struggling both within and without, I confess that by the end of the 1980s, I was exhausted.

And here came my second big experience of dumb luck. Around 1990, casually, friends called: "Something surprising seems to be happening in women's lives in Eastern Europe with the end of communism." Thank goodness, this time I didn't say I was too busy. Instead, I was ready for what has turned out to be a new adventure, traveling with feminism. But, as always, I wondered what this would mean. This question, and the adventure, have lasted me thirty years.

Visitors is a record of the next phase of my life as a feminist organizer. It tells the story of how I stumbled onto the fragile feminist movements that saw first light in East Central Europe after the fall of communism. Invisible at their start, attacked almost before they existed, these movements went against the grain of much that was happening after the fall of the Berlin Wall in 1989. The arrival of so many new freedoms was dramatic—but a roar of popular sentiment was proclaiming, too, a nostalgic desire for traditions repressed under communism, the return of the family patriarch and the Church. New opportunities were everywhere—and women benefited—but counterpressures kept pushing them back. As a workers' strike sign put it: "Women go home. We are saving Poland." The first law passed there by the newly democratic government banned abortion, a right women had had in Poland since 1956.

East Central Europe after 1989 was, like US feminism twenty years earlier, a zone of invention. Everything was changing, every aspect of life. New laws. New possibilities. What being a woman had meant under communism was remembered as a story of exhaustion, damage, and restriction. But what being a woman might mean in the new democracies was suddenly a taboo subject, unspeakable, and those few who dared express worry about women's changing fate were greeted with ridicule, misogynist insults, and a fury threatening in its vehemence.

It was with these unspeakable women that I cast my lot after first meeting them, much by chance, when I responded to that phone call in 1990. A window for new action opened. I walked through, into a different world.

1

FIRST VISITORS

In November of 1989, the Cold War ended. A bipolar world order that had prevailed for over forty years, based on an East-West divide since the end of World War II, shifted fundamentally.

Wars end. But no one had expected this kind of fast finish anytime soon to the militant confrontation between East and West. The vast Soviet empire, though undermined by a ruinous war in Afghanistan, a crippling military budget, failing agricultural and manufacturing sectors, and growing dissent especially among intellectual elites, had seemed unassailable. Whenever one of the states within its immediate sphere of interest had attempted reform or resisted any aspect of Soviet control, Soviet or Warsaw Pact tanks had rolled in, as they did in Hungary in 1956 and again in Czechoslovakia in 1968. Everyone expected this menacing response to continue to hold the gargantuan empire together.

But in Poland a complex dance was beginning between its communist leaders and the workers developing an independent trade union—the first behind the Iron Curtain—Solidarity. Although the government had signed agreements with the workers, it and its Soviet handlers found the burgeoning Solidarity too threatening. At one point, protests in the streets reached ten million people in a country of thirty million. In 1981 the government declared martial law, arresting more than ten thousand union activists.

But this time the tanks to enforce this crackdown didn't roll in. The Soviet Union was in crisis and was trying to right itself by moving to restructure. In 1985 Mikhail Gorbachev, a reformer who was to rescue the empire from what we know in hindsight was imminent collapse, was chosen as party secretary. His new programs—more political openness (glasnost) and a range of economic reforms (perestroika)—would reveal structural weaknesses beyond repair.

In Poland, where the imposition of martial law had further weakened the already failing economy, wiping out any remaining trust in the existing political system, the authoritarian regime agreed to talk with its subjects at a Round Table in Warsaw. After six weeks of citizens' negotiations with the ruling party, which had the entire nation watching with suspended breath, the communist government agreed to hold elections, the first real elections in Poland and in the Soviet Bloc in nearly half a century. Martial law crumbled.

Like dominos, in 1989 the other countries of East Central Europe broke away. East Germany would no longer maintain the brick-and-mortar wall between East and West Berlin that had for decades symbolized an absolute divide. By 1991 the Soviet Union came apart, its constituent states tearing away like so many fractious children, each with its own understory to tell an amazed and gazing West, none of whose pundits had predicted this.

Back then, my partner and I didn't have a television, so we did not watch the fall of the Berlin Wall. I have always regretted not seeing the physical fact of crowds of people tearing down the Berlin Wall, then pouring through these very recently fortified boundaries to reunite with long-lost friends and relatives—and to inhabit an entirely new reality.

IN THE AUTUMN OF 1988, an acquaintance called: Could we put up two Yugoslavian visitors, graduate students in Boston who wanted to see New York, but who had no money at all? True, our Manhattan apartment was often a boardinghouse for itinerant feminist organizers and experimental musicians, a combination that could lead to some odd moments in the kitchen at breakfast time. But I thought, *Really, Ann, you've got to draw the line somewhere. You've never even heard of these people, Sonja Licht and Milan Nikolic. You don't know a thing about life in Yugoslavia.* Yugoslavia was special, no? Their dictator, Tito, had protected them against total control by Stalin? They had some kind of economic independence? My very ignorance prompted me to say no.

I can't tell just how she did it, but Myrna Kostash refused to accept this answer. It was inconceivable to her that I—with my long history of political activism—wouldn't help these heroes of the dissident underground. "You'll love them," she said. I called the number she gave me to set things up, and a gravelly voice said he would pass the phone on to his wife, who handled all practical matters. Oh, no. I hate when wives handle "all practical matters." My eyes rolled. Another gravelly voice with the same thick accent got on, and we worked out the details.

They came a few days later. My partner, Daniel, and I opened the door to a man as big as a mountain and a woman half his height and spherical. Together, they filled the whole entry hall. Myrna was right. Almost immediately, passionately, we loved them. We had so much to say to each other that those four days could only be a beginning.

To return to that moment requires a difficult mental transit back to a world that has disappeared. These were graduate students, with few resources. He had spent two years in jail, first as one of the leaders of the 1968 student movement and, later, as one of the Belgrade Six, dissidents whose professors had been kicked out of the state university in 1975 and started a free university in 1976. In a basement interrogation room, Milan felt his heart stop. He was sure he would die there. When he got out, there was Sonja, his long-standing friend, in solidarity, and they were together from that time—keeping their heads just above water—taking little jobs at research institutes or applying for stipends here and there.

They were both researching the political stalemate in Yugoslavia. Milan's dissertation about the unsustainable life they were all living had been used as evidence against him in his second trial. But, as we sat together, laughing, eating too much, drinking, we had no inkling of the scale of the changes that were coming.

Suddenly, a year after this wonderful visit, it was 1989, and all the countries tightly controlled by the Soviet Union were about to be freed. These two embattled creatures so dear to us became well-known above-ground activists and pundits, visible to the world, controversial, struggling in a new, careening reality that brought them fame and infamy in a crumbling post-communist Yugoslavia. Now, instead of not being able to go anywhere, they traveled everywhere. We followed their astounding new trajectory in newspapers and human rights reports. At the same time, they had to figure out how to live this new life with new daily habits, new kinds of work. The context for even the smallest acts had changed fundamentally. For Sonja and Milan and for everyone around them in half of Europe and all of the former Soviet Union, these ubiquitous changes in fortune felt remarkable at first, yet also general, shared. The fall of communism scattered all lives to the winds. But soon the deck was reshuffled, and people found themselves with quite separate fates in a world that dealt very different hands to different people. Although, amazingly, there was little bloodshed, everything changed—in meaning, and in the horizon of expectation.

In 1989 we simply watched. That other life, through the looking glass, had always seemed remote, and we continued to see it as far, far away. My partner, the composer Daniel Goode, and I had in fact been behind the Iron Curtain once, briefly, in 1984. I am grateful for this chance occurrence, this small glimpse of the "then," the before. Daniel was invited by an underground music collective, Group 180, to give a concert in Budapest. (They were free to make any wild sounds they wanted, but words were carefully vetted—so they used none.) In passing, we stopped in Berlin and went through Checkpoint Charlie to our first East.

We laughed when they searched us on the bus and confiscated Western magazines. In those days, we were innocent of such daily mechanisms of control. Surely, we thought then, it's impossible to maintain Eastern virginity from Western depravity through such flat-footed means. Now, looking back with not a scintilla of laughter, I know that the blackout on ideas and images actually did work—to an extraordinary degree. But, also, it didn't. A vacuum had formed, which everyone sensed. The West glistened or glowered, but it was there, perhaps above all in its rigidly maintained drama of absence. And the dissidents we were later to know were constantly punching holes in the scrim with the sharp tap-tap of an underground samizdat typewriter, bringing east the forbidden words of the West.

Arriving in Budapest, we had all the now-mythical experiences of American first contact. One of Daniel's composer friends picked us up at the train station in a Trabant, into which our substantial Western luggage, including a fancy double clarinet case, could barely fit. He kicked the car and laughed. "Plastic." True, the sound was like striking a milk carton. And then there were the beautiful gray buildings, without any commercial signs and pocked with the bullet holes left from the war and from the uprising of 1956; the student hostel with the loudspeaker constantly making announcements, which we couldn't turn off; the difficulty in finding a towel or a restaurant; and on and on, the canonical memories of the relatively rare visiting Americans of that time.

We made a point of going to the May Day parade—May Day, that romance of Western leftists as the day of workers. We marched along with swarms of workers carrying brightly colored placards. This sentimentality of ours for celebrating "the people" aroused the contempt of the marginalized and disaffected musicians we were visiting: Didn't we understand how manipulated such mass manifestations were? We did understand. But how to explain life on our side of the looking glass, where trade unionism was steadily dwindling? May Day! A holiday that had come to mean nothing in America, just as—for such different reasons—it meant nothing here about workers' freedom to organize. With mutual disregard, we and our hosts collided in the empty space between us.

Daniel's paternal relatives were from Debrecen in East Hungary. Escaping both from communist parades and dissident disdain, we drove there to discover the name Guttman on the World War I memorial plaque still visible on the closed synagogue wall. (We found the place through a priest who said he knew a nun who knew where the Jews still were—two of them, sitting like ancient trolls guarding their piled-to-the-ceiling archive.) Four of the Guttman sons died at the front within a few weeks in 1915; the fifth, Daniel's grandfather, had emigrated to America.

Through friends of friends, we were invited to spend an afternoon in the country with a couple and their young son, two members of one of the many nationally sponsored orchestras that made Budapest the envy of the starving orchestra scene in New York. No contempt from these two for us ignorant Americans. Only envy for a storied American consumer paradise. These people seemed incapable of responding to Daniel's questions about music; they were technicians happy to have fairly decent jobs. Instead, they wanted to tell us about the extraordinary machinations they had gone through to get the car—not a Trabant, but something fancy and West German; about the miracle of acquiring this cottage, their *dacha*; about how long it would be before they would be able to add a washing machine. Because we sympathized, felt uneasy at the narrowness of these obsessive topics, then guilty for the luxury of not having to spend so much mental time on such longings, we leaned over backwards to respond to every thought or wish, with the result that they asked us to spend the whole day talking to the ten-year-old so that he could improve the English they were pushing him to learn. One day, perhaps, he would escape to the West. Dazed and exhausted by performing for so many hours in our own language, we staggered back to the hostel and fell into a deep sleep.

Before leaving Hungary, one last social encounter: a dinner party with the young musicians and artists we so admired. One was living in an unregistered rooftop aerie he had built (a consumer culture *refusnik* without *dacha*), and the others, whom we were visiting that evening, living in very grand, high-ceilinged rooms, now shared by several families of four, but clearly once the drawing room and dining room of that ghost, a haute bourgeois household.

We were very late, and when we finally arrived, we entered to an embarrassed hush. Was it because we were late? We apologized, explained, begged to be forgiven. It turned out that in our absence, the eight at the table had been dishing a book I had given a member of the collective, a recent anthology of feminist writing about sex that I had edited with two friends, *Powers of Desire: The Politics of Sexuality*. Without much politesse, this independent and brilliant company let it be known that nothing could be more foolish than feminism.

Here at last was a situation with which I was familiar enough, given my experiences in the early 1970s talking to strangers about why feminism might be worth a moment of their time, and given, too, the more recent reality of anti-feminist backlash in my very own so-divided country. And, to a point, I empathized with their skepticism. The year was the iconic 1984, and here we were eating a meager dinner in a totalitarian country. Scorn was our new friends' shield against the absurd claim that Americans had any-thing to complain about. They oozed irony at the mention of political life in any form. Politics was contemptible, something in which a repressive state and its lackeys indulged, while they were struggling for meaning and beauty in privacy. There, at that dinner table, every contradiction and uncertainty I was later to know was spread before me—though I had no hint then that later such confrontations would matter to me, and that for many years to come I would be struggling to understand the depth of experience that lay behind such talk.

I knew it was in vain to be defensive—or even to argue. In-stead, we talked about our different situations. The women were on three-year maternity leaves, while the men, tone deaf to their wives' anxieties about this and covertly critical of my childless-ness, suggested that we repair to a curtained alcove to worship the baby. I did what I have done so many times, under many quite different circumstances: I listened, I asked, I confessed that I had my private reasons to explore the meaning of my own discontent. Did they recognize any of this? Or maybe not? Gradually, the at-mosphere warmed—not toward ridiculous feminism, but toward me. We had what felt, finally, like a decent, respectful conversation about the political waters in which we were all swimming.

The evening ended well. But it never occurred to me that we would have anything more to say to each other—ever—or that I would be returning here any time soon. Why would I dream of entering this sophisticated dissident world where my life work, feminism, was such a joke? Or revisit the frenzied world of material yearning, where one couldn't imagine discussing any ideas at all? And the world of those singing, marching workers? What were they thinking? Nothing seemed more irretrievable. We went home, sent all the books that the artists we had met at dinner said they longed for (I remember Edgar Allan Poe was one request), and never heard from them again. No doubt those books never arrived, ending up on some apparatchik's shelves. Or maybe our friends of that memorable evening lacked the postage to respond. We thought: *point final*. At this the patron saint of hindsight is laughing.

2

AIRPLANE

In 1991 I became a frequent visitor to East Central Europe as a feminist organizer. I was not alone. On the plane from New York City, where I was born and still live, I was surrounded by others on similar maiden West–East voyages. With excitement, we were each carrying our own messages to an until so-recently isolated world.

HORDES ARE TRAVELING EAST: The priest in the seat in front of me is a missionary, expansive and happy now that the Church can return and save people from godless communism. He's in agreement with his seatmate, the fundamentalist woman with crisp gray curls, that the days of abortion rights common throughout the region are numbered. They share glee across their many differences. Across the aisle, the Häagen Dazs salesman is happy to describe to me this potential large market for delicious, deadly, high-fat ice cream, richer than anyone in these straitened lands will ever have tasted.

Closer to me is the political scientist. With him I share a particular American past; in spite of our differences, we've lived through the sixties, seventies, and eighties as people disappointed by the defects and failures of progressive movements in our country. Now we're both wildly excited about the prospects opening here for new freedoms and new politics. To varying degrees, all of us on the plane see the newly open East as a field of dreams, an unknown, an opportunity, a memory, a bazaar for selling new ideas and desires. But the passage through the looking glass will be more transformative than we can know.

The political scientist, who at home has had to include a grudging respect for the feminism permeating the US air since the 1970s, has unselfconsciously dropped his always-lightweight feminist baggage in the ocean. When we arrive on the other side, he is unencumbered and speaks of human rights and enlightenment values without mentioning the inconvenient critiques of these traditions made in the US for decades. For him, it's a fresh start. The rebellions that arose in the West among those who felt that theirs was a damaged citizenship are reduced to a buzz of complaints, which may indeed not make immediate sense where we are going.

I, too, am about to change. I have been a feminist activist since 1969, but like the professor, I cannot bring my activist past here in one coherent piece. But if religion, business, and liberal sentiments can travel across the ocean, why not me, too, with my feminist critiques of those fast-arriving meanings from the First World? And in addition to my killjoy doubts about the imports of the others, I'm also carrying a burden I know I mustn't jettison: the horror (and to many of my new friends, the wonder) of what the US has had the power to do in the world. Like all the others on the plane unavoidably wrapped in this tricolor flag, I never lose my worry about being like the missionary or the salesman, but at least I am the constant critic, a person from the aisle to the left, the one always slowing down her own sales pitch with doubt, with fear of the bad American habit of invasion.

Our plane arrives, and all meanings shift. The women who meet me on the other side of the customs barrier are a small minority in their own countries. They have no authority, and their feminist ideas lack all political legitimacy here. Contact with the West, even with a powerless visitor like me, marks a kind of elite status, but this very tie is also a reminder of their isolation. At some level, the West was always already here, and now its new representatives are landing. I start my travels along with those others, often as ignorant as they, curious to see the lands where so many dreams of the Left lie buried, and eager to visit the once-forbidden Araby.

3

IT BEGAN

The American New Left was thrown sideways by the precipitous fall of So-viet communism, a basic change in its maps of the political universe. Now it seemed everyone wanted capitalism. But the disoriented Left, so used to a bipolar world, had no alternative model strong enough to rebut the global market, which, in 1990, seemed to be a sweeping, engulfing reality, offering few entry points for resistance. The Left had only the wishful slogan of the World Social Forums: "Another world is possible."

Western left feminists were reading in the press how many of the supports women—and everyone—had had under communism were being swept away: universal daycare and health care, guaranteed housing and jobs. Would the new system based on a free market provide these things? From the American perspective, there was no reason to hope they would. But to whom would one now complain? The weak and poor post-communist governments? All political levers were changing. What would left interna-tionalism look like in this new situation? Power was moving—in 1990, no one knew quite where.

IN THE SPRING OF 1990, at the yearly Socialist Scholars Conference in New York, the Yugoslavian writer Slavenka Drakulić electrified a plenary session by waving a sanitary napkin at the crowd of US leftists assembled there picking through the shambles of the Berlin Wall and the scattered pieces of the leftist discourse they had known all their lives. After assuring herself that the men in the audience knew just what this object was, Slavenka offered her own take on the failure of communism: If you wonder why state socialism didn't thrive, why it commanded so little loyalty, she said, just remember, along with all the other reasons you will no doubt find, that this object of simple convenience was not available in Yugoslavia. We were modern women. In our daily lives, we constantly felt it to be demeaning and galling to lack laundry soap, washers and dryers, tampons, decent clothes, children's toys. And the state had the capacity to meet these so-called little domestic needs of women, but our convenience was never a state priority. (When I first heard about Slavenka's startling speech, I had the thought that I wished laundry soap weren't on the list of things that mainly women need. It was a thought that foreshadowed the feeling of hundreds of conversations I was later to have with women in East Central Europe.)

The American feminists in that audience recognized Slavenka. An eager but tense dialogue between socialism and feminism had played in their heads for years. A small group asked to meet with her, and I—invaded by post–Cold War anxieties, and dispirited, too, by the stalled state of US feminism—was invited along. With hindsight, I see that that little meeting was the beginning of the Network of East-West Women, the organization in which I still work today.

Slavenka is a charismatic being, one of the few who had cata-
lyzed a feminist movement among the intelligentsia of Yugoslavia
in the 1970s. When she asked what we Western feminists were
doing while women in post-communism were swiftly losing the
social supports they once had—did we understand they would
not thrive in the new order of runaway markets?—what could
we say? Well, I remember what I said: humble-pie words to the
effect that it would be officious for Western feminists, often in
basic disagreement among themselves, to pretend to know what
to do in this situation. After all those years in anti-imperialist
struggles, the idea of "Western help" sounded sinister to us, completely contaminated. Did she know the terrible thing she was
asking for?

What a look she gave me! Disdain and that elegant, ironic
glare I have come to know so well in my subsequent travels. Slavenka was withering: Male dissidents got help constantly from
men in the West, she said. They were translated, lionized, given
prizes, respect, and money. Meanwhile, what did you feminists
ever do to support our uphill efforts to build feminism in the
seventies? Nothing. I felt lucky she didn't know the whole truth,
which included our ignorance that they had had a movement at
all and my certain knowledge that we would never have supported
elite, anti-communist intellectuals like herself in the 1970s. Still,
she did guess some of this: "You were too pure, too critical of your
own government to care about us. You thought helping us would
just seem like one more case of US anti-communism."

Although many US leftists can plead innocent to these Cold
War attitudes, I cannot. I admitted them. I feared above all that
strand of feminism that has on occasion cooperated with the
powers that be. It had all happened again and again. In the nineteenth century, middle-class English feminists had sought to re-

fresh their movement by traveling. After an exhausting fight at home against the forced medical examination of prostitutes, they won. But what next? Genteel as they were, they had no way then to take a next step toward a general freedom for women of all classes to roam the streets of London.

As historian Antoinette Burden and others have observed, the burnout of that generation of English feminists was a factor in the new drive of women's energies toward altering the fate of women abroad. The white women at the center of the English empire looked about them and saw that their "dusky sisters" were being maltreated by their husbands. Here was a crusade much more likely to be approved by their otherwise recalcitrant husbands at home. Women's Movement concerns about women's purity and independence became complicit with colonial control. Among Second Wave feminists, an understandable progressive reaction to this horrifying colonialist feminist history was to stay at home: Work out your own impasse with those around you.

But there had always been another story, running alongside: the dreams of the Left, the *Internationale,* and a solidarity that was the opposite of colonialism. In the early eighties, I had gone to Nicaragua with a women's law group; perhaps US feminists could contribute to crafting a new constitution? I had sat in the mud outside the US cruise missile base on Greenham Common, England, to join an international women's uprising against nuclear weapons. In other words, I had been a feminist activist who traveled to connect related desires, to build strength through solidarity. Nineteenth-century activists had not all acted as imperial patrons, after all; as historian Bonnie Anderson chronicled in *Joyous Greetings: The First International Women's Movement 1830–1860,* contact across borders had strengthened and heartened feminists who were sometimes isolated in their own societies.

These two different traveler's tales were both playing in my head at once as I listened to Slavenka's angry critique of Western feminism's failure to connect with struggling feminists in Eastern Europe. If I bought her argument, I said, irritated in my own turn, were there in fact any real and practical moves US activists could make now, in 1990? Without skipping a beat: "Put us in touch with each other; there are feminists in the region, but they are isolated from each other." (Later I was to get two letters that said, "I am the only feminist in Romania.") But why, I asked her, should Western women be the ones for this task? Slavenka pointed out our resources—not just money but also telephones, paper, photocopying machines, our huge civil society with the space it allows for independent action. But I pushed on: Who knows whether the US experience, including all this space and money, will be relevant? Although we have built an astonishing mass movement, we have never managed to get government-supported daycare or cheap health care or guarantees of employment like yours.

And here beginneth the first lesson of the visitor's dilemma, with this staple of the East-West dialogue as I was to come to know it. As Hungarian feminist Eva Toth has put it for the Eastern side: please, "no envy, no pity." You in the West don't understand what we had, or what we didn't have. Your envy comes from ignorance about what our social services were really like, and your pity is also misplaced; you patronize us for the very survival tactics we most admire in ourselves.

In that first encounter, Slavenka put aside my anxieties about the differences and inequalities between East and West with a grand sweep of her hand. "Don't worry," she said. "Just help us Eastern feminists to meet. We promise not to listen to you."

This is just the sort of invitation I seem unable to resist.

And so we began. A small group, friends in the Women's Movement in New York for two decades, began to organize a meeting where Eastern and Central European women who considered themselves feminists—in any sense of the term they chose—could meet each other. Our proposal's title was "What Next?"

Slavenka worked on her end to help us find the people and a place to meet. She had written a piece for *Ms.* about these rare creatures, rebels against both former communist regimes and the blithely sexist new world order that was suddenly upon them. We used the snowball method, rolling out from that first list of names—from Bulgaria to Hungary, Romania, Czechoslovakia; in the end, feminists from eleven countries would attend the meeting, which took a year to put together.

The former USSR was not included, partly out of a need to set some limit, but partly because Slavenka was adamant that Eastern and Central European women did not yet want to meet with Russians, not even—and we argued about this—Russian feminists. So, it turned out there was an imperialist to resent. But it was not (yet) we Americans. In that moment between two breaths, some Eastern women saw Western ones as relatively benign, as the bearers of a way of life that might give clues to the future.

4

MONEY

In the early nineties, many US agencies and private foundations, fearing that East Central Europe might quickly revert to communism, chose to put their attention and money on building new social and political structures that would replace the rigidities of communist organization. Some were agents of a free market, establishing new banking and legal practices and importing neoliberal economic theories; but some also wanted to change the texture of social life fundamentally, funding all kinds of activities that were loosely bundled together under the capacious term civil society.

It would be civil society that would make new rights like freedom of speech and assembly into something real, a way of life that could support what were being called the "new democracies."

In only a few years, this stream of money dwindled to a trickle. It became obvious to American funders, both public and private, that communism could not make a comeback. Markets were going to sweep all other considerations away. The window-dressing of support for social initiatives was quickly discarded: Why bother spending dollars to foster the fledgling efforts of social solidarity? So funders, even some of the most progressive, dropped East Central Europe and left it on its own to develop whatever civil society it might. Neoliberal democracy seemed to be the inevitable direction. Certainly no one *dreamed in the early nineties what would in fact happen—that reactions to globalization would later take authoritarian, populist forms quite different from the old communism everyone had feared.*

OUR NEXT TASK WAS to raise the money for our meeting. US women who wanted to come to this newly possible international exchange, this indeterminate conversation between East and West, would have to find ways to fund themselves. We calculated we would need twenty-five thousand dollars to gather, house, and feed fifty women from the region for three and a half days. The first Gulf War was just starting in 1991 as I began to make cold calls to foundations. Let one exchange stand in for most of them:

> "You want to do what?"
>
> "We're US feminist activists who want to bring Eastern and Central European feminists together to discuss 'what next?' The collapse of communist governments is bringing basic changes at a dizzying rate. New constitutions are being written as we speak; abortion rights women have had for decades are being threatened by the churches, the new nationalists; the story of what gender means is being rewritten *right now*. Feminists in the region are isolated and without resources. They need to meet each other and to join an international conversation."

This, I later learned, is the "elevator pitch." Get your message down to what you can tell a funder encountered by luck between the tenth and the ground floor.

"Don't you know there's a war on?"

I began to ask myself: *Is my unabated intensity about feminism from 1969 until now, in 1991, a weird aberration no one shares? Has the fascination I continue to feel rendered me grotesque?* "There's a war on." In this atmosphere, I didn't want to be dismissed for parochial pleading while the world burned. After all, men's lives in East Central Europe were being instantly, deeply, happily or disturbingly changed, too. Under communism, there had been a community of suffering and endurance. Why did I think women would want to interrupt the solidarity of shared survival by choosing to separate from men and registering specifically women's complaints?

No doubt defensively, I explained as I called prospective funders that it wasn't I, the feminist, who was now separating men and women. Gorbachev had just written in his new book: Women are tired; let them go home. And new nationalist groups like *Vatra Românească*, the Romanian Hearth movement, were saying that under communism women had been leading unnatural lives; it was time for them to return to their true function. I would try to talk on—as there were many, many more examples of the invention or resurrection of divisions of gender and class—but I rarely got beyond this point in the argument. The answer was always no. Urging urgency had no effect.

One program officer was particularly rude. Who was I to call her? What was my standing? I backed off, hung up, stewed for a moment, then called back.

"I've called for an apology."

"You already apologized."

"No, I'm calling to get an apology from *you*. We're independent activists out here struggling to support new social movements. We're your reason for being. Treat us with respect and appreciation. Be humble. All you have is money."

Amazingly, this outburst worked—briefly. She had no money for my weird one-off meeting with its unquantifiable aftermath. But, as bullies so often do when confronted, she came off her high horse and offered some brief lessons on the possible.

One last snapshot of trying to raise money for our quixotic undertaking: In 1990–1991 one of the few Eastern European feminists we had all heard about, from an article she had written in the feminist journal *Signs*, was spending the year in a Midwestern university. In her "Legal Regulations of Abortion in Poland," she asked the question, "Will abortion create a feminist movement in Poland?" (The answer was, and remains, yes and no). On what was just beginning to be a grapevine, I heard she was there and called her at once to invite her to the (still imaginary) conference. And could she stay with me when she passed through New York?

It was exciting to have this calm, elegant, gracious person in my house. A lawyer and Warsaw University professor, Małgorzata Fuszara was getting involved in the writing of a constitution for the new Poland, watching every move of her mostly male colleagues with eyes that missed nothing. She wouldn't let them guarantee state protection for "the child" at the moment of conception; she wouldn't let them slip in invidious clauses that would enable gender inequality in future laws. We talked and talked. How could the conference support such efforts? Maybe through exchanging cross-border information about newfangled forms of discrimination swiftly on the way? We really didn't know. For Małgorzata, who was already a well-known and effective feminist activist, the meeting probably couldn't offer much. It was simply an open door, a brief moment of (possible) connection, and yet—to my delight—she agreed to come.

While staying with me, Małgorzata was invited to our biggest progressive foundation to discuss the new Polish political scene and possible future grants. (She was disbelieving when I said this foundation was named for a car. How could these socially productive millions have originated from a car?) She asked me to come with her. Maybe we could get some very small bit of these millions to help pay for the conference.

The foundation building was a dream of good architecture, good taste, order. The pious quiet intimidated us; we couldn't hear our footsteps on the rugs. When we were ushered in to see the program officer, Małgorzata explained why she had brought me with her: The conference I was planning was a specific, timely intervention. Could the foundation give us a small sum to help it happen? I know much more now how utterly offensive to the etiquette of big foundations were, first, my surprise appearance and then, Małgorzata's specific request. We had hoped to jump over the wall of slow and responsible calculation. How about a few thousand dollars from discretionary funds?

This program officer was angry and rude. Her secretary had brought us three coffees, but she told me to leave at once. In shock, I rose to go. "You can take your coffee with you," she said. "No thanks."

That cup of coffee still sits steaming in my mind. Although money helps, it can never be the point. The Women's Movement uses funds but can't really be funded; it is never merely a collection of projects. Much later, the Network was to get small grants— from the car foundation and other fine and generous sources. But, on paper, this first gathering we were planning didn't look like much. The intent of the meeting was, simply, to meet, possibly even to foster ongoing relationships in the region and beyond— who could know with what long-term consequences?

Certainly, in the autumn of 1990, stalking out, leaving that cup of coffee behind, I had no idea what connections were possible or would be desired. Surely this program officer would disparage me to Małgorzata. Surely Małgorzata would see my dismissal in disgrace as a measure of my value as an ally. In shame, anxiety, and suspense, I went home and waited for her return. How would this dignified and politically experienced woman greet me, see me, feel about me after such a scene?

An hour later, she appeared; she rushed down the entry steps and threw her arms around me: "I've never seen anything so awful in my whole life." We clung together, commiserating about the difficulties we faced, the humiliations of asking. The result is very simple: From that time and still, decades later, Małgorzata and I continue to work, suffering the ups and downs of our oh-so-demanding movement. Although we are often too busy to keep in touch, our loyalty and deep feelings for each other are permanent.

So, in the end, funding the conference was a matter of nickels and dimes. I shall be forever grateful to the Methodists, to the foundations of Irene Crowe and Genevieve Vaughn, and to various friends and relations. But as the time for the June meeting we were planning drew near, we had only eighteen thousand dollars. "Bring the cash," Slavenka instructed. In Yugoslavia, the black market in dollars was going wild in spring of 1991. She would change our money with a secret friend who would be able to get 20 percent more for it. And there it was, almost the amount we needed.

So in March 1991 I flew to Croatia, still a part of Yugoslavia. Since Slavenka's currency fiddle was strictly illegal, I was carrying thirteen thousand dollars in clean hundred-dollar bills in a string bag under a voluminous dress. With this we could send people travel money and put down a deposit on a hotel.

Throughout the process never did I encounter a Yugoslav dinar. Everything was German marks or dollars. I strolled into a deserted bank. "Can I buy some dinars?" "Why would you want to do that?" "Just curious. I've never seen one." "Oh, curious," the young teller said, dripping irony. He dug his hand into the till and threw a big handful of coins on the counter. "Here, be my guest." (Later on this trip, when I was visiting Sonja Licht and Milan Nikolic in Belgrade, they had a roll of toilet paper they'd made from dinar bank notes.)

So, money. The poverty of women and women's movements is well known. (Five percent of US foundation money goes specifically to support women's rights and autonomy.) Over the years, the poverty of the Network of East-West Women saved us from many illusions, among them the idea that Western sources would or could support feminist activism. We were to become nothing more but nothing less than part of an international women's movement.

But, of course, as I always knew, Slavenka's promise that Western women could supply even small sums of money without raising ire, envy, or resentment was entirely untrue. As the years rolled by, the scale and meaning of our exchanges were to change many times, but our shared experience of the giving and taking of things that were always incommensurate remains a central conundrum of all our years together.

5

FIRST TRIP, 1991

Before 1989, of all the countries in the Eastern Bloc, Yugoslavia was assumed to be the closest to the West. Through clever manipulation, Josip Broz Tito—under one guise or another dictator of Yugoslavia from 1939 and finally, in 1974, President for Life until his death in 1980—had managed to maintain some independence from Soviet control after his break with Stalin in 1948. Given this separate history, everyone took for granted that the relative freedom of Yugoslavs, the population's multiethnic composition, and the partial modernity of their economy would put them first in line, after the fall of communism, to join the European Union.

Instead, in one of the great tragedies of modern Europe, ambitious local politicians, many among them former communist officials, maximized the dormant fault lines in this ethnically mixed country, which had been cobbled together after World War I, to pull this union apart in a violent war in which some estimate 140,000 died. Further, powerful actors from abroad often misunderstood and mishandled their own interventions in the violent disintegration of Yugoslavia.

There will not be agreement about how viable this conglomerated Yugoslavia ever was—fusing Serbia (with its contested province of Kosovo), Croatia, Slovenia, Bosnia-Herzegovina, Macedonia, and Montenegro—frozen in its unity by Tito's dictatorship, but also providing a possible map for cooperation among its parts. However, no one can make much of a claim for the flourishing of the seven small and weak countries (Kosovo declared independence from Serbia in 2008) that remain after the big breakup, precipitated by manipulated and vicious ethnic fighting on a scale not seen in Europe since the end of World War II.

When I went to Zagreb and Belgrade in the early spring of 1991 I was still visiting Yugoslavia. Within the year, this Zagreb had been proclaimed the capital of Croatia, and this Belgrade the capital of Serbia, two different countries in formation, about to experience the return to Europe of concentration camps, the mass rape of women as a war strategy, and the slaughter of thousands, many of them noncombatants, tortured and killed because of their ethnic origins.

The Romania and Poland I also visited on this trip were to change seismically too in the years ahead. But for the Yugoslavs I met then and came to know, these changes were on another scale. In Serbia, the authoritarian government of Slobodan Milošević that swept into power in 1989 on a nationalist surge threatened all who resisted, especially members of the intelligentsia and media, as well as opposition politicians, murdering some of them when the regime was coming to its end. In Croatia, prominent feminist intellectuals were forced to leave the country because they wrote satirically of nationalism or were married to someone from another ethnic group.

In the anti-war movement that developed there was a group that was especially visible in its resistance: Women in Black. These were feminists who opposed the war from the start and understood the horror of what was happening, the fusion of all the worst aspects of fear, preening male pride, and vicious nationalism. Silent, wearing black, they stood on the main plaza in Belgrade and in front of the United Nations in New York, their signs proclaiming that this was an unspeakable madness. People have speculated about why they, a group of thirty or so, weren't silenced like so many others. The activist Vesna Kesić has argued that having this visible, independent group was good public relations for Milošević: He could claim to tolerate dissent.

However they managed it, Women in Black was one of the few expressions of an absolute resistance to the politically corrupt nationalisms on all sides that tore the former Yugoslavia apart.

ZAGREB

I ARRIVED IN ZAGREB in 1991 in early spring light, the city gray but beautiful in its bones. Slavenka Drakulić, her assistant Alemka Lisinski, and I met at once for our transfer of funds. I felt that Slavenka was mildly surprised that the Americans were actually doing this thing she had so grandly suggested, perhaps as a passing whim. What could come of it? The Americans would go home; the other participants would disperse to their quickly diversifying post-communist fates. Our meeting would hang in transitional space, neither past nor augur of any particular future. Still, here was the American, the cash, the growing list of invitees. We worked briskly for a couple of hours. Slavenka cooked us a delicious vegetarian casserole. Then we had nothing more to say to each other. To this star, who in 1977 had been part of the first feminist group in the region, a glamorous and cosmopolitan recent victim of state persecution as a feminist and anti-nationalist writer, and later to be one of the five "witches" the new conservative government had in its gun sites, the visiting American was an utterly uninteresting groundling, soiled by her obscure struggles at the grass roots.

She put me up at a friend's. "I don't have room," she said. "At Rujana's you'll be more comfortable." The outside of the dun stucco house looked much like the others on this noisy main street. But at the top of the stairs I entered a fairy tale. Rujana

Kren was the queen of this magic place, a delicate beauty in her own kingdom. The gray communist streets dissolved. She was an artist in silver-and gold-colored tin, sea glass, mirrors, and fantastically shaped bits of driftwood. Every surface of the stairs, the main room, the Turkish tents that were bedrooms, was covered with her sparkling work. I could barely believe what I was seeing.

This apartment offered one of my earliest glimpses of how complex the expressions of public and private could be on the other side of the looking glass. Private solutions, which radical American feminists derided as the enemy of collective change, had the reverse meaning here: In the personal lay all creativity, the warmth of mutual help, heroic success at surviving—and more, at flourishing—in defiance of the state prohibition against spontaneity.

Rujana's house was outside communism and inside her own head and in the lives of her husband and children. My few days there were life lived in an eternal present, blissful. She and her husband had bought a small garden allotment and had done such unusual plantings that their half acre had become a microclimate with sweet smells, berries for preserves, catkins, flowering trees and vines. No need to wait on line. They ate from this private Eden. Every mouthful of quince jam or newly baked bread had its source in home, hard work, and invention. Being an artist under communism—at least one who didn't use words—had been the best deal going.

We talked and talked—not about feminism at all. What was a social movement anyway, and what could it possibly do for her? To many I met on this first trip the idea of social action to change one's own life was completely foreign. Rujana's was a world that had had its deep sorrows—one of three children had died—but these were the things one endured, as one endured, too, all the difficulties of daily life, by visiting a first-flowering meadow at dawn. Denise Levertov wrote, "The eye, luminous / prince of solitude." Rujana's art and life were careful, craftsmanlike studies in timeless luminosity.

BELGRADE TO ROMANIA

Then I traveled from Zagreb to Belgrade by train, a cross-country journey impossible four months later, when the tracks were torn up between Croatia and Serbia, by then at war with each other. But it was March, and, waiting in Belgrade, there were Sonja and Milan, in a car so small that he filled the front seat, she the back. We were together again; our friendship had passed over the bridge of change and was for good.

Sonja Licht, a tireless and passionate activist finally free to act, had become co-chair of the international civic group the Helsinki Citizens' Assembly. With a driver, a bunch of us set off in a van to tour Romania, gathering information for a Helsinki report on the state of human rights: Just recently many Romanians had beaten up Hungarians, and some Hungarians had beaten up Romanians. This sort of violence was blooming out of new freedoms and new fantasies of territorial expansion. Power was being reorganized, and the race was definitely to the swift, to the cynical, to the manipulators of new anxieties.

Our van had a Hungarian license plate, and this posed symptomatic difficulties: Gas stations in Romania, already trailing long lines of waiting cars, wouldn't sell gas to Hungarians. We weren't Hungarians; we were witnesses. But, in its way, this identity was just as bad. The weasel government of Romania in 1991 wanted no outsiders to observe how they had killed their own citizens, had murdered their hated dictator Ceaușescu and his wife without trial or public discussion, but had otherwise remained essentially the same regime. Sonja and Milan made strategic choices about when it was safe to display our sign "Helsinki Citizens' Assembly" on the windshield and when not.

Surrounded by this atmosphere of distrust, we encountered more bitterness than hope. At one stop I had a talk with the kind and thoughtful dissident, Sorin Vieru. "You've been traveling," he said. "Do we seem worse here than elsewhere? Are we different?" His sadness made me ashamed, as I was so often to feel, at being the visitor who is only passing through; how could I have the right to answer such an eager question from such a deep place? More typically, a distinguished orchestra conductor we met on our way told me, as he pointed out the chickens in his backyard: "You from New York know nothing. Things were terrible here. We survived only because of *les poules*." You from New York. I don't know which he hated more, our presumed ignorance of the blighted life he had been forced to lead, or our prosperity, which we carried so lightly. But Sorin was quite different: He seemed to think outsiders might help him clarify his own distress. Always this fork in the road, this variation in temperament: the open hand to the stranger, or disgust at the stranger's privilege, easy mobility, and failure to know. Sorin was able to love even those who could not know. So I ventured an answer: "Here there's still fear." "Yes, yes," he said with excitement. "That's how it feels. Here things are still frozen." The food shocked even our Eastern European companions in the van. Cold, watery soup. (Why cold?). Thin, tepid juice. (Why warm?). Feminism? Ha, ha! I didn't mention it. A disconsolate mood communicated itself at our every stop.

But when we arrived in Bucharest, there the feminists were. Meeting with them lifted my hopes. I had often been told that feminism was a luxury people in the former Eastern Bloc couldn't afford. The small group of feminists I met in Bucharest, the most damaged city I was to visit on this trip, felt exactly the oppo-site. It was with a sense of urgency that they were building civil society. In 1991 the words *civil society* were everywhere—their meaning sometimes vague or contested but their promise galva-nizing, a counter to the prevailing enervation. To build women's independence was to contribute to a public sphere beyond the still-entrenched old government.

Driving hard through the night, on what little was left of our gas, we returned to Belgrade.

KRAKOW: SŁAWOMIRA WALCZEWSKA

Krakow was next. Once again, hidden in my clothes, I had cash, so that one of the handful of self-proclaimed feminists of post-communist Poland, Sławomira Walczewska, could travel to our conference.

I knew a great deal about the various ways American women became feminists in the 1960s and 1970s but how did it happen for women like Sławomira—always called Sławka—who dared to call themselves feminists in the early 1990s, making themselves utterly lonely in their suddenly changing society? True, they were sought out by a few Western feminists like me, but, in spite of our eagerness, we were often as unequipped to understand them as the traditionalist Poles everywhere surrounding them.

I first met Sławka on Krakow's main square, one of the grand-est public spaces in all of Europe, a great resonating rectangle. The glorious buildings—dating from the twelfth to the nineteenth century—were beautiful in an unchangeable grace but were then melancholy in their crumbling details. I had a courtly guide, Zyg-munt, soon to be one of the up-and-coming young men of the new Poland; when he introduced us, Sławka treated me to the first of many feminist demonstrations that were later to take place on this monumental stage set. Zygmunt took her hand as if to shake it, but his gesture turned into the elegant hand kiss, then still a common piece of Polish civility. Sławka's fine-boned face convulsed into a heraldic frown, a look of aristocratic defiance I have often seen since in Polish national art. She evaded the kiss as one might pull one's hand back from touching a hot poker.

Aha, I said. *What have we here?* Of course aware of the implications, I had nonetheless rather enjoyed this hand-kissing in my few days in Poland. How quaint, how covertly sexy, how far from my New York problems with the social encounters between men and women who are supposedly but not really equal. But here was someone who was freshly, absolutely furious at the everyday aesthetics of patriarchy. Embarrassed by Sławka's anger and alarmed by her strictness, I recognized this sudden refusal of ordinary, traditional life as the very stuff out of which feminist sensibility is made. Here was the raw material I knew so well, and I greeted this frowning woman with all my heart.

Since then, Sławka and I have often paced the sublime square and the streets of Krakow, discussing feminist ideas. One day early in our peripatetic career, we entered the square to the sound of ecstatic violins; a folk troupe was dancing on an elevated wooden platform. We stood watching a long time. The women in their wide skirts twirled while the men opposite kicked and leaped. Then the men swung the girls. Then they all formed squares and the men and the women crossed and joined, bowed and parted, then joined again in couples for a final march, the eternal (fluttering) feminine on the arm of the eternal male hero. As Virginia Woolf said, you know you live in a patriarchy because it is *he* who suspends *her* in the air.

When it was all over and the heartbreakingly lovely music had faded away, we exchanged such a look. "Maybe it's just impossible," she said. "This is all so old; how can it change?" We collapsed into wicker chairs at one of the outdoor cafés that ring the square, a perfect place to observe the promenade of he and she. Then, suddenly, half in ironic alienation, half punch-drunk confidence, we were hysterical with laughter. Yes, the dance was so strong, beautiful, joyous, seemingly timeless—but also so odd and unlikely. A shift in consciousness, and now, when the gestures of standard heterosexuality were displayed on a plinth, they struck us as abstract and absurd, an artificial performance where nature meets art, like bear-baiting. We argued about the boundaries of the possible for hours, but, running parallel to the talk, our laughter was a joint possession, a solvent we could not have rationally explained to anyone way then, since our skepticism put us in the realm of the grotesque.

In Poland in 1991 the relationship between men and women was the most solid, clear, unambiguous, unquestionable human tie in a time when all other relationships were being remade. To live, as Sławka was living, in active opposition to the sacred dyad was to live, like all the dissidents before her, in the belief that everything could be completely different. Her daily commitment to another reality took not only courage but extraordinary imagination.

She was born in 1960 in Częstochowa, the city of the sacred image of the Black Madonna, at the height of the Władysław Gromułka years, the end of a small Soviet thaw, the beginning of stricter times—no travel, no letters. Her father, a teacher, was an engineer and a geographer who traveled all over Poland mapping the country's underground mineral resources. Her mother, also serious about work, was a teacher in a grammar school and attended to Sławka and her younger brother. (Both parents had forged birth certificates and don't know their real birthdates. He was made younger so he wouldn't be drafted into the Soviet Army; she was made older so she wouldn't be given to a German family for adoption.)

My friend was named Sławomira after her cousin, born twenty years before, in that very different moment, 1940. Sławka's uncle was then an officer in the Polish underground army. He had moved his wife and newborn baby to a village to be near him and the partisans he commanded in the nearby forest. This uncle is remembered as a peaceful man—clever and warm. (In 1944 the Russians sent him to Siberia for several years, and, to Sławka's sorrow, he died in 1979, never to know the triumph of the independent trade union movement, Solidarity, the next year, which was eventually to change everything.) He named the baby Sławomira, herald of peace. In the winter cold of that small village, with no medical care to speak of, in the midst of war, Sławomira the First caught a common infant illness and died. Sławomira the Second was supposed to live for both girls, to have a life of scope and heft, with freedom enough for two.

Sławka stores a favorite anecdote, her key to her parents. As a university student, she longed, like so many others, to see the forbidden Western world. After a long wait and the usual finagling, she finally got a passport that made it possible to leave Poland. She was on her way to England—in her mind a state that worked, a liberal democracy, where the free Poles had found a home during the war and where freedom was still available. (She had read Orwell's 1984 in an underground Polish translation.) Getting there took three months; she had to earn hard currency on the way to cover her living expenses and to pay her parents back for the precious foreign money they had fronted for her, cash they had been stashing away illegally for years, two hundred dollars. During this odyssey, her parents sent her a letter. Her mother wrote: "Dearest Sławunia, Be careful. Wear warm clothes. Don't get ill. Be sure to eat. Come back soon." Her father wrote: "My Dear Daughter, You are now on the way to the famous Albion, the center of the civilized world. I am proud you are so brave and doing such a journey. I always wanted to go there. Good luck on your travels."

This sounds as canonical a division of male and female as you can get; it's like the dance in the square—charming, and on the edge of caricature. But in Sławka these rival states are connected. Obviously, her father's yearnings for other cultures, languages, landscapes are one part of her inheritance. She is hopeful like him, and, like him, she believes in possibilities underground. From her mother comes a feeling of female sufficiency; the power of her mother's wishes seems somehow to have suggested the magic force of women in general.

But with her mother it has always been so difficult. In Sławka's earliest memories, her mother was already begging her "to change," an infinitive with many meanings—from wearing skirts instead of the more comfortable and freeing trousers to adopting some hard-to-name daughterly compliance. Why not carry a handbag? Use pretty handkerchiefs? Why take such long strides?

Sławka used to fantasize coming to her mother as a monster and saying, "Look, I changed." Both parents were proud of her for fighting for her younger brother in the schoolyard, but they were anxious, too: Was this heroism female enough in a ten-year-old? She remembers her victories over the bullies with pleasure; one boy punched her in the face, and she responded with such sheer fury that he was scared from the field. Still, this was the end. The boys had so much training, she said; they were fighting all the time, getting practice. She nonetheless took away from this last victory that if one is fierce and brave, one can win, even against the odds; to be certain is to win.

Gradually, as Sławka became well known as an organizer in Krakow, her mother began to accept her daughter's distressing feminism as a possibly respectable identity. But just when this seemed settled, Sławka began to publicly advocate for gay and lesbian rights, embarrassing her mother all over again. Why couldn't she just be a feminist? Then Sławka brought her new partner, the witty, brilliant, and beautiful Beata Kozak, home. Beata could not be accepted or loved or recognized. And here was an end. Yet one day when Sławka was chopping cucumbers for a big soup and I asked her how she could possibly chop so fast, she gave a wry smile, her tribute to her mother, so fast with a paring knife, and to her mother's five sisters, a powerful female cabal still functioning across long distances of time and space, still loving the errant Sławka as their own beautiful, intelligent girl, who can no more be repudiated than they would cut off a hand.

Sławka and Beata lived then in an attic they renovated at the top of a house built at the turn of the century for a new kind of person: unmarried middle-class women with jobs who did not want to live at home. Sławka has written an illustrated monograph about these women's houses, and once she took me for a grand dinner at one that was still going in the early 1990s. It was like coming upon some nineteenth-century lace in a scented drawer. In fact, I now find it hard to believe that I really saw this vanishing world. Old, elegant spinsters (no term of opprobrium originally—just women who spin, or in this case work telephone exchanges) greeted us American visitors, fed us delicious food, showed us photographs of their independent youth. As we ate, portraits of permanently absent friends looked down on us, their hair piled high, their faces grand and dignified.

Simply, amazingly, Sławka had discovered the first wave of feminism in Krakow, had made friends with its survivors, had built this birds' nest at the top of one of these women's early, free institutions. (Later she wrote a book, *Knights, Ladies, Feminists: Feminist Discourse in Poland*, which describes this late-nineteenth-century feminism and the deep resistance it faced.) Sławka and Beata's aerie is a five-floor walk-up, all in wood, with windows opening into the tops of trees. Visiting feminists get to stay here, in a place where autonomous women have lived for a hundred years.

How did she ever find her way into a feminism so passionate and fully thought through where there was no one else to talk to? Of course, I remind myself: Feminism is indigenous to wherever it arises. All European countries had nineteenth- and early twentieth-century women's movements. Sławka's feminism comes from the soil right here beneath this house. A mystery remains. I ask, "Why *feminism* as a dream of liberation? How did you even hear about it? Did it come from the communist rhetoric about equality?"

Sławka considers: No, she says. Not from communism. The excitement about women's emancipation was the experience of an earlier generation. For us, men ran things and women worked too hard; for us, communism meant only one thing: limitation. But she suddenly remembers where she did first hear about feminism, in a communist magazine in the seventies, in an article by a well-known Polish journalist, Daniel Passent. He had described a demonstration in New York by US "feminists." Kate Millett had spoken, and he made fun of her remarks. She was an older woman with gray, wild hair (already an offense), and she was arguing that women, blacks, and all workers should unite. Ha, ha, a parody of "workers unite." How ridiculous, how childish.

The year must have been 1974 when Sławka was fourteen and in grammar school. She remembers her reaction to the article: "Long gray hair, telling something radical and new. Interesting." (In Sławka's English vocabulary, the word *interesting* is luminous, the highest praise.) So she decided at once to write a letter to Kate Millett. The first problem was taking the risk that someone might check the letter and see something suspicious in it. Then she had to concoct an address from the information in the article. Then she had to write something in her nearly nonexistent English: She could only send her greetings, and her wish to know something more. It was, she says, "a bottle in the ocean," and she didn't really expect a reply.

What must this letter have looked like to the people who received it, addressed to Radcliffe College, USA, around 1975? I would love to find the person who recognized its importance and went to the trouble of putting together a packet with leaflets, group flyers, feminist catalogues. I want to know all that Sławka can remember about these ephemera straight out of the prime experiences of my youth. "I still have the catalogue. I've been carrying it around from one place to another for years. It should be here somewhere, in the apartment." She gets up and as if with a divining rod goes right to the shelf, presenting me with a large-scale book, *The New Woman's Survival Sourcebook: Another Woman-Made Book from Knopf*. I'm speechless; I have tears in my eyes. A record of the passionate and chaotic proliferation of feminist activity of the US Women's Liberation Movement in the 1970s is sitting on my lap in an attic in Krakow: Where to find groups, with their names and manifestos; where to find sensitive women's health care clinics—or witches' covens; where to get help defending against vaginal infections—or rapists. Everything in wild confusion on every page. Sławka points out an article called "Feminist Fiction." "I wondered about this—what could this mean? The word *feminist* with the word *fiction*. My English dictionary didn't help. In fact, with my English, I couldn't really understand any of it." Living in a communist country, she didn't have the concept "movement" either, but she had the sense that this was something big. Interesting! And not least interesting was the cover, an image by Judy Chicago in yellow and black of two outstretched wings. This was something sexual, Sławka understood. Freedom and sex in flight.

Sławka had treasured this book all these years and fed on curiosity. "When I met you on the square in 1991 you were my first American feminist." I am secretly delighted, of course, but instantly the old anxiety returns. How does US feminism translate? Did she have reason to think it might be different from the European feminisms, which, by that time, she already knew? English and German feminisms were often more centrally, visibly focused on class. Did American feminism look good in part because galloping consumerism looked good to new post-communists? In fact, when American feminists did insist on bringing up class and the excesses of Western consumer culture, feminists from the East were often worried that this meant communism all over again. A student told me recently that if I had happened to begin the course I taught in the mid-nineties with a discussion of gender-with-class, she would have smelled Marxism and dropped out immediately. The *Sourcebook* was, among other things, a marketplace, an odd compilation of things to know, buy, do. Now that I was trying to look at the book from the outside, I was succeeding in experiencing Sławka's excitement—and bewilderment.

Finally, Sławka's feminism made use of everything and was an invention of her own. I began to recognize Sławka as one of those early, creative, organic intellectuals, like Shulamith Firestone or

Jo Freeman or Cellestine Ware or Carol Hanisch or Ellen Willis or Martha Shelley or Cindy Cisler in the US, who had started with the merest whisper heard on a street, an image noted in passing, a sense of wrongness that sought a name. Although there are two hundred years of modern feminist ancestors, in times of backlash their ideas recede from view, only to be rekindled by the Sławka Walczewskas of this world, when, for any number of reasons, the walls of the city are shaken.

She told me that, from the first, she couldn't reconcile a sense of being herself with being what a woman was supposed to be. Putting the two together was an impossibility, making self-invention a necessity. Besides, she found it unfair and mysterious that her brother had privileges she had not. There was something terribly wrong with the world. Those who feel homeless can sometimes find the energy to withhold female assent, resist taking the required path. They seek out their own company and a way to live differently. If the time is wrong, they live bohemian lives of one kind or another. If the time is right, they found movements. Being first, they pay a special price; they are ridiculed as misfits, trashed as leaders, distained as dreamers, feared as extremists. They face these first lonely humiliations, and then, if the time is right, thousands of us come tumbling after.

In 1978 Sławka, then eighteen, began as a chemistry major at Krakow's ancient university, the Jagiellonian. Although she hung on for two years, there was trouble from the first. She resisted the strict memory tasks, complained that there was no context, no meaning. On her exams, she began to talk about the social history of chemical discovery. Perhaps what this Polish romantic really wanted was to be an alchemist. Here was an early manifestation of her later infatuation with traditions of women's magical culture—a constant source of contention between her and me, not to mention a source of much mutual teasing and com-ic-ironic witch performances in the main square. How powerful can women be? To Sławka's mind, infinitely powerful, capable of completely transforming reality. However small, very fierce. However buried, precious ore.

In her small chemistry group, she told me, "the sexism was terrible." One old, internationally known professor was willing to talk to her, but ultimately, like the others, he believed that only men *need* to think. For girls it's enough to learn the formu-las. Perhaps this is the first example of Sławka's originality as a public agitator: She made an exhibition of pictures created from the chemicals in the lab, called "Chemical Abstracts." After three days, everything on the walls began to stink and burn.

In 1980 she changed her major to philosophy. Did things get better? Suddenly, as I ask her this, the dark and guilty memories of a survivor surface in her: There were twenty students, mostly men. The few women were brilliant (necessarily, in this com-petitive and elite milieu). One of them had a very high female voice. The men never heard her. A man would repeat her ideas as his own opinion and then everyone heard them. She became more and more "gray." She "died as a philosopher." Later, she became a librarian. Another gifted girl was incapable of fading; the alternative was to become crazy. She became a caricature of femininity, a sexy hoyden wearing raffish, aristocratic, hand-me-down clothes. She was trying to provoke, to capture their attention, and she ended as a grotesque all the men despised. She never finished her degree, left Krakow for the provinces, takes care of her family, and does no professional work.

Once, a couple, both philosophy students, came to class with their newborn baby. The professor (a favorite of Sławka's) greeted all three warmly, then, when it was time for the class to begin, he turned to the father: "You're staying for the seminar?" It never occurred to him that the mother might stay or that neither could stay. These stories are so familiar that they are only worth recounting for what they tell about Sławka. At a time when such sexism was so common that no one noticed, she noticed. She grieved. She observed these gendered fates with a sympathy for the women that was not to be found anywhere, then, but in her singular heart.

Her own strategy for survival was to maintain a dignified silence. A few professors recognized her talent, but most of the time she traveled under the radar of male contempt for the female philosopher (oxymoron), respecting herself for her state of exile and cunning. Still, her invisibility and her empathy with the others created a rawness, a frustration, and then a need to fight—but how to avoid becoming yet another easily dismissed female type, the Angry Woman? How to win? She decided that what she needed were words. She would organize with others to discuss, to seek the words to communicate "what is not okay."

A small group of allies began talking among themselves "about women and men" in the mid-1980s. Sławka was amazed when these new discussions aroused real opposition, anger, and resistance in addition to the usual ridicule at the university. She maintained her dignity by developing her own syllogism: Philosophy should be a discipline in which all questions are good; the job is to ask questions about *anything*. Most of her colleagues refused to entertain questions about gender. Ergo, they were bad philosophers. Initially shocked by their closed-mindedness, Sławka was ultimately freed by their attitude. Although they seemed powerful and authoritative, were they perhaps only a pack of cards? Their fear and derision disillusioned her.

By this time she had begun to meet with women in Warsaw who had organized a women's film festival. A male friend mentioned the festival to her in passing. What *is* a women's film festival? Interesting! In 1985 she found the organizers and was therefore one of the founding members of what may well have been the first independent, explicitly feminist Polish women's group, the Polish Feminist Association. The group was an informal network that met in kitchens and held discussions very like the consciousness-raising groups created by US feminists fifteen years earlier. Sławka loved the group and commuted three hours by train from Krakow several times a month; but she was frustrated, too, by the sequestered atmosphere that has always been one aspect of this particular political form. She wanted this talk to be more public and to include growing numbers of women. So she persuaded the group to conduct their first outside action since the film festival, to join her and her Krakow colleagues in organizing a conference, "To Be a Woman?" ("The question mark," says Sławka, "carries the story.") Back at the university, no one had a better idea, so by default this became the subject of the official annual conference of the Jagiellonian students in philosophy.

The year was 1987, and the conference is a key moment in dissident history—if that story is ever to include women. Poland was just coming out from under the worst strictures of martial law, and "To Be a Woman?" was one of the few public events around. But the reaction was disappointing. The question "To Be a Woman?" was odd, certainly, but no one imagined the gathering to be subversive. Nobody cared, and only about twenty women and a few men—mostly the women's partners—attended. Yet Sławka marks this moment with pride. Later, every single one of those precious few did something memorable to build the women's movement that followed.

In 1988 Sławka organized the second feminist conference, "The Place of Women in the World of Patriarchal Culture." Here was a bold step beyond the question mark. Or rather the question was now peremptory: "What about women?" The world was organized by men, for men. Is there a place organized by women, where women are heard? Are women absent from the whole history of culture?

Then, in 1989, everything changed.

The government had agreed to a peaceful transition of power, which was to be negotiated in a series of Round Tables, including both government officials and leaders of Solidarity. (As we later learned from Shana Penn, even though women had been absolutely key to the survival of Solidarity during the underground years, 1981–1989, only one woman was included in the Round Tables.)

Astonishing changes were being discussed, and Sławka was tired of organizing conferences only a few would dream of attending. Sławka and her friends wanted a more public manifestation of their worries. They decided to write to Parliament to protest a draft law that would ban abortion, something women had had a right to, free and on demand, since 1956. Here was the power of the Church, which was to become so central in all that followed, demanding a reward for its passionate anti-communism through all the years of repression. Women were an easy sacrifice to lay on the altar, an unorganized and powerless constituency, useful symbols of a return to a traditional pre-communist "normal." The irony of repressing women at the moment of general liberation was lost on nearly everybody beyond a small cluster of feminists.

Sławka and her friends wrote in their letter that the proposed abortion ban was unjust; women are individuals who have the existential right to decide about pregnancy; they are not mere means to an end. Now, how to give this letter some weight? Interesting new idea: Collect signatures! For two or three weeks, they solicited the town on the main square and at the university, and—

against the grain of self-protective habits under communism as this procedure was—several thousand courageously signed. After some days, a small group of Catholic students called in a priest who showed up at the main building of the university and asked at the petition table, "Who sent you?" (Unthinkable that these young people had thought of this blasphemy by themselves.) "Do you understand the meaning of what you are doing? Do you want people to kill each other in the streets without being punished?" In conclusion, he told them, "You will go to Hell for this." Sławka has vivid memories of this new kind of public exchange. She was ecstatic; here was freedom. She recalls how her group answered: "Nobody sent us. This is important, and we know what we are doing. As for Hell, let God decide about that, not you." (As Sławka is telling me this story, she teases me, a God-kicker, that the Goddess had given them different information about Hell.)

This letter with all its signatures went to Parliament. No reaction, of course. The first law enacted by the first free Parliament took away a basic freedom from half the Polish population. But in Krakow, thousands had seen the protesters and talked to them. A public political life had begun.

After the dramatic break of 1989, feminists resumed their annual conferences. In 1990 the title was "Motherhood: A Choice or a Duty?" Magda Środa, much later to head the government's Plenipotentiary for Equal Treatment, remembers the meeting as her first contact with feminists. This time, eighty people came. The feminist movement was becoming visible.

The first moment such a thing became legally possible, Sławka and cofounder, Barbara Kaszkur, registered an organization, eFKa (as a private joke, the same sound as the nickname for Eve, but officially the abbreviation for *Fundacja Kobieca*, Women's Foundation), which has been a force in feminist activism in Krakow ever since. It was March 1991.

This was Sławka, whom I met in that very same month of March for the first time, without any idea of her heroic history. We all decided to have lunch together right there on the glorious square, at the first ethnic restaurant in Krakow —Chinese, indicated by something that was also entirely new, a commercial sign, a red lantern. The food that came was odd. I asked if I could have rice. "With this you expect rice?" the waiter asked, with a touch of anxiety. Chinese food usually comes with rice, but not here, yet, in this changing place, an East Central Europe with which I was already in love.

WARSAW

Leaving Krakow, I went to Warsaw to see Małgorzata Fuszara, still engaged with writing the new constitution and still confronting version after version of the draft law abolishing abortion. At this point, some provisions were frightening, including jail terms for both women and doctors. We discussed whether these extreme proposals were in earnest, or were they just shock tactics to make women feel relieved and willing to accept the slightly milder legislation that, indeed, was finally passed?

This was my first experience of what was to become a common form of political manipulation. First the Church threatens draconian new rules; terror reigns; then the bishops take one step back from the worst; everyone breathes a sigh of relief; the worst has not happened.

In the middle of this ferment, the conference snowball continued to roll: Małgorzata introduced me to feminist scholars and activists at Warsaw University, among them the distinguished feminist researchers and professors Anna Titkow and Renata Siemieńska. They, too, agreed to come.

I had met as many feminist activists as I could find, had provided them with dollars to turn into train and plane tickets, and had just begun to grasp the scale of change—the shock, confusion, and hope—of those living in the countries I had visited. I went home to New York. Our small working group had just two months to put together the conference, "What Next?"

We wrote everyone on our growing invitee list an urgent question: What do you want to talk about? Only Sławka answered. An agenda controlled by participants? Interesting. But in some countries the postage to respond would have cost half a week's salary. Okay. We finally got it. No one yet had a clue about what we might do together. We created a loose, lattice-like meeting structure to be revised once we got there. Then we began to fill suitcases with feminist books—alas, all in English, the only *lingua franca* we had. I packed a kitchen timer to set limits on each speaker, which was later to offend everyone and get us stopped at every border because it looked like the control mechanism for a bomb.

6

THE MEETING:
DUBROVNIK,
JUNE 7–9, 1991

In the midst of our feverish last-minute planning for what became the found-ing meeting of the Network of East-West Women, the US State Department placed a travel advisory on Yugoslavia. I called, and they advised us to call off the meeting. A war was scheduled for late June. We had worked a year to bring this group of Eastern and Central European feminists together. Were we now to postpone focusing on women's interests in deference to what always gets named as more urgent—nationalist cries of crisis and cynically manipulated threat? Who gets to make history?

Wise or not, we refused to cancel. Participants feared, or refused to fear, according to their temperaments and histories; but finally everyone came—more than fifty women from the East, twenty from the West. They all refused the usual command to women in times of war fever: Step back; wait. We were horrified by the impending disaster but also half-disbelieving that a war could be scheduled in this way, as if by rational design. We never could have imagined the extent of the hysteria and political violence that was about to come. Instead, our meeting posed a general question with which we were to constantly wrestle in the years ahead: What is included in the concept "the political"? Feminism had made broad revisions to what politics should rightly include—the realms usually called "private," such as sexuality and the very structures of daily social life.

It was clear to all those attending the meeting that every piece of received political rhetoric was about to be tossed in the air, a crazy confetti to land who knew where. All of the women at the meeting were renegades in one way or another; all were rebels who had bitten the hand that had fed them before the fall of communism and were not going to line up with uncritical enthusiasm for a new world order either. They were students, teachers, writers, and journalists—all cultural workers of various sorts. From many standpoints, they were skeptics. In being self-proclaimed feminists, they were idealists, yes, but ironic idealists.

TOGETHER IN DUBROVNIK

IN ONE OF THOSE little collisions of history, we chose Dubrovnik ("gem of the Adriatic," travel agents say)—then in Yugoslavia, now in Croatia—as our meeting place. Some of the women participating had never been out of their own countries before, and Slavenka Drakulić urged that the pleasures of this beautiful place should be part of what we organizers were offering to women weary to the bone.

I liked her attitude. After my first trip, I was beginning to understand the complex dynamics of resistance to feminism in the region. Rest and meals cooked by someone else in the nice Hotel Lero might be as useful to such overworked and politically beleaguered women as hours of strategic conversation. Let there be pleasure—or at least a moment to breathe; let the conference proceed: As You Like It, or What You Will. (Over the years, we tried to hold on to this faith in let-it-be organizing. We shared skepticism about endpoints, which, except in our language on foundation grant applications, we always defined as unknowable.)

Since being in the wrong place at the wrong time always has tragic possibilities beyond any calculation, we were lucky: The war that dismantled Yugoslavia started two weeks after we left the city. We were the last meeting in the grand, stone International University Center before the Serbian army bombed it a few months later. (A fundraising letter came to New York, enclosing charred pages from the Center's library.)

But in early June, Dubrovnik was entirely there and ours— ancient, rich, and golden. At the height of tourist season, it was completely empty. We wandered; we bought extraordinary things from desperate Muslim shopkeepers, who, after the war, were "cleansed" from Croatia, never to be seen in Dubrovnik again; we talked about the looming changes in women's prospects. Only a few of us fully understood that for Yugoslavia this was an ending.

When I look back now on that first gathering, I am in awe of what we managed to put together, in the held breath before a dreadful war, and right at the beginning of a new era. Because we Americans were outsiders, our colleagues (somewhat) forgave us for the social ignorance of inviting women with such different histories, national cultures, and political experiences. Our lack of regional angst and our open-to-all policy, at times irritating to Eastern Europeans, enabled some revealing combinations. People met who were not otherwise destined to meet. The very young encountered politically savvy feminist veterans. Here were the East German women, lesbians in leather with metal spikes in their ears, elegant and stern as they surveyed the polyglot scene. They were drinking coffee in the courtyard right next to the women from Czechoslovakia in summer dresses with lace collars.

In a plenary session, Sonja Licht got up to say she had just come from Poland, where she had heard the Pope announce that abortion was another Holocaust. I heard one of the Czech women respond under her breath, "That Serb." I was jolted by her vicious aside, her tone of disgust, but why be so surprised? Certainly racism was right there with us in the mix, and, for brief but startling moments, the new nationalisms of now former Yugoslavia blew like a strange wind through our meeting. People stood to introduce themselves, first saying, "From Yugoslavia," then in embarrassment or anger or confusion correcting themselves: "I mean, from Croatia"—or Serbia or Slovenia.

We American organizers wondered how these often-sophisticated internationalists could be party to such reductive new identities, but we were soon to see how powerful and inescapable such ethnic sorting was becoming. Intellectual resistance made little difference; the real breakdown in communication among the Yugoslav women at the Network's founding lay just ahead and was of another order of magnitude. Ambitious nationalist leaders orchestrated the rifts in Yugoslavia. The phone lines were down; the train tracks cut. Although there was irony in trying to start an international communication network among women at such a time, the arrival of the war made it seem even more necessary. (Several Yugoslav women were to route messages to friends suddenly in another country through us in New York.)

In planning the conference, we US organizers had used a reductive sorting device of our own, the elastic and resonant identifier "feminist." At this point of intensifying division, as not only Yugoslavia but the whole region was flying apart, each country seeking some lost essence of its pre-Soviet past, the idea of an international "women's movement" was a countercurrent. Our gathering represented resistance to the prevailing ideological flow. We sought relationships built through the possibility of shared ideas, not defined by borders. During the war that was ultimately to divide Yugoslavia into seven countries, women's movements were to become one of the few political locations where the new militarism was named, analyzed in developing detail, and visibly rejected.

Looked at now, perhaps these images of us talking, drinking coffee, sucking up the sunlight in the courtyard lose their force; perhaps they figure us as fiddlers while the waiting fire was so near, consuming all relationships. We were definitely dreamers; even the most practical feminist activism includes desires that seem impossible in current conditions. We had the *wish* to talk to each other, what bell hooks calls the "integrity of intent." However hard a shared politics might prove to be, seventy skeptical, often burned out, often overwhelmed activists—some of whom had had to travel for several days—converged on the first morning.

AN AGENDA

Back in New York, we Americans had been very clear that we didn't want—or know how—to choose the meeting's themes. So we planned to begin by breaking into small, mixed East-West groups as an informal way for people to discover one another's interests and begin to know one another. A "facilitator" (dreadful euphemistic word, but US feminists were still allergic to saying "leader") explained the ideas behind this exercise, borrowed from the US movement practice, consciousness-raising. Each person in the group was to address the question: "How did your personal experiences bring you to an involvement in women's problems?"

In my particular group, both this structure and this sort of question were greeted with horror. "Why would we want to discuss our private histories with strangers?" Several simply refused to speak. Others talked about their activist or professional lives in order to push away these rude Americans with their voyeurism, their too-easy and innocent openness. So much for "the personal is political." What layers of safety and trust that US movement saying reflects! Here, on the other side of the looking glass, people who chose to expose intimate life to public scrutiny were fools.

The pernicious side of private life in the family—say, domestic violence, or just the daily, common repressions of individual will—were not themes for political discussion here, not even among these feminists, marginal and critical as they were within their own cultures. Whatever its limitations, the family had been, and remained, the key means of survival.

So the opening small group I attended could be called an embarrassing failure. But we certainly heard each other, and we organizers from the US were confirmed in our initial belief that we were not here to give shape to events. I was relieved that the atmosphere was contentious. No passive, quiet resistance here. Building something useful out of our baggy, underdetermined planning in New York became the much-debated work of the entire group.

SLAVENKA

Slavenka Drakulić opened the first plenary:

> We are meeting here a year and a half after the crucial changes in Eastern Europe . . . time enough to recognize the tendencies and changes especially in regard to women. What happened to them?

She laid out the bloody facts: Now that there were no more communist-style quotas and elections were free, the new parliaments included only a few women; the regional economies where women were formerly clustered were collapsing; the newly free states were trying to restrict abortion because they wanted more children for the nation and a safely conservative return to an older form of authority, the Church.

Boldly, Slavenka brought a then socially unacceptable critique of the new, enchanted talk about "freedom."

> As we all know, freedom has to be taken; it's not given by anyone, even by the new democratic governments. Women will, most probably, have to learn their lessons the hard way, through disappointment, unemployment, poverty, losses, and fears. If they don't make themselves into a political subject, and the agent of political change, they simply won't exist as women per se, and their particular problems will be neglected and ignored.

It was a wonderful speech—full of clarion warnings and rousing abjurations—and rereading it now, all these years later, I can hear the passion, the unrelentingly critical analysis, and the good sense that lay behind the founding of the Network of East-West Women.

> She went on:
> What exactly is characterizing our position after the so-called revolution in Eastern Europe?

That "so-called" before "revolution" was like a trumpet blast. It gave us all permission—East and West—to criticize what was happening. No one was going to call us communists here if we asked for social services or complained about the forms that some of the new "freedoms" were taking.

In another blast, acknowledging everyone's desire for new, unique identities and escape from the crushing gray of compulsory Communist Era groups, Slavenka nonetheless insisted on the need for a collective identity among Eastern European women who were actually having very similar experiences of loss wherever they were. Describing her trips around the region reporting for *Ms.*, she noted how little information women had either about their shared situation or about feminism in Western or Third World countries: "While feminists in South America and India were connecting with each other, we didn't connect." This was a call for a cosmopolitan feminism. The Network was forming to correct a double blackout: first, a lack of information in the West about what was happening to women in the East and, second, Eastern European women's ignorance of each other.

Slavenka goes on:

> Ann was very worried [and insisted] I had to mention [her fears] about imperialism. You know how Americans are very sensitive: 'Are we going to be imperialistic, because we are going to give you money?' [The group laughs.]
>
> Not necessarily. Are men not helping each other? Men *are* helping each other!—in a different name: They call it 'politics.' [More laughter].

My welcoming talk followed. I described the explosion of feminist consciousness in the US and the backlash against it. Now this backlash was deforming US women's movements, putting them on the defensive. I wish I had added that we wanted company in these difficult years of reaction, that we wanted to exchange ideas about how to build women's movements in aggressively unfriendly circumstances; but that important formulation of parallel experiences came later.

The word that went round among the Eastern European women at the conference was this "backlash." As one organizer said, "We have backlash before we even have a movement." Certainly, something unusual was happening. Perhaps because women had been so strong under communism, patriarchs seemed to be making a vicious preemptive strike against any aspirations these powerful women might be entertaining in the new order.

The news everywhere was full of prescriptions, open insults, and coaxing invitations to women to be feminine again, to step back and let men take charge at last.

Organizers were going to have a problem: Communists had claimed to "emancipate" women, so now any echo of that political project—in many ways still so unrealized—was tainted by the hypocrisies and failures of the past. People didn't even want to hear the word *politics*. I told the meeting that Slavenka had warned me beforehand: "Don't use the word *organize*; it depresses people." Everyone laughed at this recognition. Here we were, political people, facing a reactive, anti-communist taboo on politics, on organizing, on any idea of women's group solidarity. Too many ideologies had been enforced here from outside. Although feminism was in fact indigenous, it was being greeted everywhere as a rude intrusion, a pernicious orthodoxy from without. How were we to interrupt this alienation from basic questions of equality and justice?

What followed was an extraordinary three days. Sonia Jaffe Robbins, one of the key organizers of the meeting on the American end, includes in her excellent notes that I ended the opening session with an announcement that we had brought books—and, also, condoms—because we had heard of the lack of access to feminist writing and decent birth control. A voice from the back of the room called out, "Our men don't want to use condoms. Bring us diaphragms."

WHAT HAPPENED?

What happened at the conference? The organizers are often the last to know. They run around like maniacs, dealing with complaints and reimbursing travel costs. And maybe no one should seek a summing up. Endless acts of evaluation are, I think, greatly overrated. The meaning of complex events for each one there and for the collective future of those assembled is important but not reliably retrievable. Sometimes, years later, one notices what looks like a convincing link, the mark of past work on present capabilities. Like most activists, I require faith in such chains of cause and effect to keep going, but without big expectations. The variables proliferate, and the past gets ground up as part of new mixtures, making continuity hard to claim—or even to recognize. What happens later changes the weight of past events. Since so much has happened during the Network's surprisingly long survival, people who were there at the start can now claim a heroic, pioneer status no one dreamed of at the time. Memory feeds the present, but it's a rogue, a stealthy self-serving rewriter of what we knew and felt back then.

Trying to trick the rogue, I've been going around asking various people what first comes to mind when they recall the meeting. "Don't mull, just give me your first thought." Indira Kajosevic from Bosnia was in her early twenties then, and she comes out with, "My first lesbians." She explains that until the meeting, which thrilled her and turned her into a feminist on the spot and forever, she had barely known such women existed. They were myths of ancient Greece. But here they were. And what is more, when a Romanian announced that her country needed to deal with its perverts, Indira was much instructed by hearing the whole group hiss. Aha. Calling gays and lesbians "perverts" fell into Sławka's category of the "not okay."

Sonja Licht, on the phone from Belgrade, surprises me with her first off-the-top memory. She thinks of Slavenka and re- members hearing her at a conference in East Berlin in 1990, announcing our idea of having a specifically feminist meeting. The politically engaged women there were clueless, she recalls, without any associations at all with this topic. My dear Sonja, that great political head, tries to place this memory, to understand how our meeting could have gotten so much beyond this blank point. "Slavenka's question itself must have started a process. Ideas were moving fast then." By the spring of 1991 a question—feminism?—had crystallized in many imaginations from that small beginning.

Joanna Regulska remembers no one thing, only a prevailing tone: enthusiasm, hope, excitement. At the other end of the scale from the general to the specific, Sonia Jaffe Robbins, from New York and on her first trip to Europe, remembers her shock at the toilet paper. "I had always wondered about those stories of dissidents in prison writing plays or manifestos on toilet paper. Now I understood how that might be possible."

Nanette Funk, also of New York, remembers that she introduced, with great success, the idea of a rotating chair in her workshop on economics. Nanette had been traveling in both West and East Germany for many years by the time of the meeting, and has a moving memory of talking to her friends from East Germany in the courtyard. Their trip to Dubrovnik on a ferry had been their first free travel. They told her they had been ecstatic, free at last, the wind in their hair.

Sławka remembers comparing notes with another thoughtful and skillful early feminist organizer from Poland, Barbara Limanowska. They were shocked that Joanna Regulska, formerly of Poland but for decades located in the US, had the nerve to be directive while leading a plenary. "She told us how the meeting should go. This was absolutely not allowed at any women's meeting in Poland. Wow, at last—this was effective organizing!" Barbara also remembers smoking at lunch. Distressed Americans said, "But people are still eating!" The Eastern Europeans laughed at being reprimanded. Now, as they tell me this story, not one of them still smokes, and Barbara says, laughing, "Oh, that insidious American influence."

Finally, Małgorzata Tarasiewicz—Gosia to her friends, among whom I have counted myself for twenty-five years—tells me she attended a workshop for Eastern European women only. (There was a workshop for Easties only?) Slavenka addressed the group: "It's nice that the Americans have done this, but really, we should be doing this organizing by ourselves." The simple truth of this observation colors all that follows, but cannot erase any of this hybrid story.

Such is my brief research project about memory, the meeting's residue.

A large group was unhappy that the loose agenda we had cooked up in New York didn't include anything about the disappearance of women from all the region's parliaments. (No doubt as we wrote our draft agenda, we Americans had been insufficiently surprised at this, given the miserable US record.) The first free elections had had astonishing results: In Romania, the number of women in Parliament went from 34.3% to 3.5%; in Czechoslovakia, from 29.5% to 6%; in Hungary, 20.9% to 7%; in Bulgaria 21% to 8.5%. (The high number in these pairs, it must be remembered, were all quotas for women under communism; those many women had served in powerless, rubber-stamp parliaments.)

Did this dramatic change show that, left free to choose, women wanted no part in politics, and men were delighted to see them depart? Was it that politics is dirty, and men like that and can take it? Or was there a deeper psychological reaction here? Had communism further distilled traditional distrust of women when it granted them low-level public powers? A swarm of women apparatchiks had ordered everyone around, often in a

belligerent style far from feminine. Stalin had given women special, if in some ways fictive, status: milk for mother. And because
communism hadn't interrupted traditional divisions of labor at
home, women had maintained their usual power in the family
while men outside the party had power nowhere. Here perhaps
was a reaction, a gleeful stripping away of female authority.

The meeting agenda was reorganized to include a workshop
about women in state politics, which became the largest and
most intense of all the thematic sessions. Only later did I come
to recognize a silent group, an outer ring during this discussion, and begin to see who these outliers were—the radicals,
the anarchists, and the new liberals. They wanted no part in the
state, but for very divergent reasons. The idea of "the political"
was being fundamentally contested, and I recognize now that a
basic conundrum of post-communism was being enacted in that
seminar room.

The new liberals wanted the new governments to leave them
alone. Later, plazas and squares were renamed for Ronald Reagan—a hero to some of the women present. Freedom was an
escape from the stranglehold of the nanny state. These critics of
government wanted an unregulated entry into the world's marketplace. This was what the new "freedom" was going to mean.

Others, the majority in that radical company, were angry at
the state precisely because it was eagerly withdrawing from any
pretense of being a provider, becoming neoliberal and uncaring.
These women didn't want totalitarian government back but were
deeply disappointed by its various replacements. The anarchists
in the room carried this disdain for governments further. Po-
sitioning themselves as critics of the "Women in Parliament"
meeting, they scorned those who thought they could do anything
inside the state. Being included was never their objective. "Feminist politics" was by definition outsider politics, a continuous

critique and resistance. To them, the insider position meant unacceptable compromises.

But some of the radicals of what might be called the Left—though left/right distinctions were soon to collapse—were uncertain about what should become the right locations and aesthetics for activism; they saw all *refusnik* disengagement from national politics as dangerous. A new poverty was coming, and while they felt helpless to reverse this sweeping change—the creation of a steep class system overnight—they also felt the need to engage with official politics, to fight, inch by inch, for laws and public policies that would protect people from the downsides of the new order. They were recognizing with alarm that the new poverty was what the new politics was all about, a frightening reprise of the old communist willingness to be harshly instrumental.

Also standing in the margins of these hot discussions about how women should or should not participate in state politics, a few former dissidents presented a complex case. They had never expected any public power at all and had lived instead in a moral but static state of refusal—in and out of prison or exile. They had assumed life as outsiders was their unavoidable fate. What would these former dissident women among us do now, when their male colleagues were proceeding from jail to state power? Surely the purity of Václav Havel's "living in truth" would look quite different once he was the leader of Czechoslovakia ruling from inside the royal castle on the hill in Prague.

At one point, a frequent traveler to the US, I believe it was Slavenka, introduced a rival account of action altogether: independent organizations without any official standing, open to the like-minded but requiring unpaid commitment. This had been the organizational style of the early US Women's Movement, which had of course been fed by the fat of US society in the 1970s. No one picked up on this idea of an unaffiliated civil society as a possible path to influence, even power. Such a structure for public action was totally absent from these women's experience. Free time to meet, to develop new ideas, and to organize was unknown.

The common structures to come later were nongovernmental organizations (NGOs), with their need to trim to foundations' vacillating interests, their staffs paid and accountable to no one but foundation budget reviews. Some NGOs were able to mimic aspects of independent movements (I think our eventual Network was sometimes one of these types of NGOs), and they made some key contributions to political culture. Others tried to offer what governments were increasingly failing to provide—services and protections. These latter enterprises were financially unsustainable, making false promises that private entities could substitute for what governments should be doing—and suddenly were not. Whatever NGOs were eventually able to do or not do, in 1991 in Dubrovnik, they were still unfamiliar.

Loretta Ross, the only African American at the conference, famous for her work developing rape crisis centers and long experienced in many movements, from Civil Rights onward, made a concluding remark at the "politics" session: "I perceive tensions around stereotypes of socialism and capitalism. This topic does not get picked up on; in fact, it seems to be suppressed for the sake of the unity of the conference." Aha. No one responded to this bold observation of how different these women were from each other in their past political affiliations and future hopes. Loretta's words cast a stark light on how undeveloped and confusing was the post-communist political imaginary. Skepticism about prevailing ideas of what communism had been and what capitalism was promising wasn't a tone available for this discussion. Loretta heard caricatures of these two worlds, and a failure to name possible, needed continuities. I hear this now as prophetic.

Sławka was wandering around the edges of these discussions, unwilling to discuss the attractions of either socialism or capitalism and entirely uninterested in talking about the disappearance of women from parliaments. Who cared, unless a government could turn into a witch's coven of concentrated female power?

Given their history of relative success for women under communism, the East Germans were the ones with the most formed and unapologetic left position; one of them complained to me, "Where did you get all these conservative women?" Sigh. Like Sławka, I drifted around the courtyard a bit, feeling disconsolate. At that moment, during the first day, I remember being awash with doubt; the whole meeting seemed to be a hopeless shambles, a Tower of Babel; or, to change metaphors, how officious to bring all these apples, oranges, and pears together as if they could share a politics at any level. Why should they? I was no believer in a bland "sisterhood." But I had hoped to join an incipient political movement. The idea of a network had been dreamed up on the US side by feminists of the American New Left, whose political sensibilities had taken form in the 1960s. But now, like the women we were meeting, we were living through a fundamental post-communist realignment of all political meanings; we had to rethink "the political" too, in this enormous, global reshuffling.

Beyond questions of capitalist, neoliberal, liberal, moral *refusnik*, social democrat, leftist, or anarchist, the desire for as yet barely imagined freedoms in the wild wind of post-communism was scattering these formerly clandestine resisters. They had yet to imagine a politics beyond refusal, though some were beginning to see the anti-political force that neoliberalism might become. In the best case, our shared state of post–Cold War confusion might bring us together in some mutual recognition—of hope, of worry—prompting some shared analyses of the various difficulties we were all to face. In the worst case, it was all chaos and old night, shared incomprehension and failure of partnership.

I drank coffee; I confessed my acedia to my old friend in the US movement, Ellen Willis, who sighed with me. We'd been working at this for many years. In the middle of all these complex collisions, I needed to turn my chagrin into something else in order to face the next day. I calmed down. I laughed. After day one, I entered a Zen state that lasted until the end of the conference.

ABSENT FRIENDS

For most of days two and three, we seventy people separated into workshops. To my surprise, no one wanted to attend "Women and Health," even though Loretta Ross made the case for the urgency of this subject. But it was too soon. The imminent collapse of often inadequate public health services was not yet obvious—not yet the anxious topic it was to become. AIDS was barely on the horizon here, and the well-attended "Women and Sexuality" session was all about the absurdity of the sex education on offer throughout the region and about the sudden flood of pornography everywhere: new art form or primal insult? The health session seems to have gotten renamed "Women and the Family."

Again to my surprise, no one at all went to the room for "Women and Work." As I sift through notes, I see that perhaps *work* was too broad or vague a term. Only the Poles had positive experiences of the concept "independent trade union," and it was unclear what work women were going to do now, when the public sector where they were often employed was shrinking, and daycare centers were being closed overnight. For some, "work" was becoming unemployment. I wondered if feminists from the region, however radical, were members of elites not immediately threatened by the closing down of factories and public services. Maybe, but the mystery remained: Why was "work" an inert category to this group? Perhaps because the new insecurity of life on every front was the far more urgent topic, a more encompassing theme that echoed through the whole meeting. As Rossica Panova from Bulgaria put it:

> It was very easy to be protected by the system. A small salary without freedom with a small security; but there was something, and now there is not. There is no security; there is no protection; there is no salary at all.... We are absolutely lost. We have nothing to eat, no electricity. Nothing functions in Bulgaria.

In this new situation, conservatives were glorifying the family as the answer, and indeed, in contrast to the new, mean world of competition and poverty, the family did look warm and humane. The large "Women and the Family" session galloped in all directions, and *family* rather than *work* seemed to be a key word, one that feminists were going to have to confront, define, and redefine.

In these days, there were high points and low, but at moments the value of bringing people together from their often-isolated locations was obvious—for example, when Agnes Hochberg reported that, in 1990, she and other Hungarian feminists had demonstrated in front of the Polish embassy in Budapest in support of Polish women's right to abortion. They had hoped Polish women would hear about them, would know that, while they were all still floating in their separate worlds, some had tried to connect. A Polish woman in the group yelled loudly, "We only found out at this moment."

So, enough. The meeting was "this moment," part frozen in past time, part perhaps now still in motion. As of this writing, three of us at the conference have died: Agnes Hochberg (from a completely unexpected aneurism in her twenties), Rossica Panova (years later, after a long and painful struggle to live well with multiple sclerosis), and Ellen Willis (from lung cancer at sixty-four). Since they, who were so vivid in life, can no longer speak for themselves, let me end by registering what they said and did at our meeting.

Ellen, in the US the great theorist and activist of women's liberation, led a last-minute add-on discussion one evening about American feminism. Understandably, most women from the region grabbed that free night to explore Dubrovnik, but the ten or twelve who stayed to hear our American stories got to hear Ellen's love song to freedom, to ecstatic sex, and to the twenty years we'd just spent being part of astounding social change.

Rossica had asked us to fund her husband to come, because she was too weak to take public transportation. He drove her and their six-year-old son from Sofia. Already an advocate for the rights of women and the disabled, Rossi gave a talk one can read in that early, pioneer collection *Ana's Land: Sisterhood in Eastern Europe*, edited by Tanya Renne.

> In my paper I am going to present to you a personal case which however mirrors the whole system. . . . It is no secret that in order to determine how humane a system is we can judge from its attitude to the sick, the old and the children. I myself belong to the first of the above-mentioned groups. . . . Our society is still backward, retarded and uncivilized. It is run by "the law of the jungle." We take part in a game without any rules, a game in which the individual doesn't mean anything, since . . . our society consists of masses, not of individuals.

When Rossi died, the whole network mourned. She had been extraordinary, had managed to passionately and mindfully live out wifehood, motherhood, scholarship, and activism under an encroaching shroud. She lived just long enough to see some of the new forms of "the law of the jungle" that emerged in post-communism. No health care system in Bulgaria could help her in the nineties, and the Network raised money for her medicine in New York.

Finally, I have before me the handwritten talks Agnes Hochberg prepared for the meeting, also reprinted in *Ana's Land*. The only Hungarian to show up after we invited many, Agnes had been one of twenty-five founders of the Feminist Network in June 1990 in Budapest, exactly a year before coming to Dubrovnik. Every word she wrote breathes out her typical mixture of radical outrage and hardheaded pragmatism. She was always racing ahead. She never took for granted any of the ideas we Westies were offering. But, in her later visits to New York, she was always fascinated by US feminisms. She saw a strong movement against pornography in the US and a big push back against this position among the US feminists she knew. What was our problem? Shouldn't the Hungarians get on board and start anti-pornography protests too, now that one could suddenly buy Western pornography on any street corner in Budapest? Some of us Americans in the Network had a long history with this question. We laid out a map of a central disagreement in our movement; we described the positions of the sides in the US feminist sex wars of the 1980s.

Did we try to shove Agnes toward our side? I hope not, but no doubt yes, given the heat of this so-recent debate in our lives. I do remember saying something to the effect that, because of the tight restrictions on speech under communism, it was probably a strategic mistake to start a new movement with a wish to control any kind of speech whatsoever. To suggest even a whiff of legal censorship in response to the new flood of every kind of print and image would surely be the death of any claim that feminism was about liberation. Some Russian visitors to New York had suggested to us that the new unclothing of the female body, visible on every newsstand, was a metaphor for a much-desired transparency in the state. We Westies were skeptical; why not undress men? But we took in the larger point: Don't close down on any newly circulating material. Don't presume to know what new images and new words may mean. As always, Agnes listened, criticized, listened again. The exchange was volatile, exciting to both sides. "Okay, okay, maybe we shouldn't *start* with an anti-pornography campaign. Lots of other things should probably come first." Race, for example. She was shocked by US racism, was critical of racism in the US Women's Movement, and was the first regional feminist I knew to insist that anti-racism should become an important part of what feminism should mean in East Central Europe. In all this, one always felt her sense of urgency, her organizer's passion: *What world do we want?*

In the final plenary, a Pole with long experience in the US movement, the very one Sławka and Barbara Limanowska had so admired, was being very stern and directive as she tried to herd these cats toward some conclusion. Agnes rebelled; she yelled from the floor, "Why are you up there with the microphone? We didn't choose you to be our leader." I remember being both worried and delighted at Agnes's outburst. Here it was, the obstreperous feminism I knew and often loved—angry, prickly about maintaining fair process, and questioning all authority. Hungry for equality, Agnes had the nerve to be incautious, to denounce the rigidities in which everyone in the East had lived. She was breaking with old repressions and anxieties. For me, Agnes was the hero of the messy ending of our meeting.

Vale, dear, brilliant shades.

GOSIA

At the end of our last day, with an uncharacteristic sedateness, we ate a big dinner at a fancy restaurant on the water: wine, white tablecloths, four courses. We had budgeted for this surprise. But the final session—including Agnes's angry defiance of the chair and our over-the-top ambition to decide what-should-we-do-now—had ended in chaos. No clear plan for staying connected had emerged. Although we agreed we should write a press release, that last screaming plenary hadn't come near to producing words we might say, together, to a fracturing world. At this portentous historical moment, who would listen, anyway?

As the participants streamed by me through the hotel lobby on their way to the touted dinner by the sea, I sat on a couch in reception, a blank pad in my hand, with the worried look for which I am well known, the complement to my other familiar theatrical mask, a warm come-hither smile.

No one stopped. Why should they? We had just lived through an intense and often unsettling three days. Summing it up was not going to be a picnic. And, besides, only naïve optimists would think that more was to come.

Then Gosia flopped down on the couch beside me. But back then, as usual, I barely knew who this was. It was to take us Americans years more of talking, visiting, and being visited to begin to get a full picture of the past, of the difficult struggles of some of these activists.

Gosia was born in 1960 in Sopot, which before World War II was a charming watering hole on the Baltic Sea, part of the protected free city of Gdansk, where Germans, Poles, and Jews went swimming together in the long summer days of the North. Just up the road was the great shipyard where, when Gosia was in her late teens, the trade union movement Solidarity had its origins in a series of colossal and unexpected strikes against the communist state. In an amazing leap of desire, the workers were demanding not only bread but also roses, in the form of worker autonomy. (An LGBTQ choir was later to sing "Bread and Roses" for me in Polish, this song US feminists had loved since the seventies.) Resistance, dreams, and politics must have been in the very air Gosia was breathing in her hometown.

The spiraling collapse of communist regimes all over East Central Europe started right there in the early 1970s. In one of the greatest examples of successful popular resistance in the twentieth century, Solidarity, that rare and short-lived collaboration between workers and a dissident intelligentsia, finally triumphed in 1989, at which point Gosia had already been a political activist for half a decade.

Reviewing her political history, I can feel the depth of her desire to change things, and can begin to register, too, the constant hand pushed in her face, the aggressive resistance to her every move to join in the extraordinary public events of her time. She began as a student by becoming a member of the Independent Students' Association and participated in an occupation of the university: "It was a thrilling time when one could learn a lot about politics and activism." But this passionate political person, both idealist and activist, had no chance to become more than a drone in the Association: "It was not so easy to be a woman in that movement." Note well: Feminist sensibility blooms in revolutionary times when everything is moving, and feminism emerges when women are told by men not to move.

Next, she wanted to join Solidarity, which, in the early eighties, repressed under a strictly enforced martial law, remained the great hope for fundamental change. But once again, everyone rushed to inform her that this was not for her. "Solidarity is not really open and not very democratic," friends told her. "As a young woman, my job would be to make sandwiches and give out leaflets, without any possibility to get involved in decisions." I need hardly point out the obvious here, but I can't resist: The amount of waste—of passion, energy, commitment, intelligence, and endurance—that sexism causes in all political struggle is criminal and insane. But Gosia doesn't take this angry American tone at all; she tells these tales of utter misrecognition with ironic, sometimes comic detachment. After all, she plans to keep going and must preserve herself to face the relentless, continuing opposition ahead. This irony has become a precious shared possession, and our long, far-flung work together has traveled on the rails of our constant joking. We immerse ourselves in comic joy at the absurd extremes of sexism.

Friends sympathetic to her frustration about Solidarity advised her to try working with the independent, underground group Freedom and Peace, which was allied with an international democracy movement, Neither East nor West. Later I was to read this group's remarkable newspaper, *On Gogol Boulevard*, published in English to reach an international audience. Here was the ethos of the 1960s that I had sought in vain on my first arrival, in 1991: articles against all failures of democracy, East *and* West; against nationalism, racism, armies, and wars; against nuclear power; against every sort of inequality. These were young radicals joined in a sprawling, anti-patriarchal, nonhierarchical free association.

In 1986, at the founding of Freedom and Peace, feminist values were already in the mix. (The Canadian writer Myrna Kostash, the very one who later sent us Sonja Licht and Milan Nikolic, had a clandestine meeting with a bunch of these excited, radical young people in a church, where she told them about the Women's Movement. She was Gosia's first Western feminist.) In the Gdansk chapter, women and men acted with mutual respect—a performance of Utopia Gosia never forgets. Prefigurative worlds like Freedom and Peace linger in the lives they touch. Here, at last, she had found a political home.

Gosia's chapter, in Gdansk, "was completely anarchist and wild." Also effective: In one action, they actually stopped plans for a nuclear power plant by organizing an overwhelmingly successful referendum. In another, they organized a hunger strike in support of the many without passports, The Club of Those Imprisoned by Borders. In their hungry mouths, the individual right to a passport was not only a call for private freedom; a passport was the gateway to internationalism and big cosmopolitan dreams.

Solidarity disapproved; they wanted a new Polish nationalism to triumph, and armies and nuclear power stations were good ideas for a new, free Poland—so rare in the country's long-dominated history, so longed for—once communism was defeated.

And communism in East Central Europe *was* defeated, to the whole world's astonishment. And the Soviet Union came apart in the two years following, by 1991. In Poland, the Round Tables, where dissidents, workers, and communists converged to negotiate the new rules, seemed to be granting Freedom and Peace's every wish: They established partial democracy; they introduced alternative military service for conscientious objectors; they began the (gradual) opening up of borders. Was this not victory?

Of course, not to Gosia. The Church's rising power ended women's right to abortion at once. The only people who could be players in the new, post-communist political scene had to accept the power of the Church, the romance of a nationalist state, and "traditional values," meaning the return of the old and familiar He and She. For Gosia, the role of Freedom and Peace would have been important at that very moment of seeming triumph. She was disappointed at the collapse of her exciting counterculture, though she understood it: "People rather thought that finally they could have some rest." To me, this falling off of energy was so familiar: Women get the vote and everyone goes home. The moment of victory reveals activists' state of underlying exhaustion; collecting energy for follow-up feels impossible.

The new rights didn't come as quickly as myth now has it; she had to wait another year for a passport. But from then onward, Gosia has been a wild, free traveler—always mixing politics with the sheer delight of motion: visiting the strange fish in the mountain lake Issyk Kul, of Kyrgyzstan; visiting the piled-up temples of Thailand on a break from an international feminist meeting.

So, it was a new life. Solidarity was now legal and powerful. Once more, Gosia looked in that direction—and will miracles never cease?—she was invited to coordinate Solidarity's new women's section. But it wasn't a miracle, as Gosia quickly learned. Because Solidarity was receiving money from the International Confederation of Free Trade Unions, it was required to have a women's section. No problem. A Potemkin village, the women's section, was set up at once, in 1990. And why not hire a well-known activist with a good reputation to give the fantasy section verisimilitude? Their mistake was to think that Gosia wouldn't do anything. She dived into this new job with her usual intensity, and, bringing many women in Solidarity together, she began to make the women's section real. The women were eager, and Gosia was full of ideas: Let's discuss the coming law against abortion. Let's discuss sexual harassment at the shipyards. Let's discuss the absence of women in union leadership, even though some women were such visible heroes during the strikes and in the underground.

And that was the end of it. Over women workers' protests, Gosia was forced out after nine months. In 2013, as an Open

Society fellow, John Feffer conducted a series of extraordinary follow-up interviews with activists he had first talked to in 1990. It is his second interview with Gosia that I've been quoting all along here, and this is how she described to him her brief foray into the fast-morphing, powerful institutions of Polish politics— and the way it ended:

> Marian Krzaklewski, who became a leader of Solidarity, made it impossible for me to stay. He used all sorts of persecution, like calling me to his office to talk for hours explaining how wrong I was in my opinions or not giving any funds to the women's section. He was doing everything he could to block all options, so I had to leave. The women in the women's section who were acting in the way Solidarity leadership didn't like also had to stop working. They were not allowed into the Solidarity offices in the regions, couldn't use the fax machines or phones. They couldn't even participate in the trainings. It was said that they did not have the right moral spine.
>
> . . . We decided to meet one last time. . . . We tried to use the Solidarity headquarters in Warsaw. At first the leaders didn't want to allow us into the headquarters. But when they saw how many of us there were, they said, "Okay, come." One guy from Solidarity even tried to threaten me. He called me at home and said, "If you meet again with those women of Solidarity and try to do something, we will punish you." Of course I didn't care. It was quite dramatic. Human Rights Watch from New York wrote a report on that. Their representative came to Poland and wrote a report. But there was nothing much we could do. The women's section was abolished.

All this *sturm und drang* had happened only a few months before Gosia showed up in Dubrovnik for the conference. And it was this woman who sat down to help me put together the political pieces of our complex, uncodifiable meeting, a taking on of responsibility that I now know she had already been doing for years. We missed the hors d'oeuvres, but we wrote the statement and then read it to the diners, who voted their approval over dessert.

NEWW Conference Statement

The Network of East-West Women (NEWW), a gathering of women from independent women's movements in Eastern and Central Europe, along with a number of participants from North America, met in Dubrovnik, Yugoslavia, on June 7–9, 1991.

We consider this meeting the first step in establishing long-lasting communication and cooperation among feminist activists in these countries. We are determined that women take an active role in shaping the new profile of Eastern and Central Europe.

At the conference, we discussed our different and common situations, our perspectives and goals. The new movements in Eastern and Central Europe came together first of all to support each other, as well as to share experiences with North American feminists.

We expect to follow up this meeting with several projects: information exchanges, including newsletters, a computer network, an international telephone tree; actions in support of women's reproductive rights; and cooperation in establishing women's studies programs and cultural exchanges.

We also decided that the Network will meet annually, in different countries, to build on what we started in Dubrovnik. Through these projects and meetings, we hope to contribute to the development of an Eastern and Central European grassroots women's movement.

Approved June 9, 1991.

Countries participating: Bulgaria, Czechoslovakia, East Germany, Hungary, Poland, Rumania, Yugoslavia, U.S.

Ellen Willis had come up with our acronym, NEWW, and, in fits and starts, with steps forward and back, NEWW has done the things listed in this statement—and, to my continuing amazement, much more. Today, Gosia Tarasiewicz is the director of the Network of East-West Women, now located in Gdansk, Poland.

The meeting was over. Later I learned that many people had trouble getting home. Gosia and Barbara couldn't get a plane to Warsaw because all flights from Yugoslavia had been cancelled. Stranded in Dubrovnik, they saw men on motorcycles, loudly revving their engines and charging up and down Stradun, the beautiful, wide, marble street that runs through the center of the city. These men were gearing themselves up to fight. No doubt some of them were with those who died during the Serbian siege of Dubrovnik. Years later, when I finally went back, I saw blurry photos of them in a makeshift memorial museum. By then, in 2008, "feminism" had become "feminist theory." Dubrovnik was once again a mobbed tourist trap; because it was "the gem of the Adriatic," it had been restored to an obfuscating perfection and looked the same as in 1991. But it wasn't the same. The elegant old store windows displayed not the beautiful rugs and scarves of Muslim tradesmen but the now-ubiquitous corporate brands: the Gap, Lush Life Cosmetics. And everything cost the earth.

But in 1991 I discovered that we had paid everyone for everything and still had seven hundred dollars left. Those of us who lingered in the city tried to spend these magically potent dollars on yet another dinner. The restaurant we chose was delighted to feed the only foreigners for miles. They put a long trestle in the middle of the street and brought out tray after tray of fresh fish, delicious salads, chilled bottles of wine.

A war was coming. How could we just sit there? War is a crisis. Are women ever in crisis? Where can one locate "crisis" in the lives of women? So "we women" sat there, and I am so glad we did.

Only at this suspended moment did I finally take a breath, observe the beautiful evening light. As Slavenka Drakulić had insisted when she chose Dubrovnik, if we are to sustain our work-that-is-never-done through wars and beyond, pleasure is essential—the opposite of dissention and burnout—and rare enough. After all that convivial eating and drinking, there were still five hundred dollars left in the Network wallet—to be carried, once again under my dress, to Czechoslovakia.

Finally, everyone was gone. Daniel had arrived and we got some sleep. The kind travel agent who had helped us with the conference suggested we two use this small hole in time to take a bus tour: the bridge in Mostar, the magnificent Sarajevo. She gave us a big book about that city that I have never visited, with glorious pictures I gaze at from time to time. We thought about it, but I was so tired. The nearby island of Lokrum beckoned, where we snorkeled and saw fish familiar to us from the Caribbean, which had come to Dubrovnik in the holds of traders' ships hundreds of years ago. We'll see the medieval bridge at Mostar and the rich ethnic mosaic of Sarajevo next time, we told her. Wrong. Or not that Mostar, that Sarajevo. Finally, we left for what was then still Czechoslovakia.

7

CZECHOSLOVAKIA

First had been Poland, with its independent trade union movement, Solidarity, pushed underground in 1981 to emerge victorious in renegotiations with the communist regime in 1989. Fired by this extraordinary change, Czechoslovakia followed. Between November 17 and December 29, 1989, seismic public demonstrations, bigger each day, revealed the government's impotence without Soviet support, and tore it apart. This bloodless fall became known as the Velvet Revolution.

The communists relinquished power without a fight, dismantling forty-one years of one-party rule. On December 29, 1989, the Federal Assembly of Czechoslovakia unanimously elected a new president, formerly several times in jail, the dissident playwright Václav Havel. The barbed wire that had closed off Czechoslovakia from Germany and Austria came down and euphoria followed, with travelers moving in every direction.

But by the time I arrived in Prague in the spring of 1991 those early emotions were largely spent and a reaction had set in: What next? The pace of change was dizzying. One Czech student told me later that, after the first burst of enthusiasm for revolutionary change, most of the people she knew suffered some version of psychological crisis or collapse.

ORIGIN STORIES

I NOTICE I AM lingering in Dubrovnik, procrastinating, nervous about describing what happened next, my first visit to Czechoslovakia.

Being a visitor often leads to intellectual and moral confusion, but this visit brought to a boil all my doubts about what we were doing. I must confess that there might well not be a Network of East-West Women today had the arbitrary order of events been different and I had gone to Czechoslovakia first, before hearing the excitement and variety of voices at the conference. This is to say that this visit both chastened and frightened me. It confirmed my distress at moments during the conference, when international feminism seemed like a quixotic, utterly compromised idea, combining the worst of the false unities under communism with the buried imperialism in most Western do-good projects. *Pace* Slavenka: The mere arrival of an American could feel invasive. Questions about my power and my purpose were unleashed at once, sweeping me up in currents of distrust and a spatter effect of hurt feelings.

From the start, everyone in Prague kept saying, "You don't understand." This had to be true. But the Czech feminists I was meeting often said they shared this condition of unknowing. Although Czechoslovakia had a rich feminist past, they felt all that past had been hidden from them; they were starting from scratch and were just beginning to speculate about feminism's prospects here. Would it be handouts for mothers, or more radical critiques of the fast-changing drama of He and She?

In the early nineties, time rushed some into new lives and new ideas, while others resisted this wild momentum, asking to slow things down so as to think change through, to imagine new paths to link the past with the present. The arrival of flocks of excited political tourists like myself put pressure on these renegotiations of meaning.

Following fast after the Velvet Revolution and after all those other invasions—the Germans in 1939, the Russians in 1968, and those many betrayals by Western countries in the past, suddenly there was this tumbling arrival of the West, here more than anywhere else. Was it the romance of the poet/dissident president? Or the accessibility of a Prague that was so tantalizingly close and had been left as it once was because, under communism, there had been no money for either demolition or renovation? Whatever it was, when I arrived in the gorgeous dilapidated city in June 1991 there were already fifty thousand foreigners, mostly Americans, squatting in every lovely square, smoking pot, working as waiters, translators, English teachers—our massive presence evidence of our resources and easy habits of freedom. Just as a new Czechoslovakia was fumbling for an identity, these privileged travelers exuded confidence, ignorant of the Czech past and unable to imagine the weird instabilities of the present. In the face of this inundation, slowing things down and rejecting any prefabricated systems of thought were acts of self-respect. People were tired of being pushed around as Czechoslovakia had so often been pushed around; they wanted freedom from outside influences. But freedom to do what?

I went to Prague to meet one of the most famous and distinguished feminists in the region, Jiřina Šiklová. She had been unable to come to Dubrovnik, but everyone assured me that this was the person I had to talk to if I sought to know what feminism might become here.

How exciting it was to meet, just then, at the turn of everything, this humble and magnificent woman. Kicked out of the university as a signer of the dissident manifesto Charter 77, she had spent several years in jail. Hidden in her oven lay several trays of tiny, lively black figurines made from bread; sculpting them had helped her to endure prison.

My first glimpse of samizdat publishing was in Jiřina's large, rambling flat. One tall bookcase was piled with these underground texts, many of which she had typed and circulated herself. She showed me the difference between the first, quite readable carbon copy and the fourth, blurry and barely intelligible—yet still precious. I pictured how it must have been: This small, elegant woman, vibrating with energy, working as a cleaning lady by day, typing through the night to connect to what communism had strictly defined as the forbidden outside. She was a hero, but, like so many dissident women in the region, she never claimed such glamour, always telling interviewers: "I was nothing more than an unofficial Post-Woman."

On still other shelves, and in big piles on the floor: hundreds and hundreds of feminist books, some still in their original boxes, sent to the beloved Jiřina by US feminists, German feminists, English feminists, publishers with overstock, or individuals donating multiples of their own books now that the communist embargo on books was over. Here, clogging Jiřina's apartment were treasures and oddities from the astonishing explosion of writing and publishing about gender both in the West and everywhere but here. Jiřina said—was it with a tired flip of the hand?—"Now everyone sends me these books. We have enough to make a library, but no place to put them."

I was startled, since one of the founding ideas of our Network was to respond to this kind of local wish. When we had filled our suitcases with arbitrary titles back in New York, we were already aware of possible problems lurking in this gesture of largesse: Which books? Chosen by whom? All in English! What a mess. But the reaction at the conference to the jumble we had heaped on a table had been electric. Curiosity! More! We took note: Here is a possible project for the future, after we will have learned how to read each other.

But, as if in time-lapse photography, the books were already here. Nonplussed yet excited, I asked Jiřina what she planned to do with all this stuff. After long years of underground life, she was once again reinstated as a professor of sociology and social work, so the Charles University had offered her a room for her books. Maybe. We rushed off to see it. "Small" doesn't capture the minginess of the empty, whitewashed cubbyhole the university would "maybe" give.

We stood there, depressed. "I would set the library up in my flat if only we could pay a librarian to organize the collection and sit for a few days a week so people could come and read."

I didn't know anything then, either about Jiřina or about how ideas about feminism were circulating in this world. But, maybe? Maybe, like all the great dissidents of Czechoslovakia, Jiřina could simply bypass the prevailing passivity and hostility at her university. (Note well, however: No independent action is ever taken "simply" or is without strings of implications.) Why wait?

I asked her how much money she would need to hire a librarian; a former student of hers, Jana Hradilková, a glowing presence, was already constantly in and out of the flat, drinking tea in the kitchen, wanting to work. Jiřina considered, gazing upward as she converted crowns to dollars, counting on her fingers. Several hundred dollars would pay Jana to sort the books and to sit for some months.

That was the power of the dollar back then, in the region. I felt nervous. After all, I had just arrived. What could be more vulgar than immediately whipping out one's wallet? But I couldn't resist trying it on: "We have five hundred dollars left over from the Dubrovnik meeting. You could have it to set up the library." And I produced it, five hundred dollars in cash, squirreled away as usual here and there in my clothes.

Now I was to understand the truth of Jiřina's reputation as a great organizer: We were out on the street like a shot, on our way to open up a dollar account at the bank. Banking back then was a pretty precarious affair. People were waiting in long lines reminiscent of the bad old days. I got the feeling that they had been there forever and their feet had taken root in the floor.

Jiřina took one look at this discouraging scene and, as was obviously always her style, she refused to accept the status quo. I can't tell quite how she did it—a word to this one and then to that one—and we were off the bank floor, up a staircase, down a dark corridor, and into an office, where a small man proclaimed himself interested in receiving dollars. At the speed of light he had the cash, and we had a bank book for "the Gender Center" with both our names on it.

Later we learned that the bank was confused about who we were to each other; they assumed that the American with the money was in charge. When Jiřina first tried to make a withdrawal, the bank refused: "Not without the American's permission." I easily dealt with this by writing a letter of permanent access. It was less obvious how to dispel the suspicions and hesitations the tellers had about Jiřina whenever she went to the bank: What is a "gender center"? Perhaps a brothel?

Nice story, right? Funny and charming: inequality and money without tears. I've dined out on the joke: The Prague Gender Center, now a well-housed and flourishing institution with the largest feminist library in the region, was once so unimaginable in Czech society that the likeliest hypothesis made the distinguished dissident Jiřina Šiklová into the madam of a brothel.

But, in fact, my first visits to Czechoslovakia in 1991 and 1993 were low on comedy. The Czech feminists I met were often skeptical about what I, and a monstrous regiment of others like me, might be doing there, and I seemed unable to share any ironic play around the repeating mantra of how different we were. "Irony, skepticism, and suspicion" belonged only to the women of Prague while—continuing to use a Czech feminist theorist's words from the early feminist anthology *Bread and Butter*—"Western feminists rushing into Eastern and Central European countries with shining eyes sound too naïve, too excited, too active, too funny, and possibly dangerous."

Happily for me, these words were written before my arrival, but they do precisely describe me—for the first ten minutes. After that, my excitement cooled, my eyes narrowed. Prague was a minefield, and I have spent many years trying to understand the complex lay of that land. There was pain here, and hurt pride, and in 1991 I was just at the beginning of recognizing and sympathizing with these often intense emotions.

Early on, I met the smart feminist theorist who wrote that embarrassingly accurate piece about the naïve enthusiasm of Westerners. Just before we parted, she had one last thing to say, her eyes narrower than I will ever be able to manage: "Because you're American and I'm Czech, you have seven more years of life expectancy than I do." What? I remember that I almost laughed, then quashed that impulse. With all our other difficulties, now she was adding layers of cruel inequalities I could only acknowledge and greet with silence. Later, though, since I was much older than this serious young woman and not then in the best of health, I considered dropping dead on her doorstep. Ha, ha. But laughter was absolutely out during this period.

When accused of having advantages one can't help having, one has two choices: One can leave, with or without a graceful exit. Or one can stay, accepting the truth of inequality, the mean injustice of it, and the rage it can engender, while also blowing personal guilt out one's ear. "Toughen up, Ann," a gender studies colleague once advised, when we few and too-fragile white feminist professors were accused of racism—a charge that is inevitably true in our America. Good advice.

There's no reason at all for everyone to love you. Renounce that desire. Painfully, over time, I toughened up. How else can one struggle at all? And by then, I had already determined to return to this world of staggering change. My comic fantasy of leaving by dropping dead was the nadir, while far more subtle complexities of attempted connection were usual and still to come.

POOR MEN

Czech women had more than most in the region. No strangling church; no staggering poverty; no invidious myth of the sacred female; rather, an unvarnished pride that comes from being in charge in a hard situation. Sexuality was relatively unencumbered by immobilizing guilt, and abortion and homosexuality had long been tolerated. Although Jiřina had been told at school that sexual pleasure was bourgeois, and although she didn't learn in school or anywhere else exactly how one becomes pregnant, still, better ignorance than damnation.

In the pre-communist past, Czechoslovakia had had the region's most powerful, independent women's movement, particularly during the First Republic and the presidency of Tomáš Garrigue Masaryk, from 1918 to 1935, when feminism even had state support. Yes, everyone insisted to me that they knew nothing about this past; facts about past independent movements weren't part of a communist education. But, in Czech women's powerful and proud skepticism, was there not some lingering trace? The competence, hauteur, and power of the women I was meeting seemed unquestionable.

So why should women, as women, complain? For the feminists I was meeting, this question created a discourse problem, a knot that closed off any free flow of feminist anger. Feminists were asked this "why" many times, and it certainly didn't help them (or me) to answer this hard question by saying that the available account of the Western Women's Movement was a caricature: Western women who complain are spoiled bourgeois who already have everything. Václav Havel had said this. Case closed.

What was worse, it was popularly rumored that Western feminists had given up their femininity and were the enemies of romance. They failed to recognize the special magic women have. Jana, soon to be the librarian of the new Gender Center, felt just this. Pregnant with her fourth child, she was sorry for the loss of enchantment she saw in frenzied Western feminist visitors.

One woman who had an interest in feminism accused me of bringing divorce to Prague. As I had only just arrived and Prague already had a 50 percent divorce rate, I answered, with an irritation I now regret, that I must be a pretty fast worker.

Another woman provisionally curious about feminism told me that Western feminists hate men, to her a mean-spirited and hopeless position. I stumbled toward a response: "Which men?"

Hate is an ugly and unwomanly emotion. The women I was meeting felt that their problems with men lay elsewhere. In countries where everyone is suffering and impotent, it can feel churlish, selfish, even vulgar to mention that women's suffering and powerlessness sometimes take their own particular forms—that women might have grievances that would possibly separate them from men. At the same time, alongside this thrumming anxiety about losing heterosexual partnerships, I kept encountering a mutual contempt men and women often seemed to feel toward each other—he's incompetent, weak, sometimes drunk, while she is domineering, unfeminine, and, in her management skills, a covert collaborator with the state.

Although survival had required, and would continue to require, that men and women cooperate, this suture often failed—that 50 percent divorce rate. Any successful solidarity between women and men in these strained circumstances was bound to feel fragile and was likely to be treasured. In the place of the dissatisfaction and frustration women sometimes expressed about their husbands, and in spite of the fact that it was women who most often chose divorce, I kept hearing a hopeful and moving new vocabulary of "healing" and "reconciliation." This desire to repair damage was placed as a bulwark against a Western feminism that didn't seem particularly interested in rebuilding ties with men.

The irony in the region in general was that separation and difference were flowing back into daily life in other identity categories like ethnicity or nation, but gender and class were being rejected, were becoming unspeakable—pushed away as Stalinist leavings. The coming poverty of women was recognized, but didn't provide an engine for feminism. Aren't things sad enough without emphasizing schisms that, if named, will only get wider? Several asked, "Are you trying to turn women into a minority?"

Czech melancholy about a threatened duet between men and women had already surfaced at the Dubrovnik meeting, where a warm and sensitive Czech psychologist, Šárka Gjuričová, had given a talk: "Why We Are Not Feminists." I have this thoughtful essay in front of me all these years later, and it remains cogent, a tale of what Šárka saw as communist distortions: lost roles, male humiliation, female dissatisfaction, and child alienation. The communist claim that universal work would create equality of the sexes was hypocritical; women continued to run the daily life of the family while working full time; women were exhausted and often resentful of men, some of whom found helping with children and housework humiliating, out of the question.

Šárka didn't blame men for not helping enough at home; she saw it as natural. And rereading her now I find myself wondering if these strong women had held on to their domestic power and had ended, even if unintentionally, by keeping men out. Why give up the only control and value one has?

In Šárka's fervent writing, the sinewy vines of traditional gender relations creep up from below and grab both men and women by the throat. Mothers, she argued, had lost their primary identity and deepest source of satisfaction when they were forced to put their children in day-care centers, silencing "their intuitive understanding of child needs." At the same time, men, too, were lost, their occupation gone. The Czech sociologist Ivo Možný put it this way in his research about gender under communism: "The man lives in a woman's family."

Šárka ended her poignant essay by asking for the old arrangement back: "[I]t is hard to guess how deeply men were hurt and frustrated by their sudden incapacity to provide well for their wives and families. For this was no doubt in our culture as well as in most others much more than an important role. It was a way to fulfill the lot of men in this world."

It took me twenty years to figure out what I wished I had said to such passion, such yearning nostalgia. At the second Czech and Slovak Feminist Studies Conference in Brno in 2011, I argued that the Czech emphasis on the question of masculinity had later become my own, but that I saw the difficulty facing us quite differently—not a need to restore traditions of manhood, but to rethink them at the deepest level so as to restore the humanity of both men and women. I talked, too, about what I called the empathy gap, because women's empathy for men's losses under communism was fully felt, but there was no call for a parallel empathy that men might feel for the specific burdens of women. Where was the call for men to recognize how women have been frustrated and thwarted by patriarchy? I finally managed to write:

> Both sexes remain Other to each other. Both feel their own kind of contempt. And in this empathy gap, equality and mutual recognition are defeated. Of course I'm not saying empathy is a bad thing. Rather, women might well decide to empathize a bit less, while men need to learn this important skill.

Back then, we all decided to give it a rest. Later I learned that, in every founding statement or press release the Prague Gender Center put out, I, Sonia Jaffe Robbins, and the Network of East-West Women were credited with originating the idea of such a center, credited with funding it, and credited with supplying its first collection of books. It's nice to be recognized, even thanked. I confess that much later we were hurt when the feminist library in Tbilisi, Georgia, which we did in fact start by sending books and funds, had a librarian who completely scratched out our logo on each and every book—"compliments of the Network of East-West Women"—and replaced it with the library's new name, erasing what must have felt like a humiliating and imperialist origin.

But getting such elaborate credit when it is not remotely deserved felt even odder somehow. After all, two years before, Jiřina had already imagined and wished for a place where people could gather, read, and debate about women's changing situation, and Jana had long wished to be a librarian; the books had been continuously arriving since 1989 from all over the US and Europe. Why did the Center put the Network at the point of origin?

Were we being asked to take some responsibility for this alien excrescence on the Czech landscape? Perhaps the very fact of a Gender Center felt aggressive, toxic, implying complaint and signaling a desire for women's independent thought and action.

At this very time, some men were celebrating their public return to traditional styles of male power. In the press, women were reading these preemptive strikes against them, the strong women who had so recently been in daily charge. Being a powerful woman was going straight out of style. Shame was being manufactured by the minute for any woman pushing herself forward. It was those loud Americans who invented this glorious library, which was to become—however flawed in its conception, however skewed toward elites, however intellectually invasive—a point of entry for hundreds of Czech women to imagine themselves as having common interests formerly unnamable.

On one side, officious Western feminists arriving to tell you how to think, with no understanding of your different history; and, on the other, gleeful misogynists screaming in every newspaper, "Go home, harridans. Men are in charge again."

I couldn't gauge how angry all this abuse made Czech women in general. Weren't they furious at this version of a happy return of male freedom? Or were they of two minds—insulted but at the same time recognizing that all this misogyny was also a powerful repudiation of repressive communism, which they felt had hurt them, too?

IS CAPITALISM POLITICS?

Under all this noise, I sensed an uneasy displacement—of ideas, of feelings. At that suspended moment in history, between two worlds, Western feminism felt more invasive to the women I was meeting than Western capitalism. I struggled to understand how this worked. Before I arrived in Prague, Jiřina Šiklová, that soon-to-be matron of the brothel/gender center, had already written a key piece, aimed mostly at a Western audience, and much reprinted, about why Czech women might well hesitate at the brink—of free market, competitive capitalism? No. Capitalism is a given in this piece, "McDonalds, Terminators, Coca Cola ads—and Feminism?" Although Coca Cola and Terminator movies are unlovely, Jiřina expresses no hope of escaping them, no plan to criticize or boycott them. They are part of a package she cannot but accept—even welcome.

Feminism, though, is a more equivocal offering, partaking of both the communist past and the capitalist future. Rhetoric like "women are oppressed" creates in her "the same nausea that we used to experience with reference to "class struggle." And there it is! Nausea, a visceral disgust. Czechoslovakia is going to have to "endeavor to create, or assimilate itself to, a capitalist social order." Will this "assimilation" ever induce "nausea"? Sooner or later, but in 1991 there's no social or rhetorical room for such doubts. Here is the much-wished-for marketplace. It would be nostalgic (then a completely pejorative word) to work for or imagine resistance to the juggernaut that is coming—a full-blown, class-stratified consumer society.

Expressing some sorrow about how overwhelming all these changes will be, Jiřina tries to rescue from any scorn or critique the small women's initiatives emerging in this new space, most of which actively reject the word *feminism*. Our feminist movement, she argues, will move forward with no fanfare, no ideology, but "rather on the basis of solving concrete, nonpolitical, and primarily practical tasks."

In Eastern Europe under communism, intellectual rebellion lay in exactly this refusal of politics. Violence or organized public resistance wasn't an option; one would simply disappear forever.

So "anti-politics" was the only possible expression of protest, the only way to refuse to play the Communist Party's game. Throughout the region, standing outside of any then available idea of "the political" was a position of honor and courage, a shrewd strategy, which had led to an astonishing success.

But, as always, there were unintended consequences. Anti-politics failed to formulate a vision of an active rather than reactive politics for the future. Utopia was what foolish, oppressive communists had said they were after. All such grand political imaginings ("the people," "the collective good") were naïve or hypocritical, foolish or corrupt. Cynicism was a healthy habit, and imagining a free society an abstract exercise. Since no one expected things to change, "truth" was much discussed, but "the future," never. To formulate desires for the future can feel futile. Yet, without such thinking, the narratives of the past expand to cut off any view. Many in East Central Europe said after 1989 that all they wanted was to be "normal," a default position that left no room for new possibilities, and, worse, that accepted past traditions—unmodified, uncriticized—as natural.

I know I cannot imagine or adequately honor the courage and fortitude Jiřina brought to that complex former world of covert refusals and dangerous resistance. But now the scene of politics had changed. As always, admirably, she came above ground at once and began working—for students, for the old and sick, and for all those whom she saw would soon be totally ignored. She also wrote with anger about the "gray zone," those who had taken no risks to resist communism and were now rushing in to fill all the best places at the table—often treating dissidents like herself with a no doubt guilty resentment.

As she moved forward into new possibilities for action, she counseled caution, slow movements below the radar, a local and specific women's activism with practical intentions and no pretensions in any larger political context. She wanted women's activism to have an authenticity that politics utterly lacked under the top-down rules of communism. She wanted these activists— whatever their ideas—to become citizens.

Suddenly, I ask myself: *Why am I expressing doubt about these tentative moves, which privilege the local and the anti-rhetorical? What is my problem with Jiřina's call for activities unmarked by any relation to larger political agendas?* Surely, in temperament, I feel close to her desire to stay real, true to what people are feeling and wanting, resisting any rush to larger axioms or ambitions that can so soon become corrupt or grandiose. I guess my qualms arise because as I see it, each of these small new activities *does* have a politics and will take part, willy-nilly, in forming the new milieu in which everyone will now have to live. The desire to separate from larger ideological patterns and events made deep emotional sense, but this humility obscured the enormity of what was actually happening at all levels—virtually overnight.

The arrival of "a capitalist social order" is politics; thinking about small local problems rather than the new state is a political decision—with consequences. The fast redistribution of wealth and the rising discrimination against women in this process are both politics. Rhetoric about restoring families and healing the men, women, and children within them while economic supports for such a project are being eroded—is a misdirection of the eye.

The arrival of Western feminist ideas is a tiny glitch on this big new screen of action, power, and change. Why cavil at feminism as ideology with no reaction to the ideology that is McDonald's?

But this is a rhetorical question, possibly expressing an American feminist's anxiety about "the political." No matter what we said, we visitors were harbingers of the terrible strains to come. In Prague then, being in any sense "against capitalism," "nauseous" about its noisy arrival, was not an available state of mind for either men or women, most feminists included. And the popular image of Western feminism became a handy whipping boy for the disorienting arrival of the new. Western feminists like me who even hinted at a criticism of capitalism were absurdly out of step.

One could hardly say it was always all that different at home. US feminists had radically divergent takes on the interweaving of sexism and capitalism. Although many had searched, we certainly had not found a point of leverage against the common poverty and political powerlessness of women. Sometimes it was easier to say we had failed because some feminists had drifted toward an accommodating neoliberalism insufficiently critical of power—and indeed this happened. But more galling—even with an often excellent radical analysis—we were defeated. We succeeded in building diversity, a queer understanding of the instability of gender, a commitment to a labile feminism that of course would be different in every local context. But important as these moves were, they did not always add up to a systematic plan to modify capitalism's way of operating in our lives. We had sometimes tried, but often found it hard to go beyond the questions of rights or of protection against violence toward larger, structural demands. We made new space for personal freedom, but larger changes were far to seek in our own late-capitalist world.

I was a feminist of the Left; I believed that feminism could be a place to launch criticisms of capitalism, racist institutions, and cruelty to those who suffer poverty or violence—or more humbly, a place to find ideas and social structures that could be at a tangent to capitalism's hegemony over, say, family or the environment. None of this made sense to anyone I was meeting in East Central Europe—or certainly not back then.

At first I harbored a hidden hope that people who had lived under communism might have different levers to push against capitalist structures and central ideas. With what I soon recognized as embarrassing naïveté, I began by thinking of the East Central European political scene as wide open, susceptible to new invention, when nothing could have been further from the case. But no move to a linear narrative is intended here, no direct line from wishful fantasy to sober truth. Recognizing limitation is sensible, but it is also inadequate. I continued to push for a feminism capable of including and aligning with all kinds of progressive political hopes. I continued to criticize a feminism that was without ambitions for radical change.

Maybe I should have enjoyed the brief period when foreign imports were viewed with nausea. That mood of resistance was very quickly gone, including even resistance to feminism. "Gender" disappeared, not only as a piece of hated communist rhetoric, but also as a salient problem in the new order. There was so much else to worry about.

HANA HAVELKOVÁ

In those first few years, and still now, my intellectual guru in Czechoslovakia was Hana Havelková. A sociologist researcher, she visited the US, and I met her several times in Prague. We all read everything we could find of hers available in English. In addition to her subtle analysis, it was wonderful how she kept changing her mind in response to the fast-changing situation. Along with others, she started with the narrative that Czech feminists were behind ("for heaven's sake, be patient"), which often morphed into suggesting Czech women were different ("don't expect us to be like you, dear visitors; our feminism has a different starting point from yours and will follow its own unique track"). Here's my favorite example of the early Hana Havelková, an exemplary exchange between her and a US feminist:

The Western feminist bemoans the line of young Czech prostitutes along the road to the border with Germany. The Eastern feminist responds that, yes, there's a terrible new problem with the currency differential between Germany and Czechoslovakia. The Western feminist thinks, "what low feminist consciousness!" The Eastern feminist thinks, "Why do these Western feminists always see sexuality as the key to women's oppression rather than money?

This question flags an important place where Western influences were in fact creating distortions in the nascent feminist work in East Central Europe. Western foundation money, when concerned with gender at all, was usually for anti-trafficking projects, often bypassing the economic reasons behind the regional explosion of prostitution. The arrival of capitalism was creating new forms of poverty overnight, new women's unemployment, new needs in a suddenly precarious situation, all subjects that American foundations were unlikely—and unequipped—to address directly. Here was a complaint about Western feminist constructions that deserved more attention. In a strange but unfortunately predictable union, Eastern reluctance to discuss the communist formulation "class struggle" and Western acceptance of capitalism's economic inequalities as unavoidable givens created a double silence. The fast-forming class system in the East raised insufficient alarm on either side. Some Czech disorientation and depression came straight from here—from new problems arising everywhere, without acceptable names.

While East-West narratives of difference circulated and developed, Hana was already moving on. Just when we had all said to each other piously a hundred times that of course Eastern and Western feminisms were going to be different, so different, Hana turned around and said, yes, we *were* different at first, but the pace at which Czech society was moving toward Western ideas and material conditions was ending all that. We were more alike each day.

In this swiftly changing situation, feminism was going to be needed, but Hana saw barriers: Czech women had a confused identity that they needed to sort out. Communism had given them education, work, economic independence from individual men, and legal equality as citizens. But just as the idea of equal citizenship for women had become thinkable under communism, such rights were losing any real meaning for both women and men. After 1948, all became dependent for everything on the state. Civil society was expressly forbidden, and the force of this prohibition was real. After a hideous show trial in 1950, the Communist Party hanged the feminist leader Milada Horáková for imagining she could start an independent opposition to the new totalitarian regime.

Given this internally contradictory history, Hana identified two reasons why strong and often progressive Czech women didn't embrace feminism. They already had so much, and at the same time, they had never been allowed to shape or control any of it. Now, suddenly, communism was gone, and women were going to be "socially endangered," but the traditions required for a response to the threat were deeply buried. Woman as subject had been obscured by the overworked woman with no time for an abstraction called "politics."

Some who had observed this complex frame of mind, this amalgam of having and not having, had argued that the only way Czech women and others in the region would come to feel the need for feminism would be through getting "burnt skin," some direct experience of painful sexism. This idea depressed Hana. Must one wait until new exclusions and insults were acute before constructing a new, post-communist political identity, one that might include old strengths and new desires? But first, perhaps, one might need to grieve over the recent, so difficult legacy. Communist styles of living were fast departing, leaving memories of past sorrows. As one woman put it, "The more responsible women were, the more they worked, the less they were loved by their husbands and children." The unfairness of this predicament!—with its deep origins in pre-communist gender roles and their continuation in a communism that had simply asked women to do everything, both the old tasks of love and home and the new of work and social duty. Three generations of exhausted mothers. And now yet a new task: threading one's way, sometimes hanging on to continuities, sometimes letting the past go.

Hana calls for saving women's powers and independence while extricating that power from any idea that it is on a collision course with love and family. She tries to separate these chromosomes so tightly linked in popular understandings. In 1992 we all read with excitement her argument that some of the values and powers gained under communism could and should be salvaged. "It must not be forgotten that in these shaken societies the keeping alive of certain values does not lose its importance."

Here, nestled in the analysis of this very hardheaded social scientist, was a utopian wish. Women will figure it out; they will not let what they gained during communism be overrun by the new order. This had been my fantasy about the prospects for Eastern feminism too: Hang on to your dignity and power; why should new social relations entirely cancel the possibilities hidden in the past?

Perhaps in such thinking we were both poor Marxists. It was wishful to think that one could suture communist collectivity to the delights of the new chance to be separate, self-defining, even—gulp—irresponsible. But both Hana and I thought such a belief in the continuity of culture might be a counterbalance to both communism's absolute materialism and capitalism's absolute individualism. Communism had been unable to erase traditional structures of inequality, particularly gender. Maybe capitalism, too, could be resisted using the more recent emotions and memories of communist experience.

EVA HAUSEROVÁ

One final encounter in that first trip, just before leaving Prague: a visit to the apartment of Eva Hauserová. I had heard she wrote feminist science fiction, and would I like to meet her? Yes, yes, I love feminist science fiction.

That afternoon glows as a golden island floating alone among my memories of that time. Here was uncontained laughter about how it had been before: on the edge of impossible with two children and no water in a new, cement housing estate. And about how it suddenly is now: the children less often sick from bad water, allergies, and childhood diseases that require mothers to sit for hours in clinic waiting rooms. There's no amazing transformation of health care, please understand. Her children are better simply because time has made them older. But they do have a larger apartment, and . . . will miracles never cease? Because now she writes for the Czech *Playboy,* she is earning more than her husband! "Oh, wonderful, wonderful . . . and yet again wonderful." Now he has to help her sometimes with the kids, and because he helps more, she is less angry, and gets on better with him.

The kids are playing around on the floor of the pleasantly cluttered apartment, happy and not coughing. Later, Eva wrote a satire about the pronatalism of her generation in the eighties:

I love to be pregnant. This fascinating feeling of creating a new human being. It's simply great. Nothing can compare to motherhood. How wonderful it is to slip away from boring research at the Academy of Sciences to a maternity leave and to stay at home with a small sweet baby for two or three years.... I am fed up with genetic engineering, with the lab routine, the piles of new journals and publications to study.... I was educated by my parents and my school to be a scientific worker, not a woman. And suddenly it seems truly marvelous to discover this utterly new possibility to be a mother and housewife.

SELF-INTERVIEW: Are you really convinced that you want to have a child just now?

Yes! YES! Everybody has a baby, my friend from university, Lida, has a new baby now, and another friend from school, Taña, is pregnant too.... I am longing so much for a baby of my own! It was such hard work to convince my husband that we shouldn't favour such things as saving money, travelling, or developing my career. ... I wept, I pleaded, and finally he agreed. Hurrah!

(From: "Bronchitis, Laryngitis, Otitis . . . and Acute Hysteria: An Essay About the Cult of Motherhood and My Own Experience with It.")

Oh, funny girl who laughs at communism and at herself. A few years later, several Prague friends told me that Eva rarely appeared at feminist events anymore. "She's not really a feminist," one said. "She writes for *Playboy*." Ah, to be a feminist here, and in fact everywhere: it's uphill all the way.

DEPARTURES

I'm embarrassed by a fantasy I had then, and recurrently over the years, but I'd better own it at once. Those jokes Slavenka and others had made at the conference about silly Ann's fears of seeming—indeed, of actually being—imperialistic weren't jokes anymore, here in Prague, so I dreamed a mechanism of self-defense: I am a smooth stone jumping into this pond of roiling change. My presence creates ripples that travel outward, encountering many others in the seething water. But the stone itself simply disappears, its value or culpability beyond recall. As friends were constantly to remark over the years of my frequent visits, I was always leaving, a form of innocence that, for good reason, never held up in court, but also a reality of nonengagement, an absence; I vacated the scene of the crime. With whatever growing knowledge and persistent ignorance, I was gone, leaving people to get on with it in their own ways.

To be always leaving. What is the moral and emotional effect of such a stance? "People love you in Krakow," one friend said. Another said, "Well, of course. You never have to get entangled in local fights; you never have to choose sides because you can claim ignorance about what's at stake. You can rise above the grating against each other of rival personalities." Indeed, the free pass of not knowing, and leaving. Yes, and don't forget forgetfulness. What was that seething debate last summer? Who was on what side? Oh, dear, can't quite recall.

Do others—now many—who do international political organizing feel anything like this? I'm not asking about the new New Class, people circulating from one Organization for Security and Co-operation in Europe meeting to another, sitting on boards, always on airplanes on their way to the exotic locale of the next meeting. Whether or not these airport bureaucrats bring change is something I find hard to measure. No, I'm talking about people like me who travel to get involved in people's lives—

teaching, debating, investing real time, constantly returning over many years.

Sometimes we are greeted with excitement and pleasure, like long-lost relatives. The joy of arrival is unquestionable; the possibilities for being listened to as a fresh, outside voice are substantial. Perhaps this mode of being, like any other, is a complex amalgam of fine and ignominious intents. Or is the constant traveler a special case, requiring a particular moral yardstick?

An always defensive person, I kept asking myself if revisiting, for example, Prague, would be worth doing. Often I thought: probably not. If I went again, this would be a private journey, an adventure I'd be having quite without political echoes for anyone else. These uncertainties never receded as my travels with feminism got going in 1992 and 1993. Could an American voice prove suggestive? Before I leave this scene, this Czechoslovakia, one last try at answering this question.

YOUNG BOYS OF PRAGUE

My university in New York has a grant to fly in American professors to give guest lectures in Prague, Budapest, and Warsaw. The visitors have been famous philosophers, sociologists, and political scientists, and have been warmly welcomed and treated with respect. I, bringing up the tail end in 1993, am the feminist.

In Prague I'm met at the plane by a student at Charles University, where I am to teach. He explains that his professor, my distinguished host, has left the city; he won't be seeing me. I'm conducted to a department office and introduced to a tall, pale, youngish professor who will take me to the hall where I am to lecture on some current themes in feminist theory. As we walk along, he explains that, because he is an underling with no power in the department, he has been stuck with the task of introducing me; to rub it in, he's been told he has to stay and actually listen to my talk.

I'm impressed that all of these insults *precede* my saying a word. There's no way to take them personally. Here feminism is absurd, unmanly. This man is humiliated, but can't take the chance of disobeying and abandoning me. I tell him I'm very sorry he's been put in this embarrassing position on my account, and we enter the lecture hall.

It's full, about forty students, and along the back wall, to my surprise, a row of professors curious about this feminist theory, which bears a seal of approval from my well-known university.

To begin I ask a few questions to get a feeling for who these students are. No answers, as usual, so I use tricks (yes, tricks; I am already becoming the itinerant trickster, the feminist picaro). Once the boys are talking (of course boys only; my tricks in 1993 aren't yet good enough to break the strict boundaries of gender propriety), I see where I am. It's the zoo. Boys are making wisecracks about the inferiority of women, laughing at women's movements as a Stalinist joke. And besides, haven't I heard? Men are stronger. Don't I want the door opened for me? I listen, respond, play these fish on a long line.

Ten minutes into it, the faculty sees that I will not give an abstract lecture about gender. They will have to actually listen to their students, who, off the leash in this rare moment of license, are ignorant, crass, arrogant, incurious. Given the pedagogical styles at Eastern and Central European universities, these professors have never had to encounter how well or ill their students are able to entertain new ideas. The back row begins to file out.

Good. I don't want them. I'm an organizer, and before me sits the next generation. Can anything be done?

I have a plan, one of the best of my maneuvers in these early days of the post-communist melee. I continue to goad the boys to new heights of contempt for uppity, independent women.

Slowly, the atmosphere in the room begins to change. The girls are listening. They have never heard any of this rabid misogyny so openly stated before. Usually, here in Czechoslovakia, it's a background noise, a given that goes without saying. Several call out at boys they know, furious.

Now I have my audience. My lecture on feminism can begin. I analyze the remarks the boys have made, giving them a history, a social context, a psychology, a politics. Almost like cartoon characters—but surely they are not like this once outside the pack?—the men growl and laugh under their breath. After all, there is a limit on their bad behavior; the poor captive professor is still there, a witness who might tell tales to the momentarily absent higher authorities.

Meanwhile, the girls are listening. I have broken this class in two along gender lines. There will be much to think about and answer for later and unknowable fallout from this initial act of destruction. For now, I feel that I've introduced feminism very, very well. The shock and anger the women feel toward their colleagues are new. But what can they do with such emotions at this stage? Perhaps I have proved how undermining and negative feminism can be, just as some Czech feminists feared, leading to crashes that scare both sexes senseless. From the beginning, Czech feminists have been telling me that men are the problem; finding men a decent, dignified way to be is the first order of post-communist business. Certainly after this collision, I see just what they mean—and is this task so different from what's needed at home?

At the end of my lecture cataloging a wide range of expressions of sexual malaise, the classroom is a shambles and the students are standing around in groups, strong girls yelling at boys they have considered friends. The palely loitering professor approaches. "More interesting than I thought," he says. He ushers me out of the building and abandons me to the street.

8

AFTER DUBROVNIK

Here began the great era of visitors. Each country, moving at its own pace, began to allow travel. A flood of people from East Central Europe poured into the metropoles of the West: former dissidents out of jail, roaming free and lecturing; students speaking English, leaving behind the Russian they had resisted learning in school; recipients of grants often designed to seduce them by giving quick tastes of Western ideas; professors and professionals who had played it safe, Jiřina Šiklova's "gray zone," now free to travel and also to pick up the pieces of their former institutions, from factories to universities, the disjecta membra *of their former world as it was falling apart. And, in the midst of the ruck—the people we had just met in Dubrovnik at this sharp turn in the road—the feminists.*

By word of mouth, by invitation, by chance, the newborn Network of East-West Women became a way station for these first travelers. From 1991 onward, hundreds of women passed through my loft on Spring Street in lower Manhattan—arriving with jet lag from Romania, Yugoslavia, Poland, Bulgaria, Czechoslovakia, Hungary, Belarus—to meet us, the American feminists.

At the end of their journeys, the excited visitors from the East were met by people in many ways parallel to themselves, equally eager to talk, drink, laugh, for hours. This constantly shifting crowd included women from the East who had been in exile, often for decades, and were now hungry to hear about the lost home they had never expected to see again; women who had long studied and visited East Central Europe and knew a great deal about the before (but what now?); and women like me, the planners of the Dubrovnik conference from the US side, passionate feminists, curious, but often ignorant of how the dramas of gender had played out over the last forty years on the other side of the looking glass.

From the first there was a tension between this wild social rush and the quest for a viable form these new relationships were going to take. What were we all going to do together?

And in the midst of these complex, fresh encounters came the shockingly unexpected: the wars.

GATHERING IN NEW YORK

BACK HOME IN NEW YORK, the story speeds up: exits and entrances, long-distance flights, meetings, parties. The traveling political women who gathered on Spring Street had enjoyed relative privilege in their own countries. They were emerging from a suppressed life, well educated, and usually with some kind of former contact with Westerners or Western ideas. Some were certainly the secret readers of the samizdat texts Jiřina Šiklová and so many others had typed through the night, creating a canon for the critical and disaffected.

And who were the "American feminists" they met? I'm sorry to say this vexed question will never go away during the course of this story; it requires many answers. Speaking for myself, I was of the optimistic sixties generation, hopeful to the point of idiocy about the chance for solidarity among such diverse people, but sometimes successful in making connections by reason of this very idiocy. The women we were meeting had no such baggage of built-in confidence in this humming of the *Internationale*, no expectation of a glorious future, but at another level we were all engagé, and all of a related class: writers, researchers, professors, activists. In other words, we were members of elites, which in East Central Europe had often been heroic but much repressed and, in the US, much ignored.

Warmth and hilarity were the emotions of those charged times. I remember the mixture of absurdity and high seriousness of one evening, when a Romanian visitor was explaining the sclerotic politics of Romania—how it had had the least transformative and most violent so-called fall of communism of any country in the region—to fifty people who were crowded in, sharing chairs or sitting on the floor. She was eloquent about Romanian women's dangerous situation, but in the middle of her talk, she began to climb out of the large living room window behind her onto the shaky fire escape. As the host and responsible for this dangerous means of egress, I was mystified and worried: "What's wrong? Where are you going?" "I must smoke." She explained that she could keep talking to us all through the open window. "But it's okay to smoke inside. I'll get you an ashtray." By then, in the early nineties, my apartment was one of the few places in New York City where Eastern Europeans could indulge in this comforting social activity. Although the air was clouded, the atmosphere of easygoing pleasure and unhysterical acceptance offered real relief.

As I've said, my entry into feminist organizing in East Central Europe depended on the entirely mistaken idea that the shock of post-communism would awaken an idealism and political intensity similar to that of 1968 in the United States, a time of revelation I longed to revisit. This ignorance gave way to knowledge and disillusion at once, but it was too late. I was hooked by the entirely different desires and fears arising for new friends in actually existing post-communism; I stayed to slog along with them in the smoky, messy *vrai*.

Just then, we had a ruling term that could lash everyone together: *transition*. But this was an image that could not hold and was repudiated almost immediately. Transition to what? People registered an insult in any assumption that the trip from communism to capitalism-and-democracy was a clearly marked journey that all would take in hasty lockstep. So *transition* became sinister, covertly imperial. In repudiating a shared experience of transition, people grabbed on to difference, onto particularity.

This coming together and pulling apart was a drama being performed in my living room. The intensity of our shared social pleasure in each other was constantly coming up against the starkness of the bloc's divisions, the differences and isolations enforced among communism's many forms.

One evening, for example, the Romanian judge: Her priority, now that new laws might be written, was to get rid of easy divorce in Romania. American consternation! What face would feminism have in the "new democracies" if restraints on freedom were among its first moves? The judge, a serious feminist, was unmoved by this worry. In Romania it was almost always men who used the easy divorce law blithely to slip the noose of their families. Women and their children were then flung on the world without protection. The disgrace of divorce poisoned their existence. Isolated and ostracized after divorce, Romanian women might well greet the idea of "freedom" with irony. The judge was simply telling us American feminists, with our ideas of freedom permeating every other desire, that easy divorce was far, far from freeing the women in her courtroom. Confident, perhaps joyful, independence for women was too hard to imagine. The best the judge could manage for the women she cared about was protection. Feminism is a long-term social revolution. In the meantime, rules tying men down to the family looked like the only legal safeguard available to women.

Right-wing women had made essentially the same argument in the US: "Are you feminists crazy, letting men off the hook so easily? They must be forced by legal restraints to be responsible." In Deirdre English's wonderful phrase, they "feared that feminism would free men first."

Some at this tense NEWW meeting argued that, down the road, divorce would come in handy for women in Romania. In Prague, I had just seen how commonly—if sadly—women used it far more often than men. But for Romanian women, this degree of hopefulness was far to seek.

As we talked, we were reminded of the enormity of the feminist task: Everything would have to be different for Romanian women to feel more free. In real, existing "transition" to democracy, the Romanian family was absolutely necessary for survival. The stigma on nonconforming women was deeply entrenched, and women usually internalized this as a crippling shame. Being outside the family meant poverty and loneliness, with no public culture to offer avenues of relief. So be quiet, you clamoring American voices. Change for women will be step by step, starting now from where the Romanian judge is standing in front of an international crowd magically materializing in New York.

Coming from such different possibilities for a feminist politics, we often discussed what moments of collaboration we could find in this chaotic and widening field of action, this transforming East Central Europe. Another night, a woman from Poland suggested that, in all our debates, we were ignoring rural women. They were poor, and with changes in both property laws and markets, they were about to get poorer. The other women in the room were nonplussed. Here was criticism that stuck to both Westies and Easties. From wherever we had come, we were all urbane and not unmindful of our privilege. Somehow, out of a cloud of guilt and worry, someone asked, "What do you suggest?" The Polish woman was now a student in New York, but she had come from the countryside and had a concrete suggestion ready: "Raise money to buy cows for farm women."

Since as yet we had no idea what kind of organization the Network of East-West Women could be or wanted to be, both raising money and supplying cows felt remote. But we discussed it. Who would give this feminist organization money—for cows, or for anything? I said damply that we would need to study the changes coming to the gender organization of rural Poland. But the women with whom we were already establishing common ground were the self-declared feminists of the cities. It seemed important then—and still does now—to say who we were, and who we were not, which meant acknowledging our limitations.

We knew enough about ourselves to see that, given our particular talents and desires, cows could never be our project. This real distance between rural and urban culture was to have a big effect on regional and, indeed, US politics down the road. Maybe progressive city people in both the US and Eastern Europe should have been in conversation with rural people from the first—but we were not. In any case, such work was unlikely to be done well by us cosmopolitans, the loosely forming collection of people we were tentatively beginning to call NEWW. Finally, what unity we had came from our alienation as self-declared feminists from the mainstream of all our cultures. We had to hope that such outsider positions might become sources of the Network's particular strength.

As these connections among us were taking form, they were also being interrupted by the blooming of war in Yugoslavia. Now, suddenly, our values and allegiances faced urgent challenges and required more definition. Joanne Landy, a friend and colleague of Sonja Licht's, was trying to build a peace movement that would be both Eastern and Western out of her NGO, the US-based Campaign for Peace and Democracy. She arrived at a Network meeting where she demanded that the Network take sides: should the U.S.-led NATO coalition bomb Belgrade or not? Progressive Americans were split on this question. Those who used the historical model of Munich were for bombing: We must stop this Milošević-Hitler before he takes over more and more territory. Those who used the historical model of Vietnam were dead set against intervention, which wouldn't help and would only bog the US down in another endless Cold War-like standoff.

Joanne called for a vote: Would the Network endorse the Campaign's position against all bombing? The sixty to seventy women sitting there, over half from a number of countries in the region, were intimidated and uncertain how to position themselves. They began gathering up their coats and leaving. Joanne kept pressing for a vote. Finally, the minority that remained voted. I took a careful count and recount. Eighteen to eighteen! I almost laughed, though nothing here was funny. "Sorry, Joanne. I guess the Network is not and may never be a unified political voice. Turns out feminism, which we share, is not a key to all political commitments." Hadn't I been saying for years to my university colleagues who called feminism an ideology that feminism doesn't offer a consistent worldview? Feminism has never been a fixed configuration of beliefs, in every case on the side of the angels one likes. We were unable and unwilling to seek the kind of political unity that could make the Network a force in the complex local and national politics unfolding in the region. There it was: no cows, no endorsements, no specific platform for all.

But here came a case that put pressure on what we were beginning to see as a potentially fruitful disunity. Many had urged us to do a clothing drive for those dispossessed of all their belongings in the war. A majority felt that this kind of charity drive was not our kind of thing at all. But in our fat city, most of our closets were bursting with a superfluity of clothes, boots, and warm hats by the dozen, available on any street corner for five dollars. We sent out a call and hundreds of items poured in, piled up in heaps on my living room floor on Spring Street. Now came the discussion of how to get all this to those in need. Caritas? But that was a Catholic organization active mainly in Catholic Croatia. And this was founding NEWW member Vinka's moment: "If a blanket donated from Serbia were offered to me, a Croatian, I would choose to freeze to death rather than take it."

Once again, as so often, consternation. This time resistance to such bitter, virulent nationalism came from all sides. Here we could finally locate a community of opinion among those drawn to the Network of East-West Women: anti-nationalism. Vinka was alone. I can see now that in the very midst of the new urgency to break down the rigid conformities of the bloc, to separate, feminism offered the only enduring model of an anti-nationalist political practice in the region. The women's anti-war action group Women in Black became an international symbol of women's refusal to participate in ethnic hatred and nationalist violence, and while this position was particularly salient during the breakup of Yugoslavia, a general resistance to the worst forms of identity politics has remained central to feminist thinking in the region. Even as countries were rushing apart, creating sometimes jingoist national cultures, Network members chose not to join in this drive to fix identity.

This dynamic relationship to identity was hard to maintain, but I want to claim this virtue for the young and struggling Network. We performed what tasks we devised for ourselves in a lively space where universals and particulars vied for our attention. Traditionalists were claiming to reanimate old forms, full of the charms of nostalgia and certainty. To be sure, communism had entailed the loss of all traditional enchantments, but we feminists were in a position to doubt some happy recuperation of a past family romance. We were not so easily enchained by myths of loss and dreams of beauty wound around gender and hearth. Instead, we kept running, because several old worlds were just behind us, while the new made us skeptical as well, full of new traps for women. A bland consumer world was a sop that could only briefly satisfy the ones who actually have to do the shopping. The Network was always calling for a thorough examination of both past and present, always reacting against potentially imprisoning political identities. Women were going to have to invent, to resist *kinder kirche küche* on one side, and the kind of individualism that leaves each person stranded in an emptying world on the other. Both sides were full of temptation for post-communists. Young girls told us they wanted "lipstick feminism" if there was to be feminism at all—color, style, sexuality. Down with drab duty. Reenchantment of the world was going to be quite a task, and what the Network could offer was a gathering place where all could perform their narratives of the possible.

During the war, Indira Kajosevic, a founding member of NEWW, started a cultural club where people from all over Yugoslavia, now stranded in New York, could dance and eat. These warm parties were a poignant resistance to the dissolving of the Balkan folk culture in the city where, for decades, Croatians, Bosnians, and Serbs had danced together in the church basements of every borough. Although the inherent treachery of the Balkan scene was bigger than any party could touch, the Network put its heart into such efforts of vibrant community building.

SHANA PENN

After those first few years of discovering mutual ignorance, of debate, of learning, and, happily, of growing friendships, what was this organization going to become? One person emerges as key to the Network's survival beyond the post-Dubrovnik flurry: Shana Penn. If all we had had at that point were Sonia Jaffe Robbins's phone trees and letter writing and my open social gestures toward forming international feminist ties at this wild moment in the lives of our new friends, then that would have simply been the end of it.

But Shana, a longtime freelance activist in both feminist and Jewish US progressive movements, was a finely tuned racehorse of a different color: ambitious, driven, efficient, hungry for a job to sink her teeth into, for a road to meaningful work, and for some little power in the world. Shana rescued the Network from the oblivion that five out of seven such initiatives suffer. She faced head on the problem of how to conceive of a viable organization at a realistic scale, with money, projects, committed members, throughout a vast region.

Let one Shana story stand for many. It's 1993 and she and I are at the Ford Foundation, which has decided—along with the US government—that the disintegration of political structures in the post-communist countries has left a dangerous vacuum. The discourse is moving on apace. "Transition" has been replaced by a more productive analysis implied by the term *civil society*: a shorthand for all that bloc countries lacked, a public sphere neither government nor private. Such new thinking is the reason our small and still mostly formless NGO is sitting in this elegant office with this nice and equally elegant program officer.

We describe our plans for specific projects. Activists need to connect; the feminists we are coming to know in the region need to get their hands on the coming technologies. Not one of them has a computer. Email has arrived with corporations. But women as a demographic group are a hundred miles from putting their hands on such miraculous machines. Our program officer tells us he is impressed by our ideas and our growing international group; he thinks that if we keep going like this, the Foundation will want to fund us in a year. And here's the moment that captures a hundred others: With steel in her eyes, Shana says, "Not in a year. Now." How did she have the nerve? I was embarrassed, afraid of this boldness. But this is how it ended: Right there and then, the Foundation funded our first project, to put our nascent steering committee of regional feminist activists online.

In 1994 women who didn't know anything about computers converged on Washington, where Shana lived and had established a US NEWW office. In intensive workshops, they learned the new machines and sent emails. Each one received her own computer and a stipend to go home and, there, to train and connect up others. The project proliferated. Victoria Vrana, a new Network employee funded by the amazing grant, went to Bulgaria, where first she had to find electricity lines, then she had to rig odd hookups. Then, with a screwdriver, she put working computer systems together. Now there were feminist activists doing email in Bulgaria. In Victoria's hotel room in Sofia, the door stuck shut, but she was ready for all contingencies. She used her screwdriver to free herself.

These were our early heroic days, and Victoria and others were on the train to Beijing in 1995 to the key UN international women's meeting there, sending back email bulletins to what the Polish feminist lawyer Ursula Nowakowska called in her talk in China, "the non-region." Now, with the Cold War over, the women of East Central Europe and the former Soviet Union were finally traveling, entering the UN process of women's meetings that had begun in 1975. Proudly, NEWW was an early link. Thanks to Shana's adept, fast-moving organizing, the Network was becoming real.

At first I had nightmares that our inspired first project to put the feminist world online would lead merely to new, numbing, underpaid secretarial jobs for women. But that wasn't what happened at all. Soon, all the world needed computers. Thanks to our Ford grant, we had merely added some activist women into this new reality early, who had been slated otherwise to be the last in line.

THE CONSULTANTS

But the questions of how to structure ourselves as an organization only became more acute with each passing day of on-the-ground activity. Shana began to raise money to hire consultants to help us build a sustainable organization beyond this exciting first project. My mother had planned to leave me her heavy, hideous, diamond-encrusted necklace, which she never wore. I asked her if I could have it now. I explained we needed help to invent our identity if we were ever to succeed at raising money. Generously, she gave it to me, happily years before her death. I went straight to the diamond district on 47th Street, to the very dealer who had sold my father this ungainly object forty years before. With the nine thousand dollars he paid me we hired consultant after consultant, asking them how to structure something so all-over-the-place. How could the Network be democratic when it spanned such great differences of space and context? How could it give its own small shove to direct change, to help include feminism as an element in such astonishing transformations?

I have before me notes from that time in the mid-nineties and several formal assessments of what the Network should do. One consultant told us sternly, "Activism isn't a dinner party." I remember feeling shamed by this admonition. But, finally, I fought back: "For now, maybe really knowing each other and staying connected *does* look like a dinner party, a continuous one like in *Alice in Wonderland.*" In another "confidential analysis," once again a consultant put the situation starkly. Either the Network is simply an enabling structure for individual women and their projects, or it generates policy and goes after funding to realize particular local goals. It's obvious from the tone of this report that a humble enabling of ideas without any centralized purpose would be a minor undertaking, that more ambition was called for.

Reading this report now, I am reminded of some of the American personality disorders encouraged by the expanding capitalism of the eighties and nineties, the belief in an infinitely expanding pie for those willing to be entrepreneurs. The Network can hardly be said to have lacked grandiosity in its idea that it could contribute some momentum toward change, but at the same time, it always failed at "goal setting" in the sense of choosing a unified policy to pursue. Goal setting wasn't right for us. Let feminists on their home ground do that. What we could do was join feminists together in the process of defining their proliferating projects. We were indeed what the consultants accused us of being: a talking shop.

A curious split in the record occurs at this point. In several swift conclaves in New York, startup themes for our work were named and embraced quickly, without fuss, and without any help from consultants. They each emerged with a sense of urgency shared by Easties and Westies: law, media, consciousness-raising/education.

Law took off at once because Julie Mertus was an expert on the politics of the Balkans, a passionate US feminist lawyer, and efficient activist involved with the development of NEWW in the nineties. All through the region, new laws were being passed by the hour. Countries were writing whole new constitutions—reconceptualizing the state, the citizen, the very concept of freedom. As an organizer Julie was capable of galvanizing energy around these multiple crises. Were women going to be state actors, active citizens, free to control their lives under the new governments? The answer was blowing in a new wind of reaction, traditionalism, deadly nostalgia for a caring woman who will be there for you from cradle to grave. There was no such thing then as a "feminist lawyer" in the region. Such a person would need to be invented in response to local emergencies, just as this creature had recently been invented by Western women's movements. So, law, and urgently. By June 1994 we had a grant from the Soros Foundation to meet in Budapest in a graceful palace to talk about pulling together a regional coalition of feminist lawyers.

By contrast, our media project died almost at once. We had submitted a grant application to the Soros Foundation, which was rudely rejected by everyone including Sonja, now head of the Soros Foundation of Serbia. Based on the marvelously effective model of our still-growing online project, journalists from the East were to become interns in Western media outlets to learn the mores of a free press. This sounds officious as I write, and, indeed, this project, initially organized by me and Sonia Jaffe Robbins, didn't have a chance. In hindsight, though, I wonder:

Did US media have anything to offer in fact? Because of the deep-rooted US values of a free press, I now think maybe yes.

Consciousness-raising/education had a very different fate: It was to become my home for the next twenty-five years. Out of this theme came the Book and Journal Project, still based in New York on Spring Street and still working, and the dozens of courses, long and short, that I and other NEWW members have offered from Poland to Albania to Hungary. Finally, this project always included the fine art of the party with a small *p*, the recreational life of a thriving network that hangs together over time and fosters the conversations that build a culture. At our twentieth-anniversary party, a small affair in New York, a Hungarian activist, shy during the public moment for speeches, sidled up to me later. What had the Network done for her? "It's the consistency." I'm satisfied with that small summing up. Right now we remain a replenishing resource. Our earlier website, full of feminist news and ideas, received hundreds of thousands of hits per month. Our social media pages now are followed monthly by thousands of people.

All this is by way of saying we had no problem finding consensus about things to do. Our collective talents and our work coalesced, and we wove strong ropes of activity.

But that curious split in our history: About structure we could never agree at all. It is no exaggeration to say that during the early years of the Network, between 1991 and 2004, before its Western sources for support dried up and we moved to Poland to profit from the new, rich stream of European Union money, Network members attended hundreds of meetings to discuss how to structure ourselves, without ever agreeing. I have notes from those meetings that could paper a large room in hell. Are we a membership organization? At one point we had a directory with two thousand names. But with email and the new mobility, what did this list mean? And what member would ever pay dues—to whom exactly, in what currency?

Were we a cluster of feminist NGOs affiliated in some way? As the legal fellowship program grew, we did link ourselves to particular organizations to which our young lawyers were to return. But what did these organizations do for the Network, or vice versa?

We made an elaborate steering committee on which Eastern Europeans were the majority. But what did this mean when each country was represented by only one or two people, and the common ground of regional interests could not and should not be assumed? Our steering committee met all over the region, in New York, in Washington, without once figuring out its responsibilities or organizational purposes. We had online meetings of the steering committee which stretched out over weeks and, Sonia Jaffe Robbins tells me, were mostly frustrating or inconclusive.

From my many experiences on the Left, it shouldn't have been a surprise to me that structure and the flow of power and money it stands for should have been so endlessly divisive, even while our projects flourished on the side. To give but one example among a multitude: For NEWW to get a tax-exempt number to receive grants, the law required that we have a board of fiscally responsible US citizens. But, as Nanette Funk argued, this put the charge of the money in US hands. "But, Nanette," some of us argued back, "the International Steering Committee (in whatever of its many avatars) will make all money *decisions*." "No," said Nanette. "While the Americans control the funds, the Easties have no real control." "But, Nanette, to get grants we need a 501(c)(3) tax exemption as a nonprofit. The Americans won't have to have any say." "But the hand that controls the funds . . ." Well, you get the idea. Sometimes we made ad hoc solutions. Each project had a director, and funds were to be distributed by that person as dictated by that particular grant. But, as any worthy Marxist can see, that didn't solve the money question theoretically.

In the end, the problem was solved another way: After the mid-nineties, we never raised any significant grants again. We have never had much money, and, as I remember it, it was Shana's friend Marjorie Lightman who was the first paid consultant who made a difference. She noted the Westies' ongoing angst about always being the ones with resources, able to get grants, in control of projects. "Funding," she said, "is not what you are about." She pointed out that if the Network is basically a foundation, it's dead on arrival. How prescient she was; Ford and so many others soon abandoned ship after starting regional "pilot" projects such as domestic violence shelters that were in no way locally sustainable. "You are different," she said. "You want to be part of an international women's movement." Translation on the ground: collaborating on raising small sums of money, people in the Network were to exchange what they could to foster feminism in a number of locations. NEWW was to be an association of activists, nothing more, but, certainly, nothing less.

STRUGGLES WITH STRUCTURE

Obviously, this was a sophisticated group of people endlessly wrangling in our organizational meetings. We were of the Left— though this meant different things for the Easties and the Westies steering the organization. We had read our Marcel Mauss, *The Gift: The Form and Reason for Exchange in Archaic Societies*, and knew that a gift unreciprocated is toxic, the source of the resentment and hatred always lurking among unequals. We knew perfectly well the centuries-old track record of "helping" as an essentially colonial project.

An Austrian graduate student, Veronika Wöhrer, wrote about us in this early phase of self-definition, finding a basic split in our consciousness, from the first meeting in Dubrovnik onward, between advocating for an equal relationship between West and East and giving the gift of Western books. Did these books become the gift that creates inequality because it can never be repaid? Wöhrer questions why Easties weren't asked to bring their own feminist texts to the meeting. I can think of a number of reasons why this would have been near to impossible for Easties to do, but it's a good point nonetheless. The Western women believed we had so much after twenty years of runaway feminist publishing that we concluded that "we" were the rich ones and that "they" had less. Wöhrer wonders if Western books were wanted, given this imbalanced exchange, and makes the obvious observation that the gift of Western books led to a constantly West-aggrandizing process of canon creation.

Slavenka Drakulić had produced this tension from the beginning by saying, first, "Help us. You have so much more," and, second, at the conference, that what the Americans had done was "nice" but, of course, the women of the East were going to have to carry on this struggle for themselves, and on their own terms. Freedom, she argued, is not something an outsider can give. She saw a long, hard slog ahead in which Easties' suffering would awaken them to their own particular need for feminism.

Underlying this question of "help" and its dangers was the myth of the frozen communist years. We were told again and again that *all* radical thinking and resistance had been successfully closed down under communism, so indeed feminist ideas were going to come from the West. As I recall, both Easties and Westies accepted this model in the early nineties, but by 2000 many thinkers in the region were vigorously undermining the idea of inactive, frozen decades. The prodigious Hana Havelková got a big grant to study women's activism of all kinds from 1948 to 1989; scholars at the Central European University began the unearthing of individual stories of resistance and layers of communist commitment to what they had called "emancipation." Eventually, scholars in the East were to develop less static versions of their own past.

Although, as Wöhrer says, we at the Network bore gifts of books, the Book and Journal Project expanded early toward giving tiny grants for research, translation, demonstration leaflets, and a wide range of publishing projects. We also began sending the results of such work to other countries in the Network to break down the continuing poor communication that weakened all cross-border international ties.

Another donor devised something they called "the feminist shelf," a standard collection of twenty or thirty books to be given to each former bloc country. But this idea was the opposite of the intent of our Book and Journal Project, which sought from the beginning to respond to specific requests. I remember Czech activist and scholar Jitka Málíková's early response to our book project: "Send us books by African American feminists. Their situation is much closer to ours than that of you white visitors." And we did, by the hundreds.

By noting how far a few American dollars could go in the early nineties, Wöhrer sees the Network as enjoying how small an effort could benefit the poor have-nots and "salve our conscience." Here comes my first strenuous objection. We were movement people seeking connection. Guilt over our greater coffers was muted, first, by our other intentions and, second, by our parallel poverty as a small, underfunded groupiscule.

Always eager to question my own enthusiasms, let me offer a counter-anecdote that somewhat supports Wöhrer. Delina Fico, an Albanian activist who has participated in the Network from the beginning, tells me that at an early board meeting, Lepa Mladjenovic, a board member from Serbia, announced that the New York–based feminist bookstore Bluestockings was in dire straits and was asking the community to step up with donations to save it. Lepa proposed that the Network of East-West Women should buy all our Book and Journal Project books from them, even though this was more expensive than ordering wholesale, in order to support the store. Alas, I have no memory of this debate. I wonder what position I took. Delina doesn't remember the details, but in the end, although we bought many books there, we didn't shift the bulk of our ordering to Bluestockings. Did I point out that at that moment we didn't have a dime to spare? Did I accept that the Network's financial support would indeed and always be only a one-way street, contributing only to the region? Now, for the sake of this argument, I wish we had made at least a token donation to Bluestockings. That would have been a way of saying that Easties were willing to defer some of the funds intended for them to Westies, that both sides had equally open hands, wanting to help each other, no matter what the sum.

The psychoanalyst and feminist theorist Jane Flax has helped me shape my anti-guilt argument. When I brought her the question about the inevitable guilt of those who have more wealth, she offered: "Guilt is itself a privileged position, because this feeling contains the idea that you *could* do something but have chosen not to. Guilt exaggerates what you have and leads you to underestimate and devalue the resources of the so-called needy. When people are motivated by guilt, others don't trust them because guilt can run out; the guilty person hasn't figured out what's in it for them."

Here we arrive at the crux of the matter. Those who gesture toward helping when people have to help themselves are asking for trouble. But US feminists were in our own state of difficulty.

We needed a new path toward effective organizing. The powerful US backlash against feminism, which I date roughly as at full strength by the early 1980s, was fracturing US feminism, putting it on the defensive, flattening its more radical wishes, depleting its energies. Network women were among the many who began to seek new ways to fight and new locations for their feminist aspirations. Now American feminists began their extensive travels. It was our hope that now we would have fresh company in thinking about what feminism can do for all projects of liberation. We would not be missionaries to disempowered people bearing a prepackaged, condescending message, but allies in a movement so far-reaching that there was room within it for many different meanings and kinds of struggle.

The next question was what forms this new feminism would take in the region to maximize viability and minimize inequalities. One couldn't organize in loose free associations. In East Central Europe in the early nineties one had to formally register a group if it was to have any chance of cohering over time. Some organizational glue was necessary, and it was the NGO that presented itself as the only way to establish an ongoing group without necessarily rigidifying one's intentions.

The NGO got its odd name from its liminal position between government structures and private enterprises like corporations and foundations, an indeterminacy that means that it can be a citizens' group formed to do almost anything: help soldiers' mothers; fix the environment; change local laws; substitute for the failures of more official structures. In post-communist countries, thousands of groups loosely known as NGOs have proliferated since they could register post-1989. They have seemed useful to a wide variety of actors for their flexibility and their responsiveness to immediate conditions and desires. As the NGO form has proliferated, particularly in Africa, South America, and then ubiquitously in the post-communist countries, a large social science literature has grown up critiquing this model for political organizing.

The case against NGOs: NGOs are tainted by the compromises they make to raise funds; NGOs are ad hoc, undemocratic structures with no accountability to whatever constituencies they claim to serve; NGOs are always complicit with prevailing power structures in order to fit in and gain approval. In fact, when they challenge the values of states, even indirectly, they are often attacked and even outlawed, as they have been in Russia. Hence, they are never more than mild; unwittingly, they are weak in order to survive in the melee of politics. Some NGOs, those that tried to supply the social services the new post-communists were cutting, were doomed to failure. They couldn't possibly substitute for the disappearing welfare state. However inadequate it had been, the so-often-hated nanny state had provided health care, full employment, education, housing. No NGO was of a scale to repair the loss of such comprehensive social safety nets.

Other NGOs, like NEWW, which were much less ambitious, could sometimes be more effective. We focused on specific tasks, some of which had a natural end, while others ramified over time. To this day, and increasingly, the controversy about NGOs continues, with detractors pointing out such organizations' lack of accountability and democracy, while defenders, among them the Network's own Nanette Funk, insist that NGOs have been key steppingstones toward a functioning civil society. Nanette makes the important argument that in situations with no traditions of voluntarism or charitable giving, NGOs were the only available form for independent action; they were gathering places where growing inequalities might be undermined. Often started by elites, they as often sought the breakdown of unjust divisions and unfair distributions.

I was less worried about our shaky NGO status than by our other structural claim: the Network. What is a network? Around this time, the anthropologist of law Annelise Riles began her work on networks, studying the women's groups in Fiji who were preparing for the big, culminating UN women's meeting in Beijing of 1995. I found Riles's work devastating. She was looking at groups mired in bureaucracy, whose main activity was to perpetuate themselves. How I recognized this account of spinning wheels! I lived in fear that all this work we were pouring into structural questions would render us merely self-referential, mild, even precious.

In the brilliant *The Network Inside Out*, Riles writes:

> Although my subject is the concrete activities of those involved in . . . transnational issue networks, throughout the book I take the Network as a broader class of phenomena. By the "Network," I mean to refer to a set of institutions, knowledge practices, and artifacts thereof that internally generate the effects of their own reality by reflecting on themselves. In a recent article, Scott Lash has called for a new kind of critical theory suited to the information age that grasps the aesthetic dimension of "reflexive modernity" in order to bring into view modernity's "doubles." . . . Likewise, George Marcus has written that "[t]here appears to be no real or powerfully imagined 'outside' to capitalism now, and where oppositional space is to be found, or how it is to be constructed within a global economy, is perhaps the most important fin-de-siècle question of left-liberal thought."

Every sentence here filled me with alarm. Networks tend to become about themselves. They usher in a safe and ultimately conforming activism for "the information age," shuttling this so-called information without any force of intent. They depend on the status quo of money and power to perpetuate themselves, and they can never get outside an essentially liberal frame to suggest, far less enact, the existence of real resistance.

Riles describes a poignant circle her typical "Network" travels. First, it struggles to establish itself—in her research case, to "help women." But so many structural problems confront this hard-to-define task, above all the difficulty of getting money to keep things going. Then comes a feeling of distress: "We are not helping real women." How can one get back to the essential goal? One can try to account for every penny. Where has the money so laboriously raised actually gone? And one can reach out for contact with the real by gathering data. Data about the needs of women will demonstrate that the Network is a needed institution. But can data collection make the Network "real?" Riles doubts this circular movement can make it out of itself into actual intervention. I tried to measure our Network's practices in relation to the fundamental problem Riles posed: A Network is a series of nodes shuttling bits along pathways—but with what ends in view?

I gave a talk at around this time at an international law conference in Washington about the Network of East-West Women, in which I expressed my own anxieties about being exhausted by endlessly redefining the problem, "women," and trying to bolster our own engagement in this overwhelming and elusive topic.

My examples of possible failures of feminist organizing in East Central Europe proliferated: "Gender" was being imported as a new fashion to be used as an overly simple explanation for complex problems, particularly crowding out the unpopular communist category of class. To avoid the failures they now faced, some Eastern feminist NGOs were constructing themselves as enclaves, retreating from making any demands on the new states, which they often assumed were just as toxic as the old. Using Western grant money, they could sometimes withdraw from the dangers of the difficult and unfamiliar post-communist political scene; but enmeshed in that alien money, they felt trapped or distorted by the new bureaucracy of Western foundations. One dispirited Russian feminist organizer told the English anthropologist Julie Hemment, "We used to live from party congress to party congress. Now we live from grant deadline to grant deadline."

In my talk, the nagging list of feminist failures continued: In the excitement of the ideas of flexibility, mobility, and self-expression, feminists weren't attending to the underlying truth that post-communist work opportunities were for the swift and young. For others, new poverty was blooming overnight, and work was becoming precarious. This list of mine was a hit at the conference, especially with the fine men who had invited me to speak. What's wrong with feminist practices is always a congenial theme.

But at this very conference, the wonderful Annelise Riles was to speak about her research on Fijian women's networks. I rushed from my own bloodbath to hear her with real trepidation. Her talk was witty, full of satirical descriptions of projects that can't get beyond their own self-propagation. To become legitimate, they must work in an essentially liberal framework in which capitalism and its values are a given, never a target in themselves.

Since on the US side our Network had come from radical feminist women of the New Left, nothing would be more depressing than to find ourselves enablers and abettors of a merely liberal post-communist order. Could our criticism of the status quo devolve into a mere inclusion movement, stripped of any strong critique of the new post-communist governments? To be sure, the women we were aligning with from the East had a complex history in relation to left thinking. One of Poland's leading feminist activists has told me that she would never have taken my course about feminism at the Academy of Science in Warsaw if she had dreamed that I had all these Marxist books she later discovered in my living room in New York, or that the feminism I was teaching her was critical of the growing neoliberalism so dear to the new democracies of East Central Europe.

Had our East-West work been at cross-purposes all along? And what would Annelise say about all that? I listened and vibrated with her every critique of the damp concept "network." During the question period, I decided to be brave and identified myself as a founder of the Network of East-West Women. What did she think of *us*? She asked me to repeat our name, then she said we were an exception, hardly spending any time on ourselves as a project, but building activities that were "real," not mired in the need to self-justify. I was delighted. According to this guru of "the network," this Annelise, we managed to grapple with "the real." Of course, as a consequence of where we put our energies, we never managed to raise much money!

In the years following, others were to provide support for this relatively positive view of our small-scale modus operandi. I mention just one here because it's a comparative study that shows that the decisions we finally made were unusual. In the collection *The Powers and Limits of NGOs: A Critical Look at Building Democracy in Eastern Europe and Eurasia,* Patrice C. McMahon has a chapter about women's NGOs in Poland and Hungary, in which she distinguishes the Network as less committed than others "to a particular goal or strategy." Hardly praise one wants to write home about, though the "terms of involvement" she defines seem to me to worm their unexciting way into the heart of the matter: Other organizations are "proactive," while the Network of East-West Women is "reactive." Others import their founding ideas, while the Network works from "domestic generated ideas." Most seek to fund "short-term" projects, while the Network assumes everything is ongoing and "long term." Large grants, which most see as proof of success, are way beyond the Network's scope; the Network settles for a "large number of small grants," which are sometimes sufficient for a task at hand but which can also be seen as seed grants, a sort of immediate support and tip of the hat that signals to other funders that an interesting larger plan is under way.

The one place where McMahon's scheme and my understanding part company is her assignment of "process (seminars)" to the others and "product (research)" to us. No, just the reverse. We created as many locations for dialogue as we could, while never researching the results of our encounters. The one exception I can recall proves the rule. A consultant pushed and shoved us into doing a "needs assessment." We duly sent out some boring questionnaires. "What support would help your group the most," et cetera. The answers were predictable. "We need money. We need more staff. We need . . ." But ultimately "need" has no helpful predicate. Instead, for example, this is how the Book and Journal Project worked: A small group of us responded to specific requests that looked like feminist undertakings that were doable, given a particular group's capacity. We hardly ever said no until the money we raised ran out. Our grant limit was twenty-five hundred dollars, though most were for much less.

Our biggest contribution to the funding world, though, has never been much remarked upon. Although requests to the Book and Journal Project required a brief but full description of the reason for the plan and how it could be realized, as well as a clear line budget, the final report required only a thank-you letter to use with funders: "This is how we spent our Network grant. Thank you very much." As the drumroll of bureaucracy built up after 1990, some organizations used their grant money to hire staff who did nothing but write the increasingly elaborate final reports required.

When I describe our very different practice in the Network's Book and Journal Project, people have sometimes worried: "Aren't you afraid to be cheated?" "Well, at this scale, no one's getting rich off us!" I know of only one case, an American project director, possibly desperate, who took the money for herself. Apropos of cheating, a bunch of friends, activists in Romania, told me the following anecdote: They got a grant to hold a big meeting. First they had to show receipts for every penny. (*Hey, that candy bar on the bill wasn't for the group and must be reimbursed by the eater.*) Then they were told that the grant was for a two-day meeting, and they needed to submit photographic evidence that the meeting actually took place as planned. Alas, my friends were strapped for time, for space, for food, and needed to do all the work in one day. What to do? Ingenious women! Each brought a change of clothes. They photographed themselves in one set of garments during the morning, another set during the afternoon and party. Now this strikes me as an example of a kind of cheating that these obviously dedicated feminists might be likely to do. But what the relationship must have been—or became—between this funder and these recipients is something nasty I don't want to contemplate.

BIG DATA

The issue of "research" still rankles, and I find I have a head of steam about this question. Let me fulminate: In the early nineties, I went to a research conference about women in East Central Europe at Rutgers. There were interesting papers, some given by my new friends in the region. The Hungarian group were outliers; one young sociologist from Budapest in particular argued that her statistics showed that women were faring considerably better than men in the transition. She had an intriguing reason: Women were always service workers, and the move all over the region from industrial to more service-based economies was giving women a real advantage. I talked to this speaker afterward because the tone of her talk implied that the founding energy behind this conference, a feminist concern about women's losses during the transition to capitalism, was foolish and unnecessary. Not only were women doing fine; they were doing *better than men*. Feminist worries are kneejerk assumptions, and all this Western-based palaver about poor women is merely rhetorical and not supported by the facts—that is, her solid numbers about happy, flourishing women.

There was no way I could position myself to sound smart and convincing to this much younger woman. I don't remember the argument I made. Did I mention how women are sometimes like canaries in mines? They are the first workers out there, but when things settle they find that the lucrative vanguard has been repopulated by, gulp, men. Whatever I said, then she said, then I said, we found ourselves screaming at each other in the hall—not my kind of thing usually.

So, data. Hers. And then my analysis of how things were likely to unfold. Much more recently, I was at a meeting of UN Women in New York. Both East Central European and Asian organizers were describing their plans. One project predominated: Data collection. What!? At the reception I almost assaulted the head of this relatively recent and much wished-for new entity, UN Women, which brings the many disparate gender-based UN activities of the past under one big, coordinated tent.

"Why data collection?"

"The governments need to know where to put their funds."

"But recently there's been a global swing to the right. These governments are simply refusing to spend money on often gross gender inequality. You know how it works. They ask for 'another study.'"

The director actually acknowledged that "another study" has no other purpose but delay and, ultimately, inaction. But what to do? All UN projects are driven by the will of the member states. The will to really change how gender structures society was present in the UN in the seventies and eighties. Since then, although lip service is still paid to the gross and easily documented fact that there is gender trouble all over the world, governments are withdrawing from the project of changing women's subordination. And since 2000, one can say more: The reaction to the 1995 Beijing "Plan of Action" has been shrewdly orchestrated by churches and conservative governments. Reproductive rights, economic rights . . . But no, I can't bear to go on with the obvious list of all the freedoms for women being attacked in recent years. Read the accounts of the UN meetings Beijing Plus 5 and Beijing Plus 10—meetings meant to push the platform forward, but that devolved into multiple attacks on it—and weep. Reactionary nostalgia for a past when all was clear, including women's place, has surged since Beijing and has changed the landscape of feminist struggle all over the world.

And to counter all this, what we need is . . . data?

My own direct encounter with data came in 2011 when I was invited by a friend to spend several days giving workshops for the staff of the European Union's European Institute for Gender Equality (EIGE). I was startled to hear that EIGE had a huge budget, millions of Euros a year, to gather statistics about women's situation in European Union countries. Why so much money, when women's movements themselves were in such poverty everywhere? Slowly, the explanation emerged: Much of this money was once the EU gender budget, but conservative governments don't want to continue the feminist initiatives of the past. The EU's will toward helping women has great if slowing momentum, so the new governments weren't immediately successful in their efforts to slash the big budgets devoted to equality of gender, race, and ethnicity. To deal with this residue of past commitments, conservative EU actors moved the big sum still in the gender column, bundling it together into the data collection project that became EIGE. Did they place it in Brussels or Paris or Berlin or any other city where feminist organizing is highly visible and still on the table? No, of course not. EIGE is tucked away in Vilnius, Lithuania, and rarely visited by movement people like me. It looks expensive and is lodged on several floors of beautiful offices, all in glass. It has a large staff, some of whom I met at my first workshop. I couldn't figure out quite what they wanted to get from me. I suggested a variety of ways one might move some of this big budget into actual activists' projects for women, but I was constantly corrected: "That use of funds is outside our mandate." The meeting was sleepy and no one asked questions. Finally, I asked: "Where would each one of you like to be with your part of EIGE's work in five years?" Now energy surged, and to my amazement most of the answers were too technical for me: "I will have developed system X to interface with system Y, yielding much higher . . ." well, I don't know what. It was all about algorithms and methods of data presentation.

The next day, discouraged, I sat in the elegant central visitors' lounge, looking through glass walls at the staff all busily at work. In revolving plastic display cases, EIGE's promos and pamphlets were set out in colorful array. Such glossies are not my kind of reading, but boredom reigned. I began to read, and Eureka! Annelise Riles's descriptions of "network" promos and reports burst out at me. Smiling faces of every color. Generalities about the project of helping women. Gimmicky graphics about progress. And in among the aimless clichés some actually dangerous bits and pieces imported from various national documents. Take, for example, the booklet on "work/life balance." In some progressive EU countries, this has been understood to mean that *both* men and women are out of balance and need support to give children and work the attention they require. Men and women could share jobs or have flextime to pick up a child from school. Crèches and child health centers could be located at workplaces, et cetera, et cetera. But, instead, the EIGE brochure picked up on quite another common discourse about life/work balance in some European countries, the idea that it is *women* who have this problem. They are overworked because they have to do everything. And the solution is to "help" women to continue to do everything by giving them a variety of services, with never a mention of any housework for their male mates.

Sitting on the posh EIGE furniture reading this brochure with the smiling faces of happy women, I boiled over. I leaped up to go to my friend to complain. She was sitting right there, twenty feet away, at her desk. I forgot about the glass. I careened into the perfectly clear wall of her office. The glass must be pretty thick at EIGE; no harm done to her office. But there I was with an enormous black eye. Ice was brought from the commissary. Everyone gathered around commiserating, but some also couldn't help but laugh. A perfect metaphor can only be relished.

Gosia Tarasiewicz, now long the director of NEWW Polska, had joined me to see Vilnius, and she tended to my rather dramatic but medically undangerous wound. We walked the next day in the beautiful but still—in its post–World War II state— much diminished city, including visits to the small bridges where hundreds of newly married couples have affixed padlocks: "Juri and Katya forever." No mention of future life/work balance.

We searched in a graveyard for the tomb of the most famous medieval rabbi in Vilnius, this capital for centuries of Jewish learning. We couldn't find it, but a woman tending another grave made a weary gesture toward a modest mausoleum. She told Gosia in Russian: "Everyone comes and searches, but they never put up a sign."

Finally, with scant farewells, the EIGE people shoveled us on a plane back to Krakow, where Sławka Walczewska and Beata Kozak were waiting at the airport to collect us walking wounded. By this time, my eye had turned every color of the sunset blazing as our plane came in. But here was the ultimate happy landing, among friends, ready to eat and drink and laugh at all that had happened, including my still-throbbing metaphor.

And that was the end of my foray into Big Data. The Network of East-West Women's Book and Journal Project has supported a number of research projects over the years, carried out by feminists to further their various designs. In fact, we like knowledge quite a lot when people try to turn it to use.

NEW YORK TALES

A few years ago, one of the key Network founders, Nanette Funk, asked me: "Why don't we have those wild New York parties anymore?" "Because, alas, first visits are not repeatable, never the same river. People with contacts or resources from East Central Europe can come and go now just like everyone else." I can't bring those thrilling parties back. But I can try to remember what New York was like in the Network's early days. People simply poured in.

HUNGARIAN VISITOR

In 1995 a Hungarian journalist from one of the mass circulation women's magazines is in New York and would like to interview me. What's up with all this sex, this pornography? Where the West is, that's where her readers want to go. I feel I should warn her that US feminists are deeply divided on these subjects, and that I have been on the anti-censorship side in the long pornography debates. I joke about how my friends and I get called the "pro-sex faction." Perfect. Couldn't be better. We set up a time.

When she arrives I'm surprised. She's in her fifties, looking tired and anxious. I've been reading scholarly studies of ladies' magazines in Hungary and how they are transforming themselves now that there are things for women to buy—and the need to urge them to do so. I call up the pictures of the before-1989 hairdos in the magazines—tight, short, easy to maintain, given women's workdays from hell—and then of course the new dos, softer, sexier, and requiring all kinds of colorings and conditioners, setting a whole new standard.

This woman of Budapest standing on my doorstep has the earlier harried look, the earlier hair. I like her at once. Now I understand her worries. We have an excited conversation about how everything is changing so fast, immediately, for women and, of course, for the magazines to which these new women are so urgently turning for advice. She locates her particular glossy with a smart sociologist's precision: middlebrow, neither for the new rich nor for factory workers, but for that struggling woman in between who is gazing longingly upward in a very unstable economic situation.

We are enjoying ourselves and decide to take a walk through the busy springtime streets of Greenwich Village, chattering about the young Hungarian woman's new desire for fancier sex, more orgasms. The word *orgasm* sounds loud and clear as we hurry along, carried forward in the late afternoon rush.

I'm surprised by her lack of embarrassment. Orgasm! Impotence? Sex toys! Is this freedom Hungarian of her, or just the ease anyone might feel in a foreign city, a foreign language?

I can't remember the transition, but in some context it crops up that I am Jewish. Everything changes. Her voice drops to a whisper, her eyes dart nervously at the people near us on the sidewalk. "I, too, am Jewish." I'm shocked in turn. So this, this is what's really dirty. I ask if people know at the magazine. No, no. No one knows. I tell her to relax; she's here, in New York. But she can't get over what turns out to be our real sisterhood. We share a calamity deeper than communism, deeper than sexism, deeper than the new market forces that are pushing everyone at her job into contortions. Our time together is over, our jolly jokes about changing sexual mores are mere baubles. Having told me her secret, she embraces me with catastrophe and is gone—never to communicate with me or the Network again.

ROMANIAN VISITOR, NEW YORK

In the mid-nineties, an elegant Romanian intellectual visits me in New York. Others have urged her to see me, since by now I have friends and colleagues in Romania. But she wants me to know that my feminist project is ridiculous. I see no reason to argue. I'm only interested in debating people who seem to need or want feminism. Let the contented rest content. It's enough that we like each other; we talk of other things. She's on her way to a six-month fellowship at a Midwestern university.

Six months later, as she passes back through New York, we meet again. She is chastened by how her contempt for feminism has been received in the brilliant community of scholars she sought to know. For some reason, these American professors think gender is important, and she has been most cruelly patronized. I can't help feeling vindicated. Sometimes schadenfreude is an unavoidable emotion. But I feel bad, too. I should have tried to prepare her for the famous professors she was about to meet, should have warned her that her withering disdain for feminism would not play well at the University of Michigan at Ann Arbor.

Of course I identify with these professors. They are my group, sisters who are the hardworking bearers of a new language. But creative and brave as we have been to find new words, new things to name, let us be curious and polite. Let us listen. In this collision I'm afraid no one learned much. We are stuck with a compulsive repetition of the same cliché that women in the West and East have "different histories": Under communism "women's emancipation" got a bad name—so no one likes feminism. But how little this tells us. And is it entirely true? And with each passing year, the meaning of this "difference" changes.

In the East, distrust still lies so deep that few women would welcome an organizer or dream of joining a political group of strangers. Such tasks feel overwhelming. For now it might be more interesting to ask how the embarrassment of the Romanian professor played on her return to Bucharest. Did it become a source of usable knowledge? I fantasize various results: My interesting visitor goes home to create a new elite, using her hard-won Western ideas to outrun her university colleagues. Or perhaps she becomes a different sort of teacher, a theorist about how the local situation of women fits into larger global changes, new possibilities. This last is unlikely but, still, from time to time, feminism strikes someone like lightning.

Unfortunately, I have no idea how she finally resolved the tension of learning about feminism in this unpleasant way. As I will no doubt have to say fifty times here: I have lost touch; I don't remember her name; I can barely call up her features. There are so many encounters that I've forgotten entirely. I've lost a lot.

But here's another way to think about this regret: My failure to keep track leaves my Romanian visitor to play with her memories without Western response or admonishment. I, too, am free to imagine that my support and warmth on her second visit left a healing mark. In general, I think something of those early East-West encounters remains. We exchanged words—leaving an undeterminable residue.

ARMENIAN VISITOR, NEW YORK

When an Armenian feminist came to speak at the university where I teach, her talk had a big crack down its middle. In the first half, she spoke of women's lack of political power, their inability to demand services. In Yerevan, the water was off half the day, the elevator and lights often failed, so she had to haul her children up flights and flights of black stairs to get home. She saw women as suffering most from the collapse and from a new brutalization in the mixture of old Soviet deprivations with new free market neglect.

None of this was news, but voices from the front line of change were very important to us at that time in the mid-nineties. To those of us for whom these changes were epochal, the details of the "before" and the "after" were bearers of great meaning. We were riveted when, in her book *How We Survived Communism and Even Laughed*, Slavenka Drakulić had described the difficulties of doing laundry under communism, which, she said, explained women's complete lack of faith in the state to care and provide, a distrust that had helped crash the system. Here was feminism, the recognition that everyday life matters, that there is politics in every fold of the domestic cloth, in every trip up the black staircase.

Without transition, the Armenian visitor's talk shifted from this scene to another. She began talking about the struggling Armenian nation. Women had a huge job to do; they must make more Armenians. The state should help them do this by providing water, electricity, and child subsidies. Armenian women weren't having enough babies, were on an informal strike because of the bad conditions. Here was a crisis, resonating with the genocide against Armenians of 1915. Here was grief, the loss of the mother, the squealing of children being butchered.

Both halves of the talk were bleak. But the combination had a poignant and troubling effect. Words were blowing in from different regions of thought. A maternalist feminism that saw women as needing more help and public recognition for their traditional tasks was joined by Armenian traditions of tragic nationalism: Women must make more babies—urgently. Both these trains of thought had an essentially traditional idea of women's place in life, but the woman who demands help and support as a mother is not exactly the woman who is a public citizen in a newly independent but fragile nation. Our guest felt that the nation must support her motherhood and that her motherhood was necessary for the support of the nation—a doubleness of her activist duty that added to her desperation. I hustled her off to dinner after her talk, eager to tease the whole thing out. It was a wonderful conversation, a muted meditation on how feminist ideas travel, and how they land.

After food and wine and a mutual parsing of the mixed messages in her talk, she finally turned to me and said that her three months in America had convinced her that her feminism and the various US feminisms she had encountered had nothing to do with each other. Indeed, she found most American feminists insane. Whereas she was driven by anxiety about the children—their dwindling number, the terrible conditions in which they live—all we seemed to talk about was abortion and lesbianism!

This then was the New York of the nineties, roiling with meetings, parties, debates, efforts to raise funds without compromise and to build structure without hierarchy. My experiences in East Central Europe in those years and ongoing were very different. When I think back on all the intensity with which we lived through the constant changes and readjustments to how we were to function in the few years after Dubrovnik and realize I was also teaching full time in New York, I wonder at where this energy could have come from. Revolutionary times are like this; they create an excitement like no other. We were vociferous, radical, eager, constantly misunderstanding each other across that East-West divide but vivid with our desire to communicate. I became a teacher of feminism in East Central Europe. As anomalous a task as this was to become, in the summer of 1992, I jumped right in.

9

TEACHING FEMINISM IN EAST CENTRAL EUROPE

My university, The New School, is both distinguished and unusual. Founded in 1919 to give a home to leading professors fired from Columbia University for protesting against World War I, and shaped by the radical educational reformer John Dewey, it began with the then novel idea that adults need an ongoing education. Its graduate division, The New School for Social Research, was started in 1933 to rescue and give a place to some of the Jewish and other threatened intellectuals beginning to flee Hitler's Europe. For this work, the University in Exile still holds a glowing reputation in Europe today, where it is far more famous than in its hometown, New York.

I joined the faculty of the just-then-forming undergraduate division of The New School, Eugene Lang College, in 1986. One reason they brought me in was some knotty experience I had had starting a fragile educational experiment (Livingston College, Rutgers). Luckily, I didn't know then that the larger school was deeply ambivalent about gender studies and that, in consequence, building gender studies programs would have to be a large part of my task there.

Elzbieta Matynia was hired at around the same time, a person who was later to have such a powerful impact on my life. She had been stranded as a visiting scholar in New York because the Polish communist government had declared martial law and, in a surprise sweep, was arresting hundreds of dissidents. Friends who were still inside urgently called their friends in the Polish diaspora: "It's not safe to come home." So, like so many European dissidents before her, Elzbieta sheltered at The New School.

In these years, in the 1980s, she and I—and absolutely everyone else— had no idea that these events would lead on to others in a quick cascade, ending in the complete collapse of Eastern and Central European communism and the dissolution of the Soviet Empire. But The New School, with its unique history of European rescues, had already developed a special relationship with that closed world.

On April 25, 1984, The New School celebrated the fiftieth anniversary of The University in Exile by giving the Polish dissident Adam Michnik an honorary degree. Just then, Michnik was in prison for the fifth time for his leadership in the outlawed Solidarity trade union movement, so it was only when he was freed that a small group from The New School traveled to Warsaw to finally give him his degree in person. In a move that has become legendary in The New School's sense of itself, Michnik suggested during this visit that our university continue its support for dissident intellectuals by starting a clandestine seminar to run in Warsaw, Budapest, and New York. Thus began the regionally influential group, the "Democracy Seminars," first underground and then, after 1989, above.

It was our great good fortune that, building on the Democracy Seminars, Elzbieta Matynia became director of what was to be the East Central Europe Program of The New School (now called the Transregional Center for Democratic Studies), the wellhead of so much brilliant exchange that was to follow.

Vis·i·tor, noun, ornithology: A migratory bird present in a locality for only part of the year.

TO SIT IN ELZBIETA MATYNIA'S small office at The New School in the early nineties was to encounter what had been the buried dissident world of the entire region, now, like the feminists after Dubrovnik, roaming free in New York. The thrill of it! Sitting there, I met Adam Michnik of course, and so many more. Zora and Martin Bútora came by to explain how Czechoslovakia was about to break up. The young men of the Hungarian party Fidesz drifted in, laying claim, back then, to the title of revolutionaries. Vladimir Tismăneanu explained why Romania was doing so badly—no Velvet Revolution here, but blood and fatal stagnation. I fell in love in an afternoon with the Czech ambassador to the US, Rita Klimová. The Polish professor Marcin Król explained to us his approval of the changing university scene: Under communism, a certain number of seats were reserved for peasants from the countryside. Now he didn't have to admit them anymore. Hurray for the return of his friends, the long-suppressed elites. Sigh.

My dear Sorin Vieru appeared, grieving over Romania in his usual, moving minor key. Miroslav Kusý, from Slovakia, was so courtly when we met in Elzbieta's office, although when he learned I was a feminist organizer, he gave a gentle groan. (Adam had laughed.) I assumed his sigh was the usual disparagement of officious women, but no. This kindly man explained to me that they had all been soaked in ideology. Could they just have a moment of peace before the next intellectual contender for meaning came along? I've already explained how little I think this lurking fantasy of no-ideology could be afforded. But the warmth of some of these people! And the heroism of their recent past. Several times a week Elzbieta's East Central Europe Program hosted speakers, from Roma organizers to brand-new members of post-communist governments. I was dazzled—and also constantly instructed.

One day I was sitting in Elzbieta's office when the new idea crackling in her always-creative mind was a summer school. "Let's bring all kinds of young graduate students together from the region and from The New School to discuss this new thing, this yet to be imagined 'democracy.'" Idly, I suggested, "Why not include a class on gender?" In the context of our university, this thought could only be exotic and unexpected.

Elzbieta was surprised but intrigued. Indeed, why not? I told her about the private list I had begun keeping during the formation of the Network of all the reasons why feminism was such a hard sell in the region. Reflecting on that list now, I feel rather proud of how much I had already gathered about the homelessness of feminism, which was causing all kinds of difficulties for my new feminist friends in their various post-communist situations. I was getting the hang of the typical dialogue facing all feminist organizers.

Me: "There are problems with the patriarchal family."

The man or woman on the street: "*Are you crazy? The* family *was the only decent, private institution we had, a place of trust and resistance.*"

"There are some good reasons to be angry at some men."

"*Are you crazy? We already live in a bath of mutual contempt. It's time for some kindness and peace between men and women.*"

"Capitalism has some nasty surprises for everyone—particularly for newly unemployed, newly impoverished women."

"Are you crazy? Don't be silly. Capitalism is the name of our desire. We want what you have: hair dryers, washing machines, and lipstick."

(One American visitor was almost assaulted when she said Americans have too many shades of lipstick. Up with variety, excess, masquerade, glamour.)

"It's time to get organized."

"Are you crazy? We're exhausted from how we were constantly lined up and 'organized'! All politics was and will continue to be corrupt. Women can now preside over the private, which is the best and richest part of life. Only the worst people lust for 'politics' after what that word has come to mean."

"Women aren't necessarily so different from men, but in a sexist society, men and women have different interests."

"Are you crazy? Men and women are completely different, an obvious truth stupid communism tried to ignore. Now vive la différence. But, please, we don't want to become a 'minority' group. Horrors. Difference is our best path into the individualism you have and we want."

"Women are going to be asked to glue the changing world together without thanks or pay."

"Yes! Thank goodness. We can trust women, with their permanent willingness to nurture, to sacrifice, to love. It's getting to be a mean world out there—dog eat dog—but women can be counted on to be kind."

Here was the beginning of my growing list. I reminded Elzbieta that everything in East Central Europe was being rewritten, in laws and in daily life. Women were being repositioned as once again the symbolic keepers of the hearth. Social services were disappearing, and the pace of change in general was knocking all expectations and norms sideways. Always game and open-minded, Elzbieta included my gender course in her exceptional school's first year.

And so, in 1992, off we went to Krakow. We had forty-five students, more than half from the region; four professors; and the readers for each course—given the unusual range of participants, necessarily all in English—which were bigger than a New York phone book.

OUR SCHOOL

Krakow, my Krakow. How mine? If you visit a place again and again, year after year, you earn the right to possess it. The frowsy, rundown botanical gardens where no foreigner goes but me. The ancient rhinoceros from the Pleistocene among displays of fish bones and fossils known as the natural history museum where even my friends, some natives of this place, have had to be dragged by enthusiastic me: "Look, has anything ever looked so prehistoric? He was found in a bog right near here!" Medieval cellars deep beneath the streets, Gothic and Renaissance buildings above. The Romanesque church of Saint Andrew where the Poles took refuge from the Tatar invasion of 1241 and where, at five o'clock, I go to hear nuns chant evensong.

Hitler put Comandante Hans Frank in charge of Galicia, and of course he set up headquarters here, in one of the most beautiful cities in all of Europe. What's more, he embellished the place, building an elegant castle on the Vistula where his *Wehrmacht* officers could rest and where we, in our school, eat lunch. The windows are shaped like German iron crosses, and the view from the terrace announces sovereignty over the river, its floodplain, and all the green districts the Germans had mastered.

Five times Frank meant to destroy Krakow, but something always stopped him. Can appreciation of the city's glory have contributed to his hesitation? The last time, the Russians were approaching, and Frank had placed explosives everywhere, intending to reduce the town to dust. But the Russians were advancing too quickly; the Germans were fleeing toward Wroclaw, which they did utterly destroy, turning it into "Fortress Wroclaw," a pile of rubble meant to stop the Russian advance toward Berlin. Krakow was left standing, a miracle, to me the dearest place in the world.

Our school is just outside the city. We take our meals on Frank's wide, gracious terrace and live in a monastic dormitory at the edge of Las Wolski, a small forest, the hunting ground of aristocrats since the fourteenth century. Our rooms tend to be dark, with dormer windows opening onto thick forest, but each has a balcony for gazing into the tops of trees. My dear fellow teacher and my yearly debating partner, Jeff Goldfarb, hates the dormitory. So little light. So little hot water to fill the so-enormous bathtub.

Coming here each summer from a crowded, overlit, chaotic life in New York, I sink into the silent calm of my cell with relief. For three weeks, this is my place. At the end of the course, I am wrung out—and elated—feeling, *if this is what teaching can be, all those years ago I chose the right profession.*

WHAT TO TEACH

Sitting in this front seat, I have conversed for twenty-five years with the young activists and intellectuals of the region, a spectator and sometimes participant in the high drama of accelerated change. For the first few summers, it was plain that we were teaching a new, young elite, the children of dissidents and intellectuals who were likely to becomes leaders in the now topsy-turvy situation: their parents' generation, recently in jail, were now in Parliament.

But each year, our students from the region changed. First those who grew up in communism; then those who were teenagers when the change came and could remember their parents' struggles; then those who were children in 1989 and knew the communist years only through family lore and popular memory. As I watched from my perch, the generations flipped by at the headlong pace that is post-communism.

With these shifts came the unintended consequence that every year the regional students and the US students became more alike. Wisely, Elzbieta stirred the pot by bringing in South Africans, Germans, Mexicans. This move toward cosmopolitan inclusiveness had a sort of United Nations effect: many voices, many lands. But during these years, another tendency spoke even louder: globalization. With each passing year, country after country was experiencing privatization, a concentration of wealth, a euphemistically called "structural adjustment" away from entitlements, safety nets, and public social services.

Almost without noticing, we had all skated out onto the thin ice of a world stage—leaving behind the monumental frozen structures of the Cold War. The war in former Yugoslavia paralyzed the school for a time and short-circuited many of our hopes. But now both students and faculty were living in the future.

Although the school's growing internationalism tended to obscure this gradual—and sometimes not so gradual—homogenization, the students themselves recognized one another's references, began to cite the same textual authorities, began to share similar ideas about what graduate school is for: to build an academic career, a pathway rarely imagined in the school's first year, in 1992, but one much narrower than the wild social yearning of that initial burst of energy and hopefulness.

Very soon, the great psychodrama of the "turn," "the transition" was over, and people were adapting to new relationships with a speed that still mystifies me. How did they stuff down so much accumulated culture into a sack called "the past"? Eva Hoffman's wonderful phrase captures how precipitous it all was: "Exit into history."

Of course there was resistance to this wild career, ambivalence, even grief for many things that were vanishing from the world. As an Estonian student told me, if you get your way, professor, no one will ever make tea for anyone again. This after we talked about housework and the need for men to share it. His startling reaction to feminism is easy to understand when one thinks of how hard a loving cup of tea can be to get in both our worlds. The specter of women abandoning the tasks they do for free out of love and duty can well seem like the end of all that is sweet and milky in life. I suggested that maybe *more* people could make tea; people could take turns as circumstances required, not like now, when women make tea for others even when they are sick or exhausted themselves. But this thought did not take the justifiable fear of Western modernity away. Could I claim that feminism had increased US culture's capacity to give care? Well, we had formulated the demand. But so far no universal services, no daycare, no support for the weary tea-makers. US feminists had not won victories that cost money. To my Estonian student, feminism ushered in a world without soul.

Another student in the class, a Ukrainian, irritated by this exchange about tea, countered with a story. She worked in an institute where she was the only woman researcher. One day the institute fellows had a party. She arrived late, and a beautiful cake was sitting there untouched. They greeted her warmly; thank God she had come; they were waiting for her to cut the cake. She had been furious, had asked them: Don't you have hands? Everyone ignored her outburst; she cut the cake.

Educated and with rising expectations, these students were trying to figure out how to make good lives in the new situation. Students' worries were constantly changing. The terms we used slid around, often badly misunderstood. Curiosity could collapse into consternation often enough, and the conversation could at times reveal our incompatibility: Americans' privileges and obtuseness; Easterners' irony, suspicion, and political cynicism.

But none of our difficulties muted the excitement. We had never met like this before. Elzbieta arranged for encounters of great intensity and, the first few years, everything we said to each other was news.

Looking back on my course notes and readers, I see that I was trying to offer "feminism" as a zone of fascination. The idea was to make the familiar, the traditional, the unremarked upon into the strange. Why do we live as we do? And how subject to change are our common arrangements?

In the sixties in the US, feminism had become an explosive political movement, one in which I had staked my whole being. Pretending objectivity would be in bad faith. But I detested the idea of feminism as a single body of doctrine or a panacea for all the world. Feminism could not be confidently defined but it could be explored, its internal fault lines acknowledged, its messiness valued as a sign of its creative proliferation. Feminism could be found all over the world and its astonishing reach—in the US as a mass movement—had come in part from its flexibility of forms and intentions, making it evocative to very different people. It was this rich chaos I tried to shape into a short course.

But how to do this when the students sitting before me in that classroom at the edge of the forest were so differently placed in relation to political movements in general and feminism in particular? The US students knew a lot about feminism and it was not fresh for them. Rather, it was riddled with clichés and received ideas they had to get beyond. One might even say they presented an odd combination of the jaded and the ignorant. They were living in a time of anti-feminist backlash that had stripped feminism of its allure, but they did not fully know this. The Eastern European students knew little about what an independent feminist movement might be or do, but they did know that "feminism" in their world was a concept on the defensive, constantly caricatured as a dreary communist leftover. The backlash they faced was harsh before they had had much chance to explore what feminism might be in the new political array in which they were finding themselves.

Both groups were entering the scene of feminism without knowledge of its former periods of excitement at new revelations, or its hopefulness as a new vision of how life could be different—from birth, to love, to the texture of daily life. At this moment, feminism seemed to have no romance to offer, while, by contrast, the new freedoms were often being packaged as a happy return to the old enchantments of family, nation, and religion. In the Catholic countries like Poland, the Church glittered with meaning, opening a spiritually deep path for entering a newly uncertain and increasingly rapacious world. Family was similarly seductive, remaining a key line to survival in the new as it had been under communism. And, finally, and coming later than the other siren songs: nationalism. One could read the new, swiftly differentiating nationalisms as providing a contrast to the imposed uniformities of communism. Or one could see the new distinctions being forged among nations as a more or less conscious resistance to the global, where such entities as big business and the European Union were stealing away any sense of grounded, familiar control.

With this mixed group of students before me, I tried to offer feminism as a mode of thinking admittedly unsettling, but promising for that very reason—feminism as a source of new questions and new answers. This meant owning up to my own passion for this subject, while including a range of possible feminisms that need not resolve into one clear line of analysis or intent. I sought to surprise the Western students with feminism's range while suggesting to the Eastern Europeans a way for them to be as excited by feminism's calls for freedom as the people around them were by church, home, and nation.

As I leaf through the volumes and volumes of readings year by year, I see I kept changing my materials, often reaching for comparative pieces that destabilized feminism as a fixed subject, but giving examples of how it has sometimes led to new ideas about how change might happen. For example, early on I chose Gail Pheterson's humble little piece comparing US, French, and Dutch feminisms for the way in which she showed how each culture's starting point made mincemeat of the others. In each national context "the self" is so uniquely conceived that freedom for a female self looks completely different in each case. The feminist project is up for grabs, and these diverse students must themselves make a fundamental reckoning about what it has meant and continues to mean that we all live in patriarchies. Why are feminists dissatisfied with this condition, and how do they reach out to get a handle on something so ubiquitous and, at the same time, so dispersed and variable?

So the course ranged from the micropolitics of housework to macro questions about democracy; public and private; sexism, racism, and identity politics; the reproduction of femininity and masculinity; the body and biopolitics; the changing nature of international capitalism and how those changes might affect women at work. Each year it was more possible to add a number of pieces written specifically about women's situation in the region (for example, Maria M. Kovacs's "Sensitivities, Old and New"; Slavenka Drakulić's "On Doing Laundry"; Isabel Marcus's "Dark Numbers," about the invisibility of domestic violence in Poland; and Michele Rivkin-Fish's "Sex Education and the Construction of Post-Soviet Russia: A Call for Cultural Translation within Feminist Analysis"—these last two still in manuscript when I first taught them).

By 1997, six years into the always-kinetic life of our school, about half of the pieces in the Theories of Gender in Culture course had their origin in the region. It pleases me that each year the readings changed so much, though certain classics remained: for example, Carole S. Vance's "Social Construction Theory," bell hooks's "Feminism: A Movement to End Sexist Oppression," John Berger's *Ways of Seeing*, Guy Standing's "Global Feminization Through Flexible Labor: A Theme Revisited," Saskia Sassen's "Women's Burden: Counter-geographies of Globalization," and Shana Penn's "The National Secret," this last, a shocker about the invisible women organizers of Poland's Solidarity movement. The amount of reading was staggering, and each day one could see students at tables on the Comandante's balcony or sprawled out on the grass of the dormitory courtyard (bright with hollyhocks), the big readers before them; some were clutching dictionaries. These people were serious.

With hindsight I appreciate what forbearance the East Central European students showed me in the school's first year. On the very first day, who should appear but Sławka Walczewska? I rushed over to tell her that she would know all about what I would be teaching and that, nice as it was to see her glowing face, a class like this was not for her.

By now Sławka knew me very well, including my first-day nerves and my pervasive anxiety about feminism's capacity to be part of any and all imperial projects. With what kindness she rejected this defensive stance, standing there as we were, in the beautiful classroom with tall windows onto the forest.

She explained that she was seeking the words I would use to describe the feminist situation. Horrors, I said. You have your own words. But Sławka's reaction was—and still is—that I was wrong. Why not help with words? And what's more, our US knowledge could be a "provocation." She might be inspired, and she felt free to reject anything that didn't fit. How about a more dialectical relationship, a back-and-forth we could all use, and how about remembering that the Network's founding idea was this reciprocity, that each of us could sift what the other said—and choose.

I see that this reassurance was key to many of my later, more developed practices. In the late nineties in Kyrgyzstan, an officious young woman from the Open Society Institute told me before my lecture at the university, "Don't bring up the virginity issue here. Sex before marriage is taboo, and you should make no judgment of this culture." Ahem. I talked about the virginity requirement for marriage extensively. My highly educated translator had herself been abducted as a young girl and then, presumed to be no longer a virgin, had to marry her abductor, a man she barely knew. This had ended well because she had a son the first year, elevating her status in the eyes of her husband and his family.

I explained to my Open Society Institute advisor that the young women in this room knew all about sex before marriage. They had had foreign television for some years; they had the gossip on the block; everyone knew everything. That an American visitor has a strong negative opinion about these matters is not exactly news either. Each one there had the freedom to take it or leave it. No one is bound by what the blundering American has to say. Needless to add, I was quite a hit in the university town of Osh.

So, with Sławka's kind permission to unapologetically make my introductory case for talking about gender and feminism for three weeks, the first class began. Several already well-known feminist organizers from the region were there, with scholarships from the Network, making the dream of international reciprocity feel very real. Among them was the amazing flash of light from Serbia, Lepa Mladjenovic. How grateful I am for what Lepa did for me then, just starting out as I was: "Ann, you talk too fast. English isn't our language." Or: "Ann, you are not listening well enough. If you listened better, it would slow you down." Or: "Ann, that Romanian at the back hasn't said a word. Attend to her." This Lepa, the brilliant organizer, lover of all women even when, like me, they make so many mistakes, has been an inspiration to several generations of activists. When I went to Kosovo just before the war, there she was, building bridges between Serbian and Kosovar activists. "Ann, you are staying at the wrong hotel. Albanian citizens of this very town are barred from visiting your hotel." Or: "Ann, stop saying you have a big grant for law projects. It's not *so* big and it probably makes no sense right here, now, in Pristina." As Lepa's viciously oppressed Albanian friends in Kosovo instructed me: "Law! We have three law regimes to fight against—the Serbian repression; then the repressive law of the fathers in our families; then the repressive law of our mothers-in-law. Does your big grant take aim at any of that?"

Really, without Lepa, I would have made many more mistakes; without Lepa, I wouldn't have understood the yawning depth of these mistakes. In that first class, in Serbia, in Kosovo, and wherever I have encountered her, she has given her instructions without rancor, always with warmth, without shaming devices, instead with love. Racketing along in high spirits, flashing a big safety pin on her jacket ("lesbian chic"), always in the right without making others feel bad, Lepa is one of the great organizers it has been my good fortune to know.

In the next school year, 1993, the Polish Parliament moved to ban abortion, a right women had had in Poland since 1956. Right away, pharmacies of "conscience" followed, refusing to sell contraceptives and suddenly illegal morning-after pills. Małgorzata Fuszara and all my friends had fought hard, gathering enough signatures to hold a referendum, but, illegally, the government quashed this call for a public vote. To reward the Church for its stalwart anti-communism, legislators pushed the draconian anti-abortion law through. Archbishop Glemp was standing at the door of the Polish Parliament, the Seym, while the vote against the right to abortion, almost unanimous, was cast.

Sitting in New York, I was mildly hysterical. Polish friends told me to calm down. "We're experts at evading laws; laws mean nothing." I rushed to push back: "But now, in a democracy, you *need* the rule of law."

In emergency mode, I went to Warsaw with a kit prepared for me by Karen Ramspacher, a young activist I knew who was starting menstrual extraction gatherings in New York, since abortion was being threatened in the US, too. For a cost of about five dollars, I had a jam jar, a connecting tube with a suction device and nozzle to insert in the uterus and vacuum out menstrual blood and anything else, like a blastocyst that might be about to implant there.

In the office of the Polish Feminist Association, a small group attended my lecture/demonstration. I explained that menstrual extraction took practice and that they would need a doctor or nurse to work with them at first, but that the procedure was very safe. Looking at the blood in the jam jar, you wouldn't know if you had been pregnant or not, but in any cycle, if you were worried, this process would give you peace of mind.

Everyone was stunned. Then much talk about their talent at building clandestine underground movements, and indeed, soon after the new law, newspapers began to offer what was covertly signaled as "abortion tourism." Buy a plane ticket to Prague, stay in a hotel for three nights, then come home. Problem solved, and money in the pocket of a Polish travel agent and a Czech doctor.

Wanda Nowicka, head of the International Planned Parenthood Federation, was there, and when we discussed that memorable meeting some years later, she read the exchange differently: not that people were so blithe about breaking the law, but that such direct references to the female body were terrifying. "The body," said Wanda, "is something none of us wanted to talk about."

When it came time to teach in Krakow that second summer, in 1993, I was still in a swivet about the dreadful new law. How could I teach while a pregnant student could be in such trouble? I decided to put on my own demonstration: At the pharmacy in New York I bought packages of twelve condoms for each student, nice ones, with lubrication. On the first day of class I explained that where abortion is illegal, I couldn't teach without protest. Students were surprised, some nonplussed, some delighted. I made this action every year thereafter and only once did a religious woman from Estonia refuse to take the package, putting her hands under the table and angrily shaking her head as I circled the room.

One year, a Ukrainian student asked for condoms, even though he wasn't taking my gender class. Here he was, his wife and newborn far away, and he wanted to take advantage of this lovely opportunity, *jeune filles en fleur* all around him at the school. I was startled by the openness of his request, his assumption that I wouldn't object to his planned philandering. Aren't feminists part of the sexual revolution? Not one to say no to sexual desire, I pondered. "Okay," I said, "but there's a catch. Your wife is all alone at home with a new baby, not much freedom. I'll give you the box of condoms, if I can also express mail a box to your wife." He was horrified. "This is no joke!" (Remember, feminists have no sense of humor, so of course not.)

Another class: Our subject is motherhood, and at this moment the particular question is, *Who will take care of the children?* We go around the room asking how each one imagines she will balance childcare with work. A lot of the Americans say they don't plan to have children, a useless answer considering that 95 percent of American women eventually try to have children, and 90 percent succeed. By contrast, those realists, the women from the region, assume they will have children, and all give the same answer to the childcare question: Of course their mothers will take care of the kids. It's hard breaking this confident chain, a sort of group complacency that all is well and the American feminists are making a fuss over something the agile managers of the East have solved long ago. But Kinga from Romania is an outlier. She comes out with, "But Ann said that now older women might stay active in the world. They won't just be exhausted all the time. They'll even have sex." Embarrassed silence. Surely their mothers won't have such a life. As everyone knows, they will retire five years before the men who will then die early; they will take care of their grandchildren.

I am amazed that Kinga has linked our discussions of women's and men's different life courses—not to mention our discussions of pleasure, choice, and sex—with the childcare question. How gratifying for the professor. "But Ann said . . . !"

Now the question has to change. Can we continue to expect women over fifty to spend the rest of their lives as their children's willing servants? Will they have other desires, better health, more mobility? Right now it doesn't look that way. Only young and pretty women are getting the new jobs (in Russia, job ads openly specify "long legs"). Older women are bitterly complaining at being supplanted much too soon. Still, "Ann says . . ." There is reason to believe that my young students may not be able to rely on the traditional solution even a few years down the road. For better and worse, families are moving, changing, sometimes falling apart. That screech owl Ann, who visits but once or twice a year, may be a harbinger of instability, changing wishes, different choices. Everyone is sitting very still contemplating Kinga's intervention. Ann says the future may include sex and action for older women and, since Ann is active in the world, lover in tow, obviously sexually active too, and, in some cases, older than their mothers, no one feels free to say a word against this thinkable future. A worried silence closes this motherhood episode.

In the mid-nineties, I lend my Polish student Basia a copy of *Our Bodies, Ourselves*, the great, collectively written health bible of the US Women's Movement. She returns it the next morning, like a pestilent object. "What's wrong?" A fervent response: "How can you call your movement ethical with this emphasis on pleasure and choice?" Aha! I spend some moments digesting this critique. "Funny, I never ask myself if my movement is ethical. It's just not my word. Although in my activism I do seek the good in some sense. How do I define what I think will make things better?

Political activism does require constant value judgments and some kind of faith."

We're so invested in this conversation that we are drilling holes into one another's eyes. "If pleasure and choice aren't part of an ethics for you, what words would you use as guides for the good?" Without skipping a beat: "Duty and sacrifice." And there you have it, a ground base beneath hundreds of conversations I've had in Poland over the years. Without ruling out the possibilities in values like duty and sacrifice, how can one lobby for the return of abortion rights if everyone's sense of women's goodness and rightness revolves around women giving up a claim to their own, independent destiny? But this small story has a sequel. Eventually, Basia wrote her dissertation about feminism. She now teaches courses in gender studies. I don't know what feminism and gender studies have become in her hands—and I don't presume to care. They are her new basis of professional identity and social action. Let versions of feminism travel around, borne by the flood of urgent new thinking and bound no one knows where.

Another summer in the mid-nineties, Reka is in my class. She is smoldering, privileged, and Hungarian. The gender material in my course clearly fascinates her and disturbs her. She is active in discussions, but I sense that she is feeling this excitement somewhat against her will. Finally, we get talking. When she leaves the school, she is going home to marry an American living in Budapest. It occurs to me that her anxiety lies here; the gender class has been clouding her enthusiasm for this next move. I say nothing, of course. An automatic suspicion of any and all marriages is the sort of programmatic feminism I detest.

Yet, clearly, there is a drama unfolding here, and, in some way I have not sought, I am a player. The fiancé is coming to visit. Reka has written to him about the class. I tell her I look forward to meeting him, which by now, my curiosity aroused, I certainly do. But the boyfriend doesn't come to class; he is here in our castle, but makes no effort to see me. In chance encounters, Reka seems slightly embarrassed. It occurs to me that her fiancé is a rival! Never have I put any feminist pressure on Reka, so the idea that I'm toxic comes from this invisible other. Is he paranoid, or, my god, here's another thought: She has told him all about the class—floating around key words such as *housework, motherhood, public life, independence*. I review these themes. As an American, he has of course heard about them. But his Reka, his foreign bride, has had no such questions running in her head until now. Living in Budapest, he has been able to find an eager, uncomplaining, uncontaminated mate. But no! She had to go off and take the gender class! (Ads on the Internet offer American men Russian brides: thin, because, the ads explain, they are hungry and without cars; compliant, because without choices; content with little, because innocent of feminist demands.)

After a few days, I am sure I will not meet the intended; our battle will remain safely invisible. But then, quite by chance, I run into the couple on that greatest of meeting places, Krakow's main square. The fiancé steps away, leaving Reka to greet me and gesture toward him. The game's afoot! I warmly insist on meeting the man she is about to marry. We walk over to him—and he cuts me dead! Now Reka is very embarrassed indeed. Who is this churlish fellow she is about to marry? He has acted like a naughty and sullen child. Alarm bells. I am feeling very concerned about Reka, but none of this is my business. The fiancé goes back to Budapest and the gender class continues, including occasional and always interesting challenges from Reka.

After the last class is over, I am sitting on the grass, exhausted but satisfied. We have discussed so much, learned so much from each other. I'm rehearsing in my mind a classroom exchange with one of the older students. The subject was sex, and she told us that once after an arduous summer work detail, her period stopped, and, although she had never had intercourse, she assumed that she was pregnant. Such was the state of sex education in Czechoslovakia in the 1950s. They had taught her at school that sexual pleasure was bourgeois. Musing over such moments of revelation, I am suddenly interrupted by a stormy Reka. She plunks down beside me and begins in on me at once: "What am I supposed to do with all this stuff we've discussed? How can I go home now, knowing all this? You don't realize the harm you have done. You should consider the consequences."

I am taken aback. Here is a serious charge. Where do all these hard-won feminist insights come from? How is one to construct a life in the glare of feminist questions—however open ended—while one must still live in the same Budapest, with the same people, and the same local prospects for independence?

Reka was enraged and I was instructed. *Lente, lente.* No believer in safety in the classroom, I nevertheless formed new resolutions: Every class must not only include respect for the gendered lives people are actually living, one of my long-held values, but must also be taught at an emotional temperature that leaves room for the specific difficulties each one might well face at home. Every class must open up imaginable paths people might—but need not—take. An engaged feminist life has to be made thinkable as a response, say, to no abortion rights, or to gross unfairness in the workplace, or to lack of choice in sex or work or marriage. After Reka, I moved more slowly—until the students themselves accelerated way beyond lonely desperation. (By 1997, when I taught an intensive seminar at the Academy of Sciences in Warsaw, the students were ready for anything. In a card they all signed at the end of the course, they thanked me "with expressions of irony and transgression.")

I apologize to Reka and tell her she is raising a question at the heart of any translation of feminist ideas from place to place. Context is all, I tell her. Make a good life in the situation in which you find yourself.

Reader, she married him. But that isn't the end of Reka's story—of course not. Two years later and I'm once again sitting on the grass outside our classroom, and here is Reka, paying the school a visit with a beautiful toddler in tow and, a surprise, a lovely bracelet, a present for me. I hug her, exclaim over the beautiful boy. But her misery is palpable. So? Once she was pregnant, her husband was never home. He skipped out every night to hang with his friends. Once the baby came, things got even worse. He was actively hostile, called her a nag and a ball and chain when she asked him for help. She bore this for some months, then left him. Now she's a single mother looking for work. Luckily her mother helps her. Tears, terrible tears. It's ridiculous, I know, but I almost feel responsible. How could the old sob story be so unchanged? The compulsive repetition of women's entrapment nauseates me.

But then I say to myself, *Enough indulgence in the downbeat Reka that lurks in my own personality, too.* I rouse myself to face her sorrows. "Hey!" I say. "Look at this wonderful child. What a treasure you're taking away from the wreckage. And what a fool your husband is to want no part of him. And look at how young and smart you are. Your whole life is before you. No more one-act plays for women. You're not ruined. You are just at the beginning."

We discuss her depression, her prospects, her various support systems. Together we look for a secret source of vitality, the start of desire. I can see that aloneness is too bleak, and I feel this terror of the loss of a safely partnered life myself, a vulnerability in my own and many women's lives. So no lecture now about glorious independence. Instead, I promise that she can choose a very different mate next time. Love, friends, work. We both want them all. We embrace and I wish her well.

FEMINISM'S TRUTH CLAIM

Life in the Krakow school continued, in the gender course matching tales like Reka's of female limitation with wild moments of female aspiration. By the third year, the Eastern European students who arrived had already heard about feminism as a potential source of post-communist thinking. For the Russian student who felt insulted at the idea that she might want to take the gender course—was the registrar saying she was ugly?—there was another student avid to take the course to hear about what a concept like "women's movement" could possibly mean.

While I was trying to teach this wide range of feminist constructions, it was no help that my colleague Jeff Goldfarb was arguing in print and conversation both with me and with students that feminism is of small use in the context of East Central Europe. With his passion for democracy, he had long studied East Central Europe in chains and, before 1989, he had assisted dissidents to meet secretly with Western intellectuals as a founder of the underground Democracy Seminars. But to him, feminism was not part of that project, because he understood it as an ideology—in other words, as a fixed belief system with nameable ends. From that fixed point it was a short step to the idea that feminism would not be valued—or even needed—in East Central Europe, where the ideology of communism had created in the region a disgust with single-line theories of human history, the "isms."

We argued and argued.

Jeff: An ideology like feminism makes a universal truth claim.

Ann: What truth claim does feminism make? Feminists disagree fundamentally about what feminists want. For example, is it respect for gender difference or the dissolving of the gender distinction? Context alters content.

Jeff: Feminism makes a truth claim.

Ann: But what is that truth claim? What do you fear? The collapse of all gender differences? Or the collapse of the public/private boundary that allows you to keep basic divisions of labor that feel sacred to you? Tell me your fantasy of what feminists want. *(I do see I've given myself more lines than Jeff.)*

And on and on. My struggle was to make a (non-truth) claim for feminism's urgency and relevance here, where we were teaching, and everywhere, while skirting any universalizing of feminism. Balancing on this tightrope, every year, we debated before the whole school, and each of us was, charmingly, convinced that he or she had won. We got so used to each other's arguments that one year we decided to enact our debate as farce by switching sides. I gave Jeff an earring to wear, and I put on his baseball cap. We did well by our adversary's arguments for a time, but then something ticked one of us off, and we returned to our usual positions, with Jeff confessing that wearing an earring made him uncomfortable anyway. Our debate was performance art, and once or twice we put on our play in a café in Krakow.

I had no argument with Jeff's observation that feminism was going to be a hard sell in the post-communist world. Had I not made that point myself to Elzbieta Matynia, with my list of the "difficulties," soon translated into Polish and Russian? Here is how Ralitsa Muharska put it in her 1994 piece in my course reader, "What Kind of Feminism for Bulgaria?":

> In terms of culture, Bulgarians have only recently begun looking upon themselves as individuals, this through the refutal [sic] of their collectivist upbringing of the past. Being a member of a group is beginning to be perceived as a sign of not being free. The euphoria arising from the novelty of the changes having already spent itself, the tendency now is for people to retreat from organizations, in many cases because they are disappointed, but also because the need to belong is loosening its grip on them. This new attitude has started to act as an inhibitor to the process of group formation. A contradiction has thus arisen between the individual's distrust of collectivism and the consciousness of women of their interests as an underprivileged social group. This contradiction is having a destructive impact on fragile new groups, including women's groups. ... In fact, an activist may often be regarded as either hiding dishonest intentions or of simply being insane.

This, I think, puts Jeff's point nicely. A feminist is swimming against the heavy pull of changing currents of feeling; she appears perverse, eccentric; she is alone.

(Sława gloried in this singularity, writing in 1996: "Let's stop looking at each other and asking the question why there is no us. Playing at staging our own funeral is in the long run boring and futile. Let's do what needs to be done." And Beata comically reversed this discussion of absence by marveling, "How is it possible that feminism in Poland exists at all?")

Pretty soon, Jeff wrote up his argument for why there was not and would not be any significant feminist movement in East Central Europe: "Why Is There No Feminism After Communism?" This article is admirably respectful to my side of the debate; we share a listening stance; but that mode (which Jeff calls civility) doesn't seem ever to change what we each feel driven to say to the other.

So how to teach? We had to step out of the terms of the debate, to recognize that our differences are carried along at different emotional temperatures. Jeff's great wish is for a neutral public sphere we all can enter together—just what I cannot grant him. For Jeff the disappearance of East European women from the new, post-communist public sphere is a phase. He's calm about waiting it out. My classes about feminism lack this calm. This difference in feeling is the crux. What I taught at our school is that, as Sławka would say, "Patient waiting is what is not okay." The civility Jeff wants is a form of distance, a relinquishing of outrage. At our Krakow school, I walked the line. Feminism is fueled by obstreperous outrage, but, burning or not, life at our school was pretty civil. There was passion—but always for open debate.

It heartened me to see that Jeff, too, was no stranger to outrage in his turn. One of our few African American students hated Krakow, a provincial city where sometimes people pointed at her in the streets. The racism was terrifying. She decided to leave the school early. This space many of us in the school enjoyed was what is not okay. She decided to give herself a farewell party—women only. At this, Jeff's outrage bloomed at last. The shock of being excluded! His daughter was with us that summer, and he told her that if she attended this party that excluded men, she would be going against her father's deepest and most treasured beliefs in a civil, open society. (Did he feel the same way when SNCC threw out whites? Surely the parallel was evident?) As I so often am, Jeff was furious. I asked him if he felt a similar rage when he looked at the US Congress and saw only men. I feel rage like yours, I said, when I look at our own government. Feel the burn.

But was I not, too, like Jeff, capable of unacceptable calm? Shouldn't my love of Krakow have been ruined by its racism and anti-Semitism? Identity is emotional temperature. Those who attack identity politics as divisive are cool. With injustices organized around identity comes the burn—and passionate, partisan politics.

WOMEN ARE PEOPLE

Between sessions in Krakow, I lecture around the region. In 2011 I speak to seventy graduate students in the Social Work Department at the university in Shkodra, Albania. I have a fine translator, and this gives me peaceful intervals to observe the class, mostly women but with a good sprinkling of men. In this small city, feminism is still interesting news.

By this time, I have some idea of what might be useful to say as introduction: Women are people. To illustrate this deceptively simple point, I tell them a story about a Ukrainian student I had some years earlier. He had faithfully attended my three-week course, Gender: Stable and Unstable, but had sat inert, speechless. Naturally, by the end, I was curious: I asked what the course had meant to him.

He told me that his mother had raised him and his brother alone. She had worked hard and made many sacrifices. Everything she did was for them, the sons, to push them forward in life. He had never given her constant struggle a thought; he had assumed it was her duty. Now, after the class, it seemed possible that this had been love, something special. "I'm going to have to thank her now."

The arrival of feminist sensibility! (I had a private moment of communion with that mother. She wouldn't have recognized me, but nonetheless I was a fly on the wall the day her son thanked her.)

Editing out my huge teacherly pride in this story, I elaborated with a sense of urgency: These students are to be social workers in a new Albania, where all social service systems are crumbling and everything is going private. I described how we all tend to assume that women are here to take care of us—feed us, clean up after us, give us support and solace. Women are our servants. We never think about it. It's their duty, so we never say thank you. Women, I tell them, will be expected to take up the slack, fill the empty spaces in the new Albania.

I've talked for twenty-five minutes, a short time by Eastern European standards. Students expect a long, at least partially unintelligible lecture to demonstrate seriousness, after which they usually file out. Instead, I open the floor for discussion. After all these years I'm not surprised when not a single hand goes up. Inured to what I know to be both learned passivity and active fear, I wait. Mira Danaj, my smart translator, understands; she says nothing. We wait.

Finally, about halfway back in the crowd, a young woman raises her hand. This is rare. It is almost always men who talk first.

"I do everything for my brothers. My mother is dead. I cook for them and clean the house. They tell me things they want done and I do them. I couldn't possibly change this."

I ask her, "What would they do if you ever refused, said you were too busy?"

"They would hit me." Suddenly, she and I are alone, our eyes locked as our dialogue proceeds.

"Would they hit you *hard*?"

A flurry of anxiety at this question. "The point isn't that they would hit me. It's that they would stop loving me."

Here we are in the unexplored country of feelings that feminist sensibility cannot simply fix. I take a deep breath and launch in: "It's no part of the feminism I care about to expect you to give up the love of your brothers."

Her relief is palpable. She bursts out: "They sent me here to school. They protect me." Service and protection. Gratitude and love. These are old bargains, I say, rich, warm, familiar. It would be a vulgar and stupefying feminism that ignored the quality of life such traditions can sometimes deliver, especially now, in Albania, where the only religion is money, the public sphere is corrupt, and the shared social world so decimated that newly urban people throw garbage out their windows, expecting/waiting for a pickup that never comes. One adorns and cleans only the inside, the often lavishly furnished family cave. There's the family or nothing.

"*But*," I say, with gathering intensity—and here comes a message, carried a long way, across an ocean, a sea, and delivered in the shadow of a mountain range that shuts out morning light— "you yourself can know what you are doing. You yourself can understand that bargain that your family and all the world established between you and your brothers from the moment you were born. Knowing this, and measuring the gains and losses, you may decide to raise any sons and daughters you have differently.

"And you won't be alone. It's all changing now. Albanians are living in new circumstances that bend the old certainties out of shape. People hold on to the old family, but no one stays home for long. One in three Albanians, women as well as men, are away from home right now, trying their fortunes in the global economy. You may have company if you seek new paths to a good life. To me, feminism at its best is about the good life."

End of lecture. My dear young woman is glowing; there are tears in her eyes.

At this moment, I am completely happy. The connection is everything. And I have rescued feminism once again from its potential for irrelevance and idiocy. Feminism and I are alive and well in Albania.

Now, the inevitable male hand goes up. This is a sclerotic, blustery middle-aged man with a red face. Often I enjoy the crash that follows after such rhetorical heights. The return to Earth is most salutary. I am eager for whatever his question will be, hoping to make use of whatever comes: "What about the penis (pronounced *pén-is*)?" I couldn't have dreamed a more perfect sequel. For a moment, I consider various responses. But the delight of the moment seizes me and I laugh, not an insulting but a happy laugh. The whole class takes this as permission and joins in—men and women. I yell over the din, "Yes, good question! What about the body? So happy you brought that up!" A brief discussion on difference follows. Students ask interesting questions for another half hour, and then the crowd flows out, several students stopping to thank me, while the penis man rather shamefacedly comes up to tell me he knows feminism is okay. He was just joking. He's a musician and wants me to have his CD, Albanian folk music, the most ecstatic and heartbreaking in the world. And here, at the end of the line, is the dear one with the brothers. We embrace. We observe each other's tears. Whatever we finally can make of it, we will remember our exchange all our lives.

I gave many lectures during that two-week visit to Albania. The dean came to one of my master classes at the university and patiently questioned me: "You talk about care and love, but what about the important things—government and politics?" I tried to make use of this hierarchy, to theorize the effects of making care disappear in public discourse. But the dean had great authority in this classroom. I had talked too much about the private, de-authorizing myself from discussing what the dean said really mattered. Note to self: I must not discuss care as belonging to the realm of the private, a framing that permits a depoliticization of this urgent public subject.

Too many people on this trip to Albania insisted to me that feminism is the hatred of men. I got tired of this precisely articulated, often elegantly expressed repetition, which collapsed into the absurd the moment I pushed on it. I tried to develop a new train of thought in response. Could it be that women's acquiescence in their dependent position—with all its onerous duties—currently hangs by a thin thread? Men's loss of central position is easily imaginable in this time of disorder, a shift that would render the world unrecognizable. Virginia Woolf's women's mirror reflecting men as twice their size could so easily be smashed. Care and love would disappear.

Everyone here acknowledged to me that there is a lot of domestic violence (particularly among the displaced people moving from the country to the city). Why not make a fuss about how much men hate women, how hard they daily hit them? Fear that women will hate men—perhaps also be violent?—is a perverse reversal, like Eve being born from Adam's rib.

When I read my student evaluations from those years, I discover that a big part of the learning on the Eastern side arose from my teaching style. Never had their professors insisted on dialogue or built the discussion out of a collaging of students' own words.

I was later to learn that those who tried to bring home to their universities this method of constant exchange were blocked at every turn by the entrenched, traditional lecture method. Their colleagues disparaged the seminar style as unrigorous, while their students found it threatening to be constantly asked their opinions. But for a fleeting moment, we Westies, with our disregard for privacy and our lack of anxiety about having our thoughts known, barreled ahead, inviting open conflict, offering genuinely new experiences to the Eastern and Central Europeans who bravely attended our classes.

LAUNDRY ROOM LIBRARY

Prompted by the delight people expressed at the books I brought to Dubrovnik, I decided from the start to bring a wide range of feminist books to the school in luggage no longer thinkable after September 11 2001. Comandante Frank's castle on the Vistula had an elegant library, and I asked the librarian there to house my forty books for students to see. Why is it so often like this: The library was usually closed, and the librarian was a prison guard whose job it was to prevent any book from ever getting out. Perhaps fear of circulation was a holdover from communism, like the slow and painful traffic in toilet paper at the dormitory. I pulled my books out of the always-closed library, but where to put them? The dormitory laundry room, of course. Since women's work is never done, the laundry rooms of the world are always open. Students could read while waiting for their clothes to dry. The notice I taped to the wall read:

Gender and Culture Library
Welcome!

These are the rules:

1. You may borrow a book, but please bring it back in a few hours; don't leave it sitting around in your room where others can't see it.

2. If you are in the Gender and Culture class, write your name in the back cover of 3 books you would like to take home.

3. If someone has claimed a book you want, or if there are other books you would like to have sent, write your requests in <u>THE GREEN BOOK.</u>

The Green Book became a yearly tradition and was a building block of the Network's Book and Journal Project that followed. People wrote everything in the Green Book: their dream research projects; urgent needs for material for term papers; questions about feminist theory. At the end of each three-week school session, I returned to New York to fulfill the requests in the Green Book, a sort of treasure hunt, which increasingly included materials being written in the region, where circulation did indeed remain a problem.

At first, the Project was all heavy suitcases and packages sent by sea. The books to Mongolia took a year; during the war, the books to Kosovo were sent back to New York by the hostile relay station in Belgrade. By 2000 the post office had discontinued the cheap by-sea M bags we used to haul to the post office. Books were ordered online and mailed directly by air. And suddenly that earlier heroic time of fetching and carrying was gone like a dream.

10

WHO NAMES CHANGE?

Change comes, and who gets to name it? Rapid change in East Central Europe was often greeted in the West as the joyous triumph of capitalism, but in fact, beyond this unidirectional story line, many were seeking other ways to think about the future.

When I first met them in the early 1990s, my friends in East Central Europe were living through upheavals of a magnitude beyond my experience. They had to reinvent everything: What work was one to do? To whom was one now to complain when things went wrong? The world of things had suddenly exploded. What was one to want?

Now communication was allowed, but what should a public discussion look like? Who did one want to talk to, and how? The Network of East-West Women's first formal project after our founding meeting in Dubrovnik was to get feminist organizers talking to each other online. But "online" was itself just being invented. For this, one needed telephone lines, machines, and, more difficult, an idea of what such conversations could be like in a widening world.

Each day, Krakow changed, the people changed, the institutions they were imagining developed. Because of the excitement and the pace, the first *rush of feminist organizing in the 1990s was a sort of golden age. Political work developed in all directions, as people groped for possible forms such work might take.*

EACH SCHOOL SESSION ENDED with a lovely drunken bash organized by that gifted designer of events, Elzbieta. She would put on a recording of Chopin's "Military" Polonaise, and the whole school would make a procession down the winding path from the dormitory to what was for the school unusual: a sumptuous buffet and drinks waiting on the terrace below. I see in the film that Elzbieta's husband Dick Adams made of one of these magnificent parties that I am dancing along in the procession, ecstatic. How much I loved the school is there, captured for good.

Elzbieta always invited officials from the town to this final party, and, graciously, she also included the Krakow feminists. In the first year, one of her many contacts, the vice mayor of Krakow, got talking to the always engaging Sławka Walczewska and Beata Kozak. They had already established their Women's Foundation, eFKa, in 1991 but their work had no foot on the ground, no home. They wanted to make a women's center, a hotline, a library. The vice mayor was intrigued. "Okay. I'll try to get the city to rent you a space."

This moment—in which Elzbieta's connective genius, the Network's readiness to lend a hand, and the local feminists' ability to recognize the moment for action—seems exemplary to me, a combination of forces that was just what we were dreaming of. Almost immediately, the city offered eFKa three tiny rooms near the center of Krakow. Now the women's movement had its first of many homes. The Network donated a small gender studies library, and eFKa managed to get a telephone, a rare acquisition in those days. Of course the phone, meant to be a women's hotline, didn't work; but it would—eventually. I like a photograph of us all from that time: I am wearing the phone as a hat, since it doesn't yet have any other practical use. And in the background, you can see that the small office is a shambles. The Krakow feminists provided the sweat equity; Sławka, Beata, Roma Cieśla, and above all Viola Cywicka renovated the space. How right that the place had once been a laundry—that theme of women's work again—so it was called the *magiel* (the wringer).

I happened to be sitting on the hard-bottomed old couch in the newly renovated center when two students wandered in to use the library. The woman wanted to write a school paper about gender; her boyfriend was riding shotgun. She had read in the newspaper that the center had books. A flurry of excitement. Did eFKa plan to lend these books? Should there be a card file? What would be the time limit for borrowing? How would they ever get the books back? The student told us her subject (it was images of women in advertising, I believe), and we searched the shelves for good material. ("Is the gaze male?") She was the first.

eFKa has had many offices and many homes for its now large, well-organized library, following the fortunes of feminists in Krakow up and down through the decades. As the work evolved, feminist journals began here, first the scholarly *Penem Glosem* (*Out Loud*), then the more popular feminist magazine *Zadra* (*Splinter*).

Roma informs me that we first met at the very beginning of the school in 1992. She remembers that Sławka and Beata introduced us on Krakow's main square—where else? History was moving very fast then. Roma had just met her lover Viola—the minute lesbians could meet legally in 1990. Then, immediately, they started the first lesbian group in Krakow, "Lesbian Lambda," named after the gay men's groups starting all over Poland in the post-communist melee of new freedoms. Sławka and Beata had come to one of their early meetings. Soon Roma was leading a group of my students in a discussion of gay life, which, it would seem, included a visit to a gay club called Sauna, as Roma's notes tell me, "at Rejtana Street."

The amount of organizing this small gang of women did in the magic years 1990 to 1996 is astonishing: picnics, summer retreats, international conferences, women's crisis lines, constant local meetings. I still have some of the posters in the great Polish poster art tradition for the hotline, which was answered by two young psychologists. Before the *magiel*, Roma wrote in her notes to me, they had "no stable place for meetings in Krakow, just cafés or open spaces in a meadow." They reached out, building a large world, "mainly correspondence we were doing at home with the old fashioned private typing machine" and later on the phone, "important for networking before the era of the Internet."

One sentence in Roma's notes opens a door to that utopian period, for which I confess nostalgia: "We were playing together in the evenings after lectures." Several American friends have remarked that the fun I was having merely shows that I missed that common phase of having a girl gang in high school. Well, maybe.

For me, the chance for true levity came with the seriousness of feminism. The early seventies were thrilling and wild. Later, backlash slowed down that naughty élan, which, I've discovered, younger American women have no sense ever existed. To them, "Second Wave feminism" means merely racist, puritanical, and humorless. To my amazement, here in Krakow, that mad rush of energy, hilarity, and hopefulness was once again possible for a time. We—Roma, Viola, Sławka, Beata, and I—careened through the city streets, sat around in its charming cafés springing up overnight; we assessed its crumbling buildings where we plotted to establish women's centers, group houses, and, for Sławka, witches' covens. It was our city. No one molested us at whatever hour. Our freedom felt absolute and I was completely happy. Of course, such periods end, leaving behind a mythic residue in those who took part.

In those early years, we and many others were "playing"—or let me revise that, through the process of playing—were building a feminist sensibility that has endured, spread out, created currents of discussion and debate, even in what is now a very dark time for feminist desires. Although feminism had no mass appeal in the region, the variety of activists and intellectuals who entered its debates laid down a layer of thought and feeling not unlike the one cultural dissidents established in the region before the fall of communism. Feminism is a strand of resistance to current nationalisms and to what is now called "anti-genderism"—the idea that gender is fixed nature and mustn't be touched by politics. But even the term "anti-gender" is on the defensive, and nods to feminism's power to disturb. We were at play; the game was to imagine something new. The richness of that freedom keeps reinstating its allure for new young women unsatisfied with the traditional offers of hearth, church, and nation.

During this Age of Gold, the Network of East-West Women was bursting with energy. Under Shana Penn's ever-accelerating leadership, our first big project bloomed into being: We put our ramifying international steering committee online; by extension, we got all our members talking to each other, wherever they were. It's hard to remember this now, but the web, as we know it, was just coming into existence as we started this work. Sonia Jaffe Robbins, one of the writers of the computer users' manual the Network produced, remembers that they were putting the guide together just as the Internet itself was becoming a mass medium.

Shana's grant design was simple and elegant. We would choose already well-connected feminist activists with good English from all over East Central Europe. (Later the service was also in Russian.) These first few came to Washington DC for about three months for an insanely intensive training program: learning computers, learning the Internet, learning the mechanics to connect others. These exhausted women, stuffed with new technical knowledge, got a computer to take home and were to travel from country to country like Johnny Appleseeds, wiring women up. I've already told about Victoria Vrana's struggle in Bulgaria, to which Sonia's notes add this further detail: people kept stealing the new phone lines installed for the modems, for the copper.

It made perfect sense that Roma, with her talent for building groups and connecting the once invisible or closeted in the tumbling new realities around her, would be chosen for the first Online Project cohort in 1994. She has told me what a struggle it was. In spite of her very fine English, like me she is slow at new languages. The computer turned into an alien she struggled with daily. It was a great relief when Viola came to have Christmas with me, Daniel, and Roma in New York. Because of Viola's homophobic family, they had never been able to celebrate together what in Poland is a gorgeous extravaganza of a holiday. Daniel and I bought our first Christmas tree for them, and the ever-handy Viola constructed beautiful ornaments for it.

In spite of the pains of computer life (ones I still experience), Roma was to write at the end, "It is a special feeling that I can use high technology that is very progressive, very new." Zsuzsa Béres of Hungary's then flourishing group, NaNE: "We're very excited about this sort of flow of information around the Universe!" Albania had not yet joined the international telephone system and had no international country code. Sonia tells me that when she asked when Albania would be added, the US international operator had never heard of the place. And finally, again, Bulgaria, from one of the founders in Dubrovnik of NEWW, Christina Kotchemidova: "Electronic mail will help us overcome our sense of isolation from the modern world and from other women around the globe."

Soon we were holding our steering committee meetings online. The limitations of that fantasy, "around the globe," were to become clear, as were a thousand other problems with the wondrous Internet, but let me pause here to celebrate the hard work and courage of the more than one hundred and fifty women who were in NEWW's Online Project. It was all so new. Roma reminds me that once she was home she became one of NEWW's official online trainers. She hooked up women in Prague, Bratislava, Vilnius, Riga, and Tartu, not to mention a number of groups in Warsaw. By the end, trainings were held in thirty-one cities, and email accounts were opened for forty groups. From Ljubljana to Tver, from Bishkek to Pristina, from Vilnius to St. Petersburg, from Skopje to Sofia, they all joined in a feminism that was now traveling.

I can't follow all the afterlives of what the Online Project set in motion in those years. Picture a thousand lines crossing or the millions who later visited our message boards and websites—

now migrating to Facebook. But one story I can follow: Roma's, one of my dearest friends in the wired—or any—world.

At the end of the online trainings, each participant got an official-looking certificate to commemorate her successful completion of the course. Shana was good at such things. I seem to remember that we both signed them. Such pieces of paper are usually bound for oblivion, but not Roma's. She and a friend, a co-founder of eFKa, Barbara—or Basia—Kaszkur, who was already a computer whiz, had the idea to start a school to teach older women about computers. In context, this idea was nothing short of revolutionary. Not only women but *older* women. No group more invisible. Like Shana a gifted organizer, Barbara began to raise money to buy a few computers and to rent a cozy, welcoming office/classroom. The Network Book and Journal Project provided a small grant so they could advertise their new school in the newspapers. Brave women from this badly superannuated group came. There on the wall, framed and draped with a plastic rose, was our Network certificate authorizing an expert: Roma.

They called their school the Fullness-of-Life Academy. No doubt this intriguing but awkward name works better in Polish: *Akademia Pełni Życia*. Older women were to have a full life. Interesting. But the path was blocked in any number of ways. A professor representing the Church arrived to make sure they weren't advocating for abortion. They rarely said the computers were for women only; mostly they implied it. Funders told them, "women only" isn't "serious." In later years they even stopped mentioning women at all, substituting a category more in favor: "seniors." In fact, seniors were usually women, but not always. Roma and Basia told me funny stories about how a few men always assumed they were welcome, God's gift to all unconfident women. Roma described these guys' learning style: free, experimental, often leaving a lot of computer wreckage behind.

To her chagrin, women had their own parallel and regrettable thumbprint: They were timid, afraid they might hurt the machines. Roma had a hard time persuading them to play with the computers, to make a mess like the men. She saw that women were crippled and needed a special style of pedagogy to rescue them from shame and fear. They saw themselves as "stupid." (One woman's husband assured his wife she was stupid so often that she studied in secret, learning a lot about computers and mastering competent English, all the while gloating that he didn't know what went on in the flourishing Fullness-of-Life community.)

In the beginning, Roma and Basia thought they were helping older women get jobs, rather than stay home caring for ailing relatives or grandchildren. But this emphasis on work faded as the school evolved. Finding work for older women was not easy. But these two passionate feminists remained subversive. It was Fullness-of-Life that was central to them. Engaging with the world was a value in itself. They were taking a scythe to the stereotype that older women wouldn't be able to communicate or learn new things, or be modern. Because of computers, a chasm was opening up between the generations, and the school was fighting back against this social isolation. Women just talking together made for better lives. They came to talk—or to get help with the divorce papers.

In the early years of this enterprise, I interviewed some of these women who came to learn computing from Roma and Basia. Varied as they were, they were all seekers, looking for some reentry point to public life after being forcibly retired (five years earlier than men), or widowed, or divorced, or displaced from communist structures like state-run businesses or women's councils. Basia and Roma were eclectic in their culture building: lectures on medieval Europe or architecture or ceramics; lots of card playing. The women I interviewed found the Academy to be a free, undoctrinaire place. They came from every class. Feminism was rarely mentioned, but the founders' belief in the importance of happiness for women was a glue that held everything together. Since money was scarce, everyone played a crucial role in keeping the Academy going. They needed each other, different as they were, and the place was alight with a relaxed energy.

For some years, this was Roma's world. Then she and Basia had a falling out. I could never get to the bottom of what went wrong. "So dawn goes down to day / Nothing gold can stay."

Success and failure. But of course. Looking back in a 2017 essay, Roma says that the only place where she really feels at home is the gay and lesbian world. Other projects failed to sustain her. Identity moves around; successful communities come and go. The Church points out that God never changes—an idea at the center of its profound power. People who dream of social change are always trying to tie down what that means. Uncertainty rules, and those who want change are always imagining a world beyond the foursquare seemingly eternal dance of men and women, set to engaging, familiar music in the central square.

LIGHTBULBS AND PIZZA HUT

But change comes. Krakow, my Krakow, was changing itself summer by summer. After my initial romance with the timeless beauty of this place, it just wouldn't stay still. The builders moved in early, and the city became a vibrating site of urban renewal. "Do you mind the transformation of familiar landmarks?" I asked Sławka. "What! Everything is improving. Everyone is busy. Finally, foreign food. The sound of hammering is great!"

The mighty St. Mary's Basilica, dominating the main square, had been dingy, or one might say evocative and gray. Now, cleaned, it turned out to be bright red. Suddenly, a choice between a Mexican and a Corsican restaurant; then in the next leap, Internet cafés.

No one feared this galloping gentrification yet, but later an artist, Karolina Kowalska, was to take a picture of Floriańska, a main artery leading out of the central square, whiting out all the new commercial signs or ads. The resulting image was almost entirely white, with an occasional flash, a cornice or elaborate doorway still visible, half-buried reminders of the remarkable architecture beneath.

The slummy and half-deserted old Jewish Quarter began to offer Schindler's List tours and glossy guides to Jewish Krakow. Then came nightclubs, and tourist spots with Jewish music played dully by university students who had never met a Jew before the arrival of a torrent of visitors from Israel or New York. Of course McDonald's came, but the city fought back, succeeding at least in keeping signs with golden arches off the main square. Undaunted, my friends kept moving; when the monumental main square became a tourist trap in summer, they happily shifted to cafés in new neighborhoods in some other fast-changing part of town. The women's center kept moving, too, as rents changed.

At some point in the mid-nineties it seemed that, no matter the generation, everyone's memory began to erode. Eyes front, and no one was grieving. Occasionally, as traces of the former time began to disappear, people created little local museums of communism to hang on to disappearing objects. In Gdansk, near the shipyard, you can see a careful replica of a communist shop, only a few pieces of inferior-looking meat in the glass cases and spirals of flypaper hanging from the ceiling. I visited the place with Gosia, Beata, and Sławka, who were old enough to remember. It was moving to watch them study its details, exclaiming over tins of beans and plaster models of bad bread.

It's September 2013, and I'm throwing away my Polish hot-water kettle. This has taken a long time because of an entirely unfashionable and indefensible nostalgia for the days when one couldn't easily buy this basic convenience.

Each summer during the nineties, I would arrive in Krakow carrying this kettle, two small fans, ceramic cups, large towels, hair conditioner—I won't go on with this idiosyncratic domestic list. This was before September 11 2001 when it was possible to travel with huge expanding suitcases, which I stuffed like circus cars. Once one of my bags went astray, and my colleagues teased me about what the poor thief would find: three voluminous towels and twenty books of feminist theory for the library.

I would spend my first few days in Poland, before the students arrived, searching for still more things I needed. A Western consumer to the bone, I used to love the hunt. And everything back then was so cheap! From the straw market: a wastebasket and a woven tray. From the Old City open market, a plastic dish, a colander, a spoon, a sponge, a ten-dollar skirt. From shops with no sign or name, an electric plug, some picture wire, a small mirror. In this way, I greeted my beloved Krakow, street by street. Treasures were hidden, and you had to know where.

Then one summer, say, 2003, I told Sławka and Beata I needed to do my yearly shopping. "For what?" I produced my usual odd list, and they laughed. "It's all at Tesco's." Oh, dear. We jumped into their old Jeep, the side painted with a large picture of a hungry-looking wolf, and went to the outskirts of the city. There, a huge box store glowed under klieg lights. "How do you feel about this?" I asked them. "It's incredibly convenient." And so it proved. *Everything* on my list was there—also food, furniture, and follies of all kinds. Most people couldn't afford this new stuff, but they could yearn for it, name the brand of their desire. Only one stop. An era ended—and only one silly visitor left to grieve.

It was several years before one could begin a conversation about the dangers lurking in consumerism. Restraint was off limits in the early days, with the one exception of the clever anarchists who staged a protest at Tesco's by wheeling around the huge shopping carts, clogging the aisles, and buying nothing. Slavenka would have rebuked them: here, at last, aisles and aisles of tampons. Welcome, oh weary women shoppers.

Memory now provides this slender anecdote as a stern corrective to my sentimentality about a lost world of scarcity, B.T. (Before Tesco): Beginning in 1992, at the front desk of our dormitory, the same surly attendant was always there, giving us the kind of anti-greeting typical of the time before tourists or before come-hither marketing gestures. There was no sign at reception to say, "Welcome to our comfortable guest house right next door to one of the most beautiful forests in the world, where sometimes elephants from our charming zoo take walks." Not a hint about the noble beech trees, the glorious trails. Nothing but a hostile scowl.

This man's job was to take our room keys when we (so frequently) went out and return them to us when we (so belatedly) returned. His other task was grudgingly to dispense toilet paper, a much-valued commodity, one roll at a time. (Once I went ballistic and demanded two rolls because I was a professor. I do believe this was the only time I ever demanded more in Eastern Europe—with the exception of an embarrassing occasion in 1991 when, at a different hotel front desk in Timisoara, Romania, I asked for a second lightbulb for our room, causing the staff to howl with laughter: "We'll ask the boss.")

By the late 1990s, our once-mean front desk attendant in Krakow had changed utterly. He greeted me warmly on my arrival, giving me two rolls of toilet paper at once as a welcome gift. Although no one from the old days had been fired, everyone was doing new work—from supplying kettles to fixing broken lightbulbs. Now the world was different; visitors were different. An old depression had lifted. I inquired about this miracle. The friendly others on the staff told me with wonder, "He's learning English." It occurred to me that some of his surliness might well have come from having to serve the new, high-spirited, entitled foreign visitors who asked for things in languages he couldn't understand. So humiliating. So irritating. Now we shook hands. The new life was better. More toilet paper was better. Not being told to scrimp over every roll—obviously better.

And fast food was clearly glorious, too. Sitting in a café in the early days, I watched as a tired-looking mother paraded by, holding high like a chalice a big flat box emblazoned "Pizza Hut." Behind her, her four children, eager acolytes. At last, dinner was solved and worthy of a grateful "Amen."

In the mid-nineties, Roma and Viola take me for a picnic in the green fields that I always gaze at from our castle terrace across the Vistula. They have tinted memories of this lovely place from childhood when their parents used to bring them here on family outings. At first all is well. Here are the beautiful old trees, and here the meadows full of flowers. But something is terribly wrong. Every so often, a bulldozer seems to have dug a deep trench. Finally, a sign tells us this is to be a housing development. Roma and Viola run around, assessing the scope of the damage. It will all be gone, and soon.

But this common story of change, to Roma and Viola obviously a story of grief, doesn't end here. A few years later, Sławka and Beata declare their small rooftop aerie in the center of Krakow too small for two. They move to a bright if a bit generic housing development where they can spread out, keep their many books, cook in a big kitchen with all the modern conveniences.

The apartment blocks aren't beautiful, but they are a fresh white, only a couple of stories high, with lots of space between for bicycles and cars and even a few baby trees. We stroll around, assessing the pros and cons, and suddenly I recognize where we are. These streets have paved over Viola and Roma's green fields. Here is the same lay of the land, the same proximity to the river. I tell Sławka and Beata where we are, but they can't feel sorrow. They like it here. New things are often better—cleaner, smarter—than old things. We settle in on their big couch, watch something about feminism on a big TV, eat at the large table by the French windows. New is better.

One more turn to the story: After a year or two they move back to the aerie. New is good, but, for overworked organizers, being in the center of town is better.

By what scale to measure gain and loss? Change is a cheat—or not. And rapid change is the hardest to judge, its secret after-stories only slowly disclosed. Let me put it this way: By the late nineties, ambivalence about how to measure success was common in all locations. Where was one to locate enduring values? Shopping malls or restored synagogues? Do they inevitably go together? Who could confidently assign meaning to what was happening to my friends? They themselves were endlessly ambivalent. When a newfangled pierogi shop with twenty-five different fillings came to the Jewish Quarter, we all ate until we dropped. Variety and indigestion.

A friend told me, "We had time, before, of a different kind from now. Irritating as the details of daily life were, everything slowed us down to a walking pace—good for looking." Elzbieta Matynia remembered the delight of action outside the system: "For a short time in early spring, snails were everywhere; we used to wander through the forest gathering them; a yearly feast with no waiting on line, no money." My friend the philosopher

Karol Chrobak offered this version of the change in his life, a recalibration of public and private: "For some of us there was a deeper chance for individuality in communist times. We each made our separate life, private but full, known to our intimates. Now one must compete for outside recognition. Success, failure are public judgments. It is no longer possible to keep this privacy in the former way. One has lost privacy of self-realization." Luckily for Karol, his new public life has had many rewards. His books are published; he is a distinguished professor in Warsaw. But still, this, now, is a very different life from before.

Karol's mother, my dear friend Masza Potocka, has moved from creating and managing, singlehanded and under communism, the small avant-garde art gallery where Daniel performed in the nineties; to restoring the main museum of modern art in the center of Krakow; and now to directing her own glorious museum on the outskirts, an impressive new architectural assemblage and major Polish cultural institution, where I have given lectures about feminism. No doubt such a stunning traverse across the sky is not a typical story. Making an art world has been Masza's passion from the beginning, and no outside events either enabling or destructive were ultimately able to constrain her dance with the limitless. Constriction she turned into art; then expansion she turned into art; now as constriction and censorship threaten to return, she rises to that change too, because she sees such change as life itself, the very stuff from which new art will be made. Some temperaments make their own reality—let me hasten to add: as long as there is no gulag. And even then? I think of Jiřina Šiklová in jail, sculpting figurines out of bread. Roma too insisted on honoring her past and always resented the image of the communist years as relentlessly dark and dreary: "We were young. We enjoyed ourselves"—those picnics in the then untrammeled meadows.

Rujana Kren, she of the magic fairy house in Zagreb where I stayed at the very beginning, in 1991 offers a similar story of pleasure, dignified privacy, and coherence in the communist years—but with a darker ending. As only artists can, she had withdrawn from the drab reality of communist daily life. Waiting on line for bread? Why? When you can bake your own cakes, covered with your own quince jam. No room in the family home for two adults and two children? Construct for each one a Bedouin-like tent, covered with mirrors, refracting each other into infinite space.

But then came the end of the secret beauty of this life. The European Union required inspection of old, run-down houses and all jerry-rigged arrangements, applying new safety standards. They proclaimed that this wild house, put together by smoke and mirrors, wasn't structurally safe or sanitary. The tiny bit of money that had been enough to float the whole family including a grandchild wasn't enough anymore. A new roof was required. And the artist who had always stitched life together by the thinnest of threads was getting tired. The power of her magic was waning, and the new Zagreb was becoming an expensive place where artists need public recognition to survive. The always-beautiful letters from Rujana—with descriptions of lonely islands visited, meadows full of flowers at dawn—get sadder and sadder. The changed world has closed down the old private loopholes; Rujana's strategies of escape and quiet independence are now harder to maintain. Few people know about her artist's power, the gorgeous objects that she used to adorn her family's life. Still, she has extraordinary inner resources. May the richness of the world she is always making sustain my dear friend Rujana.

I'm reminded of two of my favorite Polish students, Tomasz Kitlinski and Pawel Leszkowicz, a gay couple, brilliant aesthetes who, at the time I first met them, were both living at home with their parents. "How has life changed?" I asked them—my perennial question in my quest to understand life over the precipice of 1989. But what I sought to know was always hard to tell. So many small shifts were slowly shaping an entirely new way of living for Tomasz and Pawel as out gay men. Finally, though, Tomasz came up with a formulation: "We never had the books we wanted. We lived the life of the mind through friendships and conversation. Everyone hung out for hours talking; every birthday, anniversary, sunny day was a good reason to meet, drink, talk. Now we have the wonderful books we wanted, but we have no time to read them. The friends are dispersed or too busy to hang out. Instead of sitting around in each other's kitchens—private, intimate— now everyone meets in noisy bars and nightclubs. Having a good time is all about dancing and drinking. There's too much noise to talk. The old easy, slow pace is gone. Somehow, daily life is completely different."

Telling this melancholy tale, suddenly Tomasz becomes aware that he is registering a loss; he hastens to say that certainly he doesn't want the old days of stagnation and isolation back. Still, while returning his thoughts resolutely to the exciting present, he lets slip, "There's a bit of desperation in social life now."

Vesna Kesić, from Croatia, a key member of the Network, was far more cutting on the subject of change. It was during the war that broke up Yugoslavia, a war that we all watched—and some Network members directly suffered—with such amazement. At a NEWW board meeting, some of us Americans were talking about trying to make "social change." Vesna leaped on us. "You Americans talk as if social change is naturally good, something you work for, as if it is not something overwhelming you can't control that changes *you*. No! Social change for us is this war."

As an activist, I've always believed you can give a shove to change as it rushes by. But sitting at my desk, writing this, I'm a different person from that activist; I'm the eternal skeptic. All

I can say with any certainty is that the quality of my exchanges with individual others has made my life better and made action more thinkable. I simply don't know if the feminist activism we have shared in East Central Europe has increased the happiness of my students and friends. And how would they, themselves, rate happiness as a goal?

Let me end this discourse about temperament and changing times with the case of Monika Ksieniewicz, wild and wonderful Monika. Tomasz likes my teaching in Krakow and invites me to lecture to his university students in Lublin. (In a recent note I learned that this lecture was "without the permission of the dean.") I go. Although it is the late nineties, here it is like the early days all over again. A full room with boys making preening declarations about men's superiority, women's place, the idiocy of complaining about nature. In other words, the usual. But, as always, I have my tricks. I use them; and we talk for a long time with not a single word from any of the many young women in the room. That silence is also as usual—though it becomes less so as the years roll by.

And I know what will happen next. I declare the formal lecture and discussion over. I wait. And here they come, the women, furtive but eager. They want to talk privately about these outré feminist ideas. Is there really something wrong with women doing all the cleaning, cooking, and care of children? By what authority can I claim there's a problem here? Such a refocusing of the lens of justice is both thrilling and scary.

One among them, with huge eyes and floppy red curls (as charming then as she is all these years later), is Monika. She has some urgent questions. Her boyfriend never helps her with anything. He won't pick up a dish or a dust rag. He's a lord of creation who depends on her for everything as, formerly, he depended on that loving slave, his mother. (I flash on one of my students in Krakow who was full of abstract theories about the strengths and weaknesses of feminism. He talked unintelligibly half the time, which greatly impressed the women in the class, until the day we discussed housework. Each student described how housework was divided in his or her house. When it was our dear theorist's turn, he said that he had only just moved out from his childhood home to his own flat. Aha! Everyone was eager to know how cleaning up after himself was going. So assertive and insistent were his colleagues, the women, that he had to admit, a bit—but not very—sheepishly, that his mother comes round, cleans the new apartment, and takes home his laundry. Pandemonium. The women never listened to him with quite the same awe and respect again. But he himself was essentially ungored. He didn't really see anything wrong with a busy scholar having a full-service female attendant.)

The peremptory Monika demands an answer: "Should I marry him or not?" I have to laugh. "A feminist is not a marriage counselor or a therapist or a fortune teller. How can I know if you'll be happy with this guy or not? I wouldn't dream of giving you advice." But this isn't acceptable: "I need help!" "Okay, okay, I'll send you some books to read."

Once I got home, I made a package for Monika. *The Mermaid and the Minotaur*, by my mentor, the feminist psychologist Dorothy Dinnerstein, of course, and what else? Pat Mainardi's perfect "The Politics of Housework"? Books about care, about balancing children and work? I don't remember, but I think Monika probably does. A few years later, she showed up as a student in the Krakow gender class. No scholar, but excited by feminist ideas, she bopped through the course happily. "Well, did you marry him?" "Of course not. Those books you sent! I read them and now I'm here taking gender class." "I'm sure it wasn't the books

that broke your engagement off. It was your own good judgment."
Who knows? Speculation is in vain.

Smart, fast, able to compromise and be practical without
angst, Monika became a player in the Plenipotentiary for Equal
Treatment, a department of Polish government that comes and
goes, depending on which party wins the election. Later she was
sent to Brussels, a feminist negotiator in that great maw, the European Union. I see her when she comes to New York to work
at the UN. She ran through a number of men, but didn't feel
satisfied for long with any of them. Had feminist consciousness
made her finicky? Had raised expectations, mobility, and startling success lifted her beyond the reach of a mere mortal man?
Like a traditional mother hen, I used to ask myself who could
be good enough for our spirited, vital Monika? Her energy can
move mountains.

Now she has married an old friend, a nice guy presumably capable of housework. In her forties, she has happily given birth to a
son. I did so want for her to have everything. She's a feminist to
the bone; her story continues. And at each turn she takes, I feel
delight. The travels of feminism: I'm constantly reviewing them—
with excitement and doubt, with hope and unending anxiety.

ON NOT SPEAKING POLISH

After we started the Network of East-West Women in 1991 about
two thousand women joined our membership list, about half
from all the countries of East Central Europe (with a few from
the former Soviet Union) and half from the US. In those early
years, there was no thought about Americans learning all or any
of these languages. Some knew one or two already, either from
their roots or as part of their earlier work in the region. But those
of us Americans without any regional language comforted our-

selves with the fact that our colleagues in East Central Europe were abandoning the Russian they had (reluctantly) learned at school. Now they were rushing to use English as the new *lingua franca*—not only to talk to us but also to talk to each other. At our meetings, English connected Serbs, Romanians, and Czechs. These colleagues had deeply resented the imposition of Russian as the master's language. In contrast to that iron law, choosing English initially felt liberating.

(In the late eighties, a Polish theater group did a public performance in Krakow. A big tall man wrapped in a Russian flag and wearing a Russian army cap walked beside a little guy with a Polish flag and cap; the big guy kept hitting and shoving the little guy as they proceeded together through the streets. This was how many Poles learned Russian. The actors were arrested, of course, and went to prison.)

From the first, we Americans understood that this precipitous arrival and triumph of a new language would soon be recognized as a form of imperialism, too. We were benefiting from a honeymoon with what in a while would be seen as a new coercive force. In a Czech film from the early nineties, a group of Russian language teachers are suddenly ordered to teach English instead. Some manage to retool quickly. The film shows them struggling with pronunciation. Others simply can't get enough English fast enough and are ruined, their occupation gone. Even with all the will in the world and under threat, trying to learn a new language as an adult pushed some of these teachers into a terrible depression. They were failures in the new life. The advantage was all to the young, their students, who were clearly about to inherit the earth.

The fact that very soon knowing English would be a necessity not a choice for any kind of international success was obscured by the warm welcome US capitalism was receiving across the region during these first days of rapid change. English was access; English was mobility; English was money. If you were young, you were on track to join the upper levels of the new class system evolving overnight; English was your entry pass.

I have always been terrible at languages. Although I am still able to discuss the weather and seating arrangements with Romanians or manage a stiff argument with Adam Michnik about Iraq in French (anti-war passion loosed my halting tongue), my one foreign language, drilled into me at school, has faded. Always mildly dyslexic, I have a bad memory that has only gotten worse with the years, along with my hearing. Sometimes, now, I can hardly make out what my American students are saying.

As long as I was visiting Romania and Serbia and Georgia repeatedly, no one could expect me to learn more than a few words in each of these languages. But after 1992, when Elzbieta started our summer school in Krakow, wherever else I went, I was in Poland at least three weeks a year, and often longer. Surely, people said, you'll learn Polish.

Two American friends tried it one summer. Both would stagger out of their daylong class looking distressed. Of course they were learning a lot of Polish, but they couldn't actually *speak,* and understanding a fast-paced feminist debate among our friends? Not a chance. I was so much older than they, so untalented at reproducing the unfamiliar sounds and remembering them. I began to collect single words and key phrases to mask some of my disgrace: *herbata* (tea), *Centrum Kobiet* (Women's Center!), *dzien dobre* (good morning), *dobranoc* (good night), *przeprasazm* (I'm [very] sorry) for all that I cannot say.

Finally, my worldly Polish friend Marta Petrusewicz decided to put me out of my misery. She argued that I would never speak well enough to really talk to people, to hear nuance, to debate. The reality was that the intelligentsia would speak to me in usually elegant English. Others I would reach only through translation. "Give up," she counseled. "Accept your limitations and do your work."

Needless to say, I was grateful for these home truths. Indeed, I was noticing that I mostly forgot between visits whatever Polish I managed to learn. And eventually I had several translators who were so good, so literary, that it was as if they were breathing with me. Again, gratitude.

But now another question was arising, far more central to my (occasional) life in Poland where I was teaching, debating, giving radio talks. The friends. After only a few years, I had friendships in Poland as intimate and deep as any I had at home. Although for all of us, feminism is funny, adventurous, wild, each one expresses our collective high spirits in a different sort of English. Roma is fluent. She was once the English speaker in an office. Gosia, too, speaks fluent English. She had a father living in the US and spent a lot of time working with the Network in New York. Sławka's English is halting; she knows a lot, but there are enough holes to prevent a fast flow. She is fluent in German.

And now the mystery of Beata. She doesn't speak English all that fluently. Her best second language is German, which she decided to learn at the age of ten after hearing some German kids at the seashore speaking with mysteriously unintelligible sounds. But she's a language artist. Her wit is stunning as she invents pathways through English, plucking words from the people around her, moving forward through sound and metaphor and gesture.

A lot of our group's constant, collective play is essentially word games. After all these years we have developed a private language. People who lack our high hilarity and comic irony are *niegazowana* (without bubbles, like still bottled water). The words *normalny* and *naturalny* are woven into English to express our own sense of the ridiculous idea that there is a single "normalcy," a stable "naturalness."

We happily make a grotesque figure of the Polish minister who didn't want the Russian submarine fleet to come to Poland because men and women lived on board together, a clearly immoral arrangement. But the fleet came anyway, and the minister went on board. He explained to the press afterward that he was no longer worried about impropriety. The Russian female sailors were so large and unfeminine that they could neither tempt nor be tempted. "Those are not women," he said. "They are whales."

Whales! Whales! Unfeminine women are whales! The word enters our vocabulary. We are delighted spectators at this constantly running theater of the absurd. And with each shared experience our language grows; our language bridges get more and more sturdy. By now we have so many polyglot words in our secret dictionary and so many common experiences that we often speak in shorthand. Neither Poles nor Americans can understand us. Sometimes, now, just a look is enough to set us off. We are whales singing messages through the viscous medium that lies between our different worlds. It's a great, crooning sound.

But, still, I don't speak Polish. I get some affectionate nagging about this after all this time. At a Krakow restaurant table with Poles and Slovaks, everyone is speaking English. I ask, "What language would you speak if I weren't here?" "We would speak our own languages. Polish and Slovak are similar enough for us to understand each other." Although English isn't close enough to any other language to give me this kind of cross-border experience, it is spoken all over the world. The American joins the party, and everyone is stuck with English.

Another Krakow restaurant table: I'm eating pizza with eight beloved Polish feminist whales. The exchange is excited, punctuated by shrieks of laughter. Everyone is speaking Polish. I can't understand a word at this pace. I am wrapped in Polish like a child is wrapped in her mother's arms while the adults talk over her head.

Could it be that I like not understanding? No reason to concentrate; no expectation that I will respond. I am resting, innocent of all words, slanders, intricacies of the daily conflicts of these loved people. Not speaking Polish rescues me from any illusion that I am an insider. Not speaking Polish removes any fantasy that I understand. I can and do know more and more about their lives, but going native is utterly impossible. I am a failure at something important; language makes its own world, and I am outside. It's best to face this fully. Not speaking Polish reminds me of what I cannot know, what I cannot do. Wrapped in a cocoon of beautiful Polish sounds, I relax and eat my pizza.

After some years, my so-much-loved gang of five broke up. First Sławka and Beata quarreled with Roma and Viola. It became a major task to stay close to both couples. Then in 1999, Roma and Viola broke up. Then, in 2014, the unthinkable: Sławka and Beata broke up. They had been so productive as a powerful team, but their lives kept changing beyond my intimate knowledge. In addition, and inevitably, detractors multiplied. After all, eFKa wasn't the only feminist group in town, and younger women were impatient with older ones, who try to hang on but, like mothers, never get it right (a situation sometimes called in New York "founder flounder").

In fact, such falling apart is the lifeblood of a growing feminism. Projects and groups split and proliferate. Love and work dance together to their own rhythm. In New York I had lived through many such movement realignments. Personality and beliefs had twined together and could never be separated. The particular "why" of each break could never be resolved, the mixed feelings and meanings never finally disentangled. Why couldn't such differences be talked through? I was at many meetings where such talking through was tried—and failed.

Is it the narcissism of small differences? Dinnerstein believed beleaguered groups suffer from cabin fever, a need to break out from the forced intimacies shared by underdogs. Well, feminism in Poland in the nineties was certainly beleaguered, and there can be no closure on that story of endless wrangling. *Zadra* magazine embraced this struggle in its very name: "Splinter." (Splinter indeed. Krakow feminists once handed out wooden kitchen utensils to men in the main square.) So many rival feminist provocations continue to flourish in Krakow.

11

SOME RETURNS
ARE IMPOSSIBLE

Before World War II, Poland was central to Jewish life in Europe. By the end of the war, 90 percent of this once-thriving community (over three million people) had been murdered.

People often assumed that my frequent trips to Poland—and all of East Central Europe—were a return to my Jewish roots. This was far from the case.

WHEN I FIRST BEGAN my work in East Central Europe, I would often point out that women were losing social supports they took for granted under communism. But the more I pushed my point about the danger of total privacy, about the need for public institutions to support freedom and general well-being, the more I got the reaction: "Are you a communist?"

Gradually, I began to see what no doubt many in the region take for granted. From the chaos of post-communist realignments a deadly triangle was emerging—not new but clarifying. First,

I was a feminist, a trailing reminder of official, party-directed women's unions controlled from above. Second, I was concerned about the loss of a welfare state. Hence, once again, I was a communist. The third corner of the triangle took me a while to understand: communists are Jews. Conveniently, Jews can be blamed for this half-century of repression, hypocrisy, and corruption.

At first this idea, that Jews were the driving force of communism, was just a rumble in my head. But episode after episode lit up the sides of this triangle: At our school, a Ukrainian student tells the Israeli political philosopher Shlomo Avineri that Jews are the architects of communism. Standing at the front in a big lecture hall, Shlomo sighs. He's heard this so many times. With a weariness few Americans can feel to the full, he begins to answer: "The Jews were besieged. They tried everything to solve their dilemma." Some, he explains, retreated into orthodox exceptionalism; they were different, the chosen. Some became Zionists; they would leave, found their own country. Some assimilated; they tried to disappear. Some left—for America or the wide world. Some embraced the communist project—either with cynicism or with idealistic hopes.

So, yes, some Jews became communists; but of course their actual percentage in communist parties was always small. In Poland, after 1968, when Władysław Gromułka charged Jewish communists with undermining his tottering rule, Jews—as always, the well-established scapegoats—were purged from the Communist Party. That small remnant of secular Polish Jews who had managed to survive the war and rise in the party were driven into exile. In fact, at that point anti-Semitism was so openly expressed—at the grocer's, in school, on the street—that in a short time almost all the remaining Jews left the country. As one of them said, kicking the door behind him as he went: "Only abroad can I be what I believe myself to be, a Pole. In Poland, I am a Jew." Goodbye, goodbye. So many layers of goodbye.

Sławomir Sierakowski, leader of the Polish leftist group and magazine *Krytyka Polityczna*, performs a piece by Yael Bartana in an abandoned sports stadium, derelict and overgrown with grass. In the video, he stands at the center of the empty space and calls out, "Jews! Fellow countrymen! . . . This is a call, not to the dead, but to the living. We want three million Jews to return to Poland to live with us again. We need you!" Alas, the very formulation illustrates the problem. Who are these "Jews" who are to come back? Will they be Poles? Orthodox? Secular? The American Lauder Foundation tried "to come back" with elegant buildings in Krakow, summer schools, exhibitions of Jewish relics, but the undertaking languished, though the Jewish Community Center, the bright young radical group Cholent, and the religious education now offered here and there are all cultural presences.

Throughout the region the Jewish cultural festivals and other acts of nostalgia can be sincere efforts, but I find it impossible to believe that there is really any "coming back," any return for the Jews to East Central Europe. The meaning of "Jew" is as unsettled as ever. Historian Jan Gross records words that can still be caught on the wind in many places: "We hated the Nazis but they did accomplish one thing we wanted—no more Jews."

In the center of Lublin there's a big bowl of green. "How lovely, a park in the center of the city." "No, no," explained my guide, Tomasz Kitlinski. "This was the Jewish quarter; it's completely gone." We visited the great medieval castle that looms above the empty space. As the Russians were coming and the Germans were rushing to depart, they killed the several hundred Jews imprisoned there, abandoning the place still awash in their blood. "Why bother?" I asked Tomasz. "When you're packing and fleeing, why take the time and trouble to murder a couple of hundred people?" "It was a utopian act." "What!" "Yes, the utopian dream, a world without Jews."

In the Brama museum nearby, a dedicated group of young Poles are re-creating the disappeared Jewish neighborhood in a room-size maquette. Using photographs, old maps, and architectural drawings, they are building a beautiful miniature with medieval crooked streets and quaint old houses. Lublin was one of the great centers of Jewish learning for centuries. I love these maquette builders, but in their miniature they show as no one else how small is the hope of any "coming back."

Always a great believer in the importance of utopian yearnings, a sort of necessary yeast for even the most mundane of political projects, I was impressed by the idea that killing the Jews of Lublin was such a project. I am Jewish, but it was not as a Jew that I was visiting.

My mother was a utopian dreamer and a political activist. At one time a communist, she was also a feminist, and a Jew. When some people hear this part of my history in East Central Europe, they put on a knowing look. Of course. Feminists are communists, Jews, or soft on Jews. So I come as a "cosmopolitan," a key word and an old stand-in for "Jew"; I am left-wing, Jewish, a feminist from that stew of races and cultures, New York City. In Eastern Europe, this history is seen as a package. I recognize the bloodlines—in both senses of the term. But since I grew up, ignorant, in this polyglot New York, anti-Semitism still can surprise me; its manifestations and relics in East Central Europe can still be a good slap in the face. The triangle vibrates and I am in awe of the endurance of this most stable of architectural structures.

In 1992 Gosia Tarasiewicz came to New York and complained to us all in the Network that Polish women were about to lose their right to abortion. "Do something!" But what to do? We planned a demonstration. Those were the too brief but radiant days of WAC, the Women's Action Coalition, which provided artists' ingenuity, sense of design, and energy to the feminist movement. From them we got numbers, and a drum corps. From the brilliant political artists who have made movement demonstrations beautiful over the years, Hannah Alderfer and Mary Beth Nelson, we got big white Styrofoam birds on long sticks and glittery blue signs in Polish and English: "Freedom for Polish Women." "The Right to Choose for Polish Women." "*Solidarności z Polskimi Kobietami.*"

"Let's do the demonstration in Greenpoint," the Polish immigrant neighborhood in Brooklyn. The Polish activists in the Network were horrified. "Are you crazy? That's a nationalist, anti-communist, very religious Catholic community. They'll kill you!" So we chose St. Patrick's Cathedral on a safer Fifth Avenue in the center of the city. Still, the Poles in NEWW hung flyers in Greenpoint. "For more information about the demonstration, call Ann Snitow," phone number supplied. I won't be doing that again! My phone answering machine took the message, delivered in a guttural, heavily accented male voice: "You lousy Jews, killing Polish babies." Who could deny it? Although many Poles participated in what became a passionate and photogenic demonstration, I was a Jew, a communist, a feminist.

The several Polish newspapers in Greenpoint, and of course the US press, paid no attention to the fifty women—and some men, too—all wrapped in blue satin scarves, carrying our floating birds and our big signs in two languages. But in Poland, several journalists picked up the story. Friends told me that people they talked to were amazed and delighted. "In New York they care about Polish women losing abortion?!"

Ever the cosmopolitan, the urbanite, I was hoping for international liberation movements while, behind my back, the triangle was vibrating, obscuring my intentions. Many friends have their own stories about how these vibrations were felt. The mother of my friend Irena Grudzińska-Gross said nothing to her daughter growing up, let Irena assume that she was a little Polish Catholic girl like everyone else. But then she didn't get to do first communion like the others. Why no beautiful white dress? There was an excuse: Her parents were communists. But at age eight, Irena was canny enough to have doubts. There was a mystery here, and it amazes her to remember that, aided by her nanny and a nun, she went secretly to get religious instruction at the convent, an elaborate subterfuge in one so young. Gradually, she began to understand that she was Jewish. The sisters comforted her that she could be baptized and saved at age sixteen without her parents' consent. But here began suffering. Her parents would go to hell. How could she save them? To bolster her struggling faith, Sister Tereza told her you must believe the saints exist even though you have never seen them, just as you believe America exists even though you have never seen it. But Aunt Hinde had sent a postcard from Los Angeles, so there was a problem here.

As a grownup, Irena confronted her mother: How could she have maintained this shameful deception? They quarreled, and, in a rage, her mother erupted: "I thought that if my children were going to be Jewish, I wouldn't have them." This mother decided that to bring more Jewish children into the world was to expose them to too much suffering and humiliation—experiences she herself had hated. Let there be an end. These children were to become dissidents, staunch resisters against communist regimes that were crushing their lives. But did they manage to deconstruct the triangle that shaped what they could say or do? Could they ever simply be Poles struggling for freedom? No. Impossible. Most of them left.

Several Polish friends find it exotic, romantic, exciting that I am Jewish. I am rare, distinguished, of course terribly intelligent. My Polish friend Anna Bikont discovered in adulthood that she was Jewish. What a delight. Now she can draw away from the racism in Poland and embrace a stunning and tragic past. When we talk, I see that her passion for rediscovering and re-embodying what she lost is very much like my feminism. Becoming a Polish Jew deeply animated her intellect and her imagination. I love her because her collision with a damaged but galvanizing identity is like mine. In writing, she can reenliven the past and revisit how that past ended, the Holocaust, but the question recurs: What is the future? In Poland? In Israel? I'm always urging her to try out the feminist corner of the triangle. I want to think feminism can "come back." This is a wish, perhaps as full of fantasy as a small maquette of women's past entitlements under communism, a model of a past full of betrayed promises. But I wish it.

Dear Ania, our emotions about identity are a fertile ground we share. Ours are the projects of an always renewing struggle: To face the identities of the past; and, my dear, we must try to imagine something beyond them.

For all these painful reasons, I have always felt that resonant as this Jewish past remains, it is never as a Jew that I return. I am a feminist activist of the Left. That's two sides of the triangle; the last vibrates, too, of course, as the festivals of identity come and go.

Early on in my travels to East Central Europe, my sister-in-law, Deborah Kaufman, remarked off-handedly, "Of course being Jewish must be part of the pull; you're returning to the old country."

"What old county?"

"Poland, Ukraine, Romania."

These are indeed my family origins. Also, Russia, because the Ukrainian branch was exiled to Irkutsk. We all began to sing that klezmer number we have on records, just one word passionately repeated, an ecstatic incantation, "Romania, Romania, Romania." My maternal grandmother came from Romania as a teenager, traveling with her sister to join relatives in New York. I was fourteen when she died and had never thought to ask her about such important things. How does a sixteen-year-old get from Moldova to New York at the end of the nineteenth century? That I wasn't curious then tells much about the depth of the break. She did tell me tales of the fools from Chelm, which she may have heard as a girl or perhaps, as I have, learned from books in a library in the New World. Beyond an extraordinary embroidery pattern book I loved—where is it now? It had patterns I later recognized on tablecloths in Romanian folk museums—knowing her didn't give me the slightest glimpse of the mental baggage she brought with her except, perhaps, her sadness and anxiety. And, in my experience, these aren't temperaments that necessarily have their origins in an uprooting journey from Romania. She was brilliant and frustrated, living an unhappy wives' tale more than anything else. Once their three daughters departed, Grandma and Grandpa separated like a shot, never to see each other again.

So, was I returning to Grandma? I think not. This feels important: Any Jew returning to Eastern Europe can so easily claim the harrowing emotions of the victim. This damaged identity, Jew, this word of insult, is always there as an entry point. But I felt this way in to be inauthentic: I was a child of privilege in the New World. Now, it is everyone's job to imagine the terrifying suffering of the Holocaust. Now, it must belong to everyone, not just one tribe; it is always, for everyone, now. It was politically insufficient to return to Grandma.

But, in the end, for my own reasons, which I hope to be able to pull together here from a complex nest of experience, I returned: To discover being Jewish in East Central Europe does matter—immensely.

RETURNING

In the early days, post-1989, the period of constant visits, dinner parties, strangers' meetings, I went to a dinner at my university president's house in honor of Sonja and Milan, packed with distinguished dissidents from the East. I was seated at a table with a couple, famous Romanian intellectuals, now, after very hard times, free at last to tilt a full glass in New York. They were warm, interested in what I was doing. I mentioned in passing that my grandmother had come from Huşi, a small city in Northern Romania. Their reaction was electric. Oh, wonderful. Visit us and we'll take you there. People in Huşi will be so interested to meet an American descendent. I felt a prick of anxiety. To dispel it, I asked, "Will it matter that we are Jews?" Without a pause, or the slightest diminution of warmth, the wife said jubilantly, "We won't tell them!"

I've told this story many times and, as Edgar says in *King Lear*, the worst returns to laughter. How funny, I can say—and feel—because I was born a Jewish girl in New York on May 8, 1943, the day of the decisive fall of the Warsaw Ghetto. "Did you know what was going on in Europe on that day?" I got around to asking my mother decades later, when I began to go myself to Eastern Europe. "Absolutely not." (Could such US ignorance of a dramatic foreign horror exist now? Absolutely yes. There is suffering all over the world we know nothing about—here at the dinner party.)

So, obviously, now I wanted to go to Huşi on my own. We went. The city's chief rabbi was well known for having bought a lot of Jews from the Romanian government, which allowed them to leave for Israel. It was Friday, the day when the Romanian peasant caretaker of the Jewish cemetery had been told to admit no one. Ten dollars was what it took to get him to change his mind. He was raising cabbages among the graves, and his laundry hung like flags above them. And there, as usual, on stones in ramshackle condition, were the names in the New York phone book: Rosenberg (Grandma's name), Moscowitz, Schwartz, Rubin, Berman. They had had the custom of putting enameled photos on the graves of the middle class, so one can gaze at the smiling faces of beautifully dressed men and women who had the good luck to die before Ion Antonescu killed forty thousand Romanian Jews in one week in 1941.

All I could recall, and I believe all Grandma told me, was, "We lived by the river." "But there's no river anywhere here." We drove around. Then as we were leaving town, suddenly there it was, the big river Prut that divides Romania from Moldova. Here she had lived as a girl. I was aware of one main emotion: gratitude for Tillie Rosenberg's brave journey. We were leaving this dreary communist provincial town. Return has never been my motive.

But anti-Semitism lives, and from experiencing it on my travels I learned something I had always longed to understand: how racism works in people who don't think they are racist at all. I described what I was observing to my colleague in New York, the poet and performance artist Sekou Sundiata. "It's not that the intelligent, liberal people you tend to know hate you or believe you are inferior. What happens among the good anti-racists you meet is a flicker of self-consciousness, a touch of anxiety. It might be guilt, but it might also just be hyperawareness. They can't make themselves not know about a difference of such shattering historical importance." Offering this, I had Sekou's full attention. Old acquaintances, we were finally, really talking, and I felt irradiated by horrible insight: Whites can work on themselves—and *must*—but racism is woven in, a helpless self-consciousness, a shame that can damage intimacy. Sekou gave me one of his sublime smiles: "That's about it." By leaving home I had discovered how my own racism showed itself, something worth looking into for every American.

After 1989 diasporic Jews began to flood into East Central Europe. These pilgrims spend most of their time in derelict graveyards and ruined synagogues. This sort of visiting provides a constantly renewed shock—and there's always more and more. (My most recent encounter with horror was the barely marked deep fuel storage pits near Vilnius, now covered with grass, a small sign to the side—only in Lithuanian—saying how many Jews were shot and buried here—about seventy-two thousand between 1941 and 1944. Visitor, you can never guess such a number from this untouched, bucolic scene.)

Famously, anti-Semitism is vibrantly alive in towns and villages throughout the region. Anthropologists go into the countryside and come back to repeat the scarifying tales still told to rural children: "Don't go out on Friday night. Jews will kill you and use your blood to make their Sabbath bread." The repertory of phobic hatred can seem endless, and of course it's exacerbated by guilt. Just like home, where whites hate blacks with a special heat because they have wronged them for centuries and built a nation on their backs. And, in both places, the fear that the wronged will rise up and retaliate can take a very literal form. We took a two-day tour of the little Polish shtetls where Jews once lived and were told that at first the Jewish visitors like us who were pouring in were feared by people in the villages:

What if these Jews want their houses back? Everything, absolutely everything, had been taken. (Primo Levi describes a dinner party in Germany where he suddenly realizes the beautiful silver sugar bowl is a Jewish ritual object.)

Once the people in the shtetl where we stayed had realized that the returning Jews were just visiting and didn't want an old wooden house on a muddy lane in rural Poland, they breathed a collective sigh of relief and inaugurated a yearly summer Jewish festival for Jewish tourists with klezmer music, men dressed in medieval black with *payas*, delicious traditional foods—all things the elders well remembered. Jewish revivalist Kostek Gebert once talked to the students in our school about how in the early nineties, a returning group of Jewish ecstatics dancing down a Warsaw street on the Sabbath caused shock to older Poles who thought they were seeing ghosts. (Later in the same talk Gebert began to speak of how wonderful it was to return to the old pre-communist family structures, the wife learning to make the traditional foods and to perform the Sabbath rituals, the husband returning to his long-repressed role of patriarch. Red light! So awed was I by Gebert's long suffering and new authority that at the time I said nothing. *Treppenwitz!* But all the Network of East-West Women's efforts since have stood against such aspects of religious traditionalism.)

Jan Gross is the most recent example of the searcher who finds horrors. In his *Golden Harvest: Events at the Periphery of the Holocaust*, we gaze at a picture of peasants standing at ease with picks and spades, an array of skulls on the ground before them. It's 1941 and they are digging up the destroyed Jews of Theresienstadt in the hope of finding gold teeth the Nazis may have missed.

The horror of the Holocaust, in spite of all explanations, the constantly reforming mystery of so much sustained cruelty, is always in the wings, waiting for its cue, but let me register here what is now more present in a daily way: either sentimentality or the vacuum of absence. We laughed what Jews call "bloody laughter" when we heard a pretty blond girl from Switzerland singing Jewish songs in a former Jewish prayer house in Krakow. The chorus of one particular song was "*Oy, oy, oy,*" trilled sweetly, without a trace of angst.

It is absence, though, that can still take my breath away after all these years. The sociologist Iwona Irving-Zarecka set out to study how the Poles manifest grief about the loss of a big part of their prewar world, the Jews. To her dismay, the sorrow she set out to study simply wasn't there.

I used to go with Sławka and Beata to do errands for *Zadra*, just to see parts of Krakow I didn't know and to experience daily life in the city. On one of those trips, we were in an old neighborhood I'd never seen before. On the plaster side wall of one of the buildings was an advertisement in a style obviously from the thirties, showing a dapper man with a tilted hat and cane, Zolberg's Haberdashery. With excitement I pointed this out to Sławka and Beata: a remnant of a Jewish shop! An authentic trace, not the usual laborious re-creation. We admired the jaunty image, with its tasteful if faded pastels. We must photograph this! But no camera that day. I let it go until the following summer and my reliable return. "Let's drive to see the elegant man selling hats—this time with a camera." The neighborhood was still run down, a backwater, with only one sign of fresh paint, the large white rectangle where the sign had been. And there was an end of it.

In my next small story of the surprising pain of absence I am all alone, wandering in the vast national museum of Krakow. Up staircases, beyond the special shows and the famous paintings, there are floors and floors of period furniture, Biedermeier breakfronts, étagères, the heavy and not particularly distinguished leavings of Polish bourgeois life in the eighteenth and nineteenth centuries. Finally, I come to a corridor that is completely dark, but I see flashes of golden objects. What is this? I gesture to the mousy lady who is always sitting in these museums. Oh, so I want to see this? She begins to turn on the lights, revealing a treasure house of Jewish objects, rooms and rooms, jumping out at me as she leads me through, turning on the lights as we go.

Suddenly, I'm furious. But we don't have a language in common. I urgently want to ask her: No one wants to see this stuff? Or, we Poles don't like this stuff? Or, we're saving electricity? It seems too obvious to need saying: The Jews have gone into the dark.

Let me hasten to say that in the daily life I live for a week here, a week there, in Poland, Serbia, Romania, I have encountered little anti-Semitism, with the occasional exception that I described to Sekou of that initial moment of anxious hyperawareness. Do people I encounter in my daily round know I'm Jewish (on both sides, and my husband, too)? There's disagreement about this. Iwona Irving-Zarecka, a great expert in these matters, assures me that everyone knows I'm Jewish. Others say no; it's not a heavy mark, not like my friend Melissa, dark, thin, intense, with an elegant curved nose, who has been heckled in Berlin. How can I know? I have only one personal story of anti-Semitism to tell.

Marta was my student in a three-week summer course in Wroclaw about gender. An out lesbian and feminist activist, she was valuable in the class, smart and usefully challenging. Some students felt that the few talkative Marta types were monopolizing class discussions, so I told them about the group process of lots. Each student gets three or four counters to buy a turn to speak. Once these are gone, no more talking until everyone has used all their counters. The strict student who had complained, very experienced in political processes and a trade union organizer, brought in her grandmother's button box. Each student got three buttons and Marta simmered down, choosing not to waste her precious buttons on brief parenthetical remarks.

The entire school went on a field trip to the Jewish cemetery of Wroclaw. We asked why this large and magisterial graveyard hadn't been destroyed like so many others. In 1945 the Germans left in a hurry from what was about to become Poland, and the Poles were relocated in the city in a hurry, evacuated from what was about to become Ukraine. Because of this dizzying turn of events, the target for the new, aggrieved Polish arrivals was, above all, the German cemetery, which, in a rage, they decimated. The Jewish cemetery had survived this delirious season of stone breaking, but it had been neglected. Now it was being restored by our fine American tour guide Juliette Golden and her Polish mate. The usual shocks were many, though more subtle here. The prosperous Jewish merchants of what was once the German city of Breslau had built large family mausoleums meant to house the bones of many future generations. But there were no future generations. Most of these stately necropolises stood two-thirds empty. I felt that special extra sorrow reserved for the victims of genocide: We all die, as the cemetery reminds us, but here there will be no more family mourners. No one visits. We are not seeing what we should expect to see, the usual cycle of life.

I picked up a stone and put it on one of the graves. Marta asked, "What are you doing?" I explained that Jews put stones instead of flowers to mark that a grave has been visited. She actually paled! Or am I elaborating in memory? Certainly, her face registered shock. "Are you Jewish?!" "Yes." Here was a moment I had long expected, had waited for, and had no intention to waste.

"Marta," I said, "we're already colleagues in the feminist movement. After weeks of class, we know each other. Do me a big favor. I *really* want to learn something that is usually hidden from me. Tell me what you just felt when you found out I was Jewish. You were obviously very shaken. Give me a true account of what it meant to you." I went on reassuring her I would be grateful for the truth, not angry at her.

So she told me: "You're extinct." "What?" "The Jews are gone." Indeed. Poland is now 98 percent Polish Catholic. The Germans and the Jews are gone, the Roma and Ukrainian immigrants undercounted and mostly illegal. The nation considers itself one, and conservative politicians are often openly proud of this monochrome.

Still, would our absence be enough to make a girl go pale? I pushed her: "Anything more?" She was reluctant, but she understood how much I wanted to know. "Well, when I was little, my grandmother used to say that all our Polish troubles came from the Jews."

"Got it. I've heard about all that of course. But you're grown up, sophisticated, and you spend your time with people very different from your grandmother. Why does this discovery still have so much power to rock your world?"

Now we were at an impasse, because she simply didn't know why she had to reorganize her sense of reality to encircle the information that I am Jewish, like a grain of sand forces the oyster to secrete a layer of protection to bring back comfort and order.

There it is, my anti-Semitism story. I greet Marta warmly when we run into each other in Warsaw. She's a hardworking feminist, and I value this. All the same, she is a silent carrier of a bacillus she has never had to notice. Since we all carry these, blame is not interesting. One might, though, be engaged by possible imaginative cures—partial as they are bound to be. Juliette and her Polish husband, different as can be, are restoring the graveyard. Overhung by great old trees, it's a beautiful place that can now reenter the culture of the city.

Needless to say, given the enormity of the record, such stories may seem hopelessly small. First, a thousand years of Jewish presence in East Central Europe are grounds for bottomless exploration. (Now you can see artifacts from this long endurance at the astonishing Museum of the History of Polish Jews in Warsaw.) Next there's World War II and the stories of Jews that wind and wind around that cataclysm. The war is an infinite pool of narrative. Sociologist Ethel Brooks has made the case that, for the minorities of Europe, World War II continues; trauma has shaped an ethnically marked world far more rigid and polarized than, say, the Austro-Hungarian Empire ever was.

We are still inside this disaster. The marks are everywhere and, in some ways, venerated; the war remains vital, still shaping day-to-day reality. In Gdansk, where the Network now has its office, bullet holes remain on the apartment building walls. The war began right here on the Baltic coast. Hitler watched his attack on the promontory of Westerplatte from the terrace of Sopot's Grand Hotel, where Gosia and I once walked in a cleansing snow that could not hide the past. He was waiting to see if any other nations would try to stop this outrageous invasion. No one came, and the small Polish resistance collapsed almost at once. The defenders mostly died, and their deaths were the beginning of a global bloodletting that will remain impossible to grasp.

Just as Hitler watched his war begin from his own *aussichtspunkt*, being Jewish in East Central Europe is a standpoint. I came to see that I was positioned to be both loved and hated entirely without reference to my own thoughts or judgments. I, who have always hated exceptionalism, who have always countered that cry, "My people have suffered more than any other people," with counterexamples of hideous disasters, I, I was forced to be exceptional. The history of Europe and the war twisted secular citizenship so far out of shape that it became clear to me that no one has quite recovered from the war. And many have retreated to their tribal corners for good.

ROZSTAJE

During the 1990s a new, post-communist kind of folk festival spread over Eastern Europe, celebrating the Jewish departed—as long as they were really and safely gone. Krakow's Jewish festival was one of the most magnificent: klezmer groups flown in from New York, singers from Israel, once even my partner, Daniel Goode, with his *Critical Mass,* a piece celebrating secular joys.

Daniel's piece was meant to remind everyone that Jews don't all wear black hats or yarmulkes, that from the Enlightenment onward there has been a sturdy tradition of secular Jews, some assimilated, others actively seeking nonreligious but traditional Jewish values like *tikkun olam*—the responsibility to repair the present and actual world we live in.

But the festival's aesthetic showed how hard it is to interrupt a romance with Jews as Others. It's as if Jewish intellectual traditions that arose during the Jewish Enlightenment, the Haskalah, had never happened, as if Jews had never really been part of modern Europe.

For me, the great festival was the recurring ethno-festival *Rozstaje*—"crossroads." It was something completely different. No doubt, my love of this event grew out of my own cosmopolitan dream, my own romance. Sławka called me in my room on the edge of the forest: "There's an Eastern European folk festival, not in any one place but all over Krakow, everywhere, for everyone. It's supposed to be like daily life from the past, with musicians playing on street corners or markets or cafés as they might have been heard and seen in the nineteenth-century city." We'd just have to walk around and hope to find something. This was vague, but interesting.

We began in the main square, still glorious then before it became a summer shopping mall. Roma fiddlers were strolling around, and dancers in beautiful-colored clothes were circling them, yelling and singing. Without a stage or any formal announcement, they wound around the beautiful space, and we followed them.

Then we turned onto side streets where Lithuanian music came from small groups on church steps. On the next corner, Slovenian girls wearing dirndl skirts were swinging around in dances that were more Germanic than Slavic. *Um-pah.* Around one corner we came on a small Serbian group playing a *kolo* so beautiful it almost stopped our hearts. Everyone was in costume, but casually, as if for a local village festival. Hybrids, these supposed peasants were wearing both farm clothes and fancy hats, some pulling along cows or goats.

Sławka and I were in a trance of joy. So many kinds of people, so many kinds of music. The world was a complex place. The tribes were different, but they were all present with no borders and linked by family resemblances. Intoxicated by the mess, we felt free to wander this world. Ethnicity and nostalgia were pleasure.

Eventually we wound up at the railway station. Performers were carrying bundles, dragging children, calling out to each other, dancing, laughing, eating. Someone had had the beautiful idea of creating a nineteenth-century station, full of people wearing long dresses, carrying period portmanteaus. Here was the past from a diorama like the ones at the ethnological museum on Wolnica Square, but suddenly alive, a lost world in motion.

We went from waiting room to waiting room. Krakow's railway station has grand nineteenth-century wooden benches in high-ceilinged rooms that are dignified, spacious, and run down, needing no additions to make them authentically of the past. And, here, at last, were the Jews, all dressed in black, the men with hats and prayer shawls; the women, solemn, in sweeping long skirts. A few in this formal company were playing music on cellos and clarinets in a minor key familiar to anyone who has ever gone to a synagogue or listened to a cantor. The others, both men and women, were revolving to this music in a slow dance.

Suddenly, I was distressed, undone. "Sławka, Sławka! It's only the nineteenth century. Why are they so sad?" Sławka took this question very seriously. We sat down; we watched and listened for a while. Finally she offered the thought that melancholy was the property of this whole world we were visiting. All the groups shared some part of it, including the wailing undertow of the Serbian circle dance that had stopped us in our tracks hours before. Sorrow was a collective experience, and the power in all this music came partly from the sorrow.

I was impressed that Sławka could claim the Jews this way. She had often told me how much the Poles had suffered during World War II. From her country house high on a hill covered with cherry orchards, the peasants who had sold her the place had watched the Nazis kill everyone in the village below and set fire to the houses. So high up, they were safe, the steep climb to destroy a few mountain cottages not worth the trouble.

We sat there on a bench in the train station and mourned for absolutely everybody, and only this feeling of community could protect me from dissolving into a lonely grief. Ultimately, our shared feminism meant something beyond tribes; in a dream, we had walked through them all, each group gesticulating like puppets on a stage set, and ended up here, at a point of convergence and departure.

We went out onto the train platform. The festival designers had decked out an old locomotive with streamers and flowers; and, blowing its whistle, it was just leaving the station. The windows were crammed with musicians and dancers, yelling and waving. In a state of wonder, with our own gesture of farewell and gratitude, we waved back.

12

WHY?

If a grieving return to the homeland wasn't my objective in organizing and teaching in East Central Europe, what then were the forces that kept pulling me back there?

Here I try to list the many streams of thought and feeling, conscious and unconscious, that may have fed my long-lasting flow of commitment. I'd like to be faithful to the complexity of all motive, including the trivial and faintly embarrassing, but instead can offer only this abbreviated catalogue.

When I was a child, my mother would intone at the breakfast table as she read the New York Times: *"Something must be done." These words trumpet the grandiosity of thinking "something can be done," and they offer one source of my constantly rekindling desire to be somehow an actor in the world.*

BABA YAGA

EVERY SUMMER IN THE nineties my father would ask, "How can you go there?" "There" meant all those countries where hating Jews inevitably goes with the territory.

I would try to describe the allure to my brilliant father. Teasingly I would ask, "Could it be that childhood tales of big forests and witches like Baba Yaga lend Eastern Europe a mythic familiarity? Or, perhaps, I am like Henry James's American girls, entranced by an old and treacherous Europe?" I'd joke, "I like ruins a lot, and Eastern Europe is full of them!" In a way I couldn't fully explain, I felt both at home and estranged there, a combination that was intoxicating.

THE NEED TO BE SERIOUS

One year, when Daniel came with me, as we sailed over France to Warsaw, he said: "Sweetheart, remember Western Europe?" True, I used to love it and hadn't been back in years. One time on my way east, I had had a twelve-hour layover in Paris. Paris! A loved place of my young womanhood. I put my carry-on in storage and took the metro in from the airport. I walked in the Jewish quarter, *Le Marais*. Quaint, and with lovely food. I ended up in the Luxembourg Gardens. It was a perfect day, and everything was in bloom. Small boys with white hats were sailing boats on the lake.

Just one little problem: It was the height of the war that broke up Yugoslavia. Slavenka had written about seeing a woman across the street hit by a wandering shell. She was blown into the air and died just a few yards away from Slavenka's feet. Slavenka left Zagreb the next day. Rujana Kren had stayed in the thick of it. She wrote about the destruction of Vukovar, a town she had loved. It had had beautiful domestic architecture. Of course, she said, they will completely restore Dubrovnik, but not these streets and streets of beautiful wooden houses.

Here, in the Luxembourg Gardens, I was surprised to find myself in tears. What's this! A romantic attachment to melancholy? An indulgence in *weltschmerz*? Or, to be kinder, maybe the stretch between a pretty garden in Paris and the shocks of war so nearby was simply too great. My imagination reeled. Where was I located in the world? Another privileged American traveler, I lost any sense of where I was.

Cultural critic and historian Paul Berman makes an interesting observation about my generation of American left activists. We were people who came of age as political beings in the 1960s. Often living in relative comfort, we knew what lay behind us as a partly unconscious inheritance, the lives of our parents and grandparents, who had faced dire circumstances—the Holocaust, the war, the struggle to establish themselves in spite of trauma. Berman speculates that this past haunted us far-less-threatened children. The young leftists Berman is describing were the lucky ones who didn't have to start over in a new country or fight a horrendous war. But we, too, wanted heroic acts and meaningful struggles, which we hoped to find in resistance to the Vietnam War. We, too, wanted to live lives of significance, facing whatever was dark in our own, easier times. We, too, wanted to be serious.

In the East, seriousness didn't need to be asserted in the same way. Difficulty was palpable, and lack was everywhere. In general, this trauma of lack could be dramatic. Traveling by car from Bratislava to Vienna in 1993, I went from bleak rundown farms with scrawny cows and goats to the border with Austria. Immediately on the other side: flourishing green pastures, fat cows, pretty painted farmhouses. Americans trot around the globe to places of horrendous deprivation, then come home again. How does one (for example, how do I) travel between such different zones of fortune and danger? My only method has been to keep making the trip.

THE LOSS OF THE LEFT

Thinking about Henry James when I look back on my travels seems apt since my optimism at the outset was utterly American. Not as innocent as Daisy Miller, I did think aspects of a defeated communism—the ones I admired—might linger, making some kind of marriage possible between democracy and socialism. Marx wrote about the extraordinary dynamism of capitalism, everything solid melting into air; but I wasn't listening closely enough. I still believe certain continuities—call them memories—might carry over, but after the fall of Soviet communism, the welfare state took a tremendous blow—in many parts of the world—a blow from which we are all still staggering.

By 1989 the growing weakness of the Left was stupefying. The feminism in which I had been living was deeply rooted in the American Left, but it was clear to me that the end of the Cold War was a thick, dark line of demarcation, separating the left movements I knew from their own past. Chains of connected cultural meanings were suddenly broken. In a day, people dropped the word *revolution* from their vocabularies. In a week, friends were all saying they had *always* been democratic socialists. The Left, a broad and, indeed, often democratic group in the US since the 1960s, was having a nervous breakdown. How were left aspirations going to be rebuilt in the midst of the awful triumphalism of the defeat of communism? The former Soviet bloc was so uniformly maligned on all sides that the Left was silenced. Anyone—East or West—who cast back a glance at advantages in the old system was accused of impotent nostalgia.

I wanted to know the future of the ideas I had been brought up with, which had shaped my activist life for decades. What was the legacy going to be? When a Romanian student told me she had never heard of the Russian revolutionary Alexandra Kollontai, I was surprised. I asked her about the early, radical phase of the Russian revolution, and she had never heard of those times of cultural experimentation. Did you read Marx in school? Not really. They had "political education," which as she described it was an utterly static account of communist doctrine. Everyone learned it by rote and also disdained it. The difference in what "Left" meant here from my experience was fascinating—and endlessly instructive. For now the work of feminism was homeless. The underpinnings that had held up this structure had taken a hit, and now everything needed to be rethought. Post-communism was a continual—and salutary—shock.

THE LOSS OF FEMINISM

In the sixties and seventies, a mass movement for Women's Liberation changed daily life in the US. By capillary action, by spontaneous combustion, from the Civil Rights Movement, the Anti-war Movement, the Sexual Revolution, the fat and freedom of postwar society—who can say in what combination—women became uncomfortably self-conscious about their lives. Women and men began talking about how they lived together. Whenever the conversation went badly—which was often—the expected forms of social life split apart. Other relationships were suddenly thinkable. White women, in particular, were feeling urgent about changing the gender contract: As their husbands and lovers in every class began to leave, hugging the dark side of the road, these women began fissioning out into lives, lesbian or straight, that were harder, sometimes lonelier, but also freer and, at times, thrilling. At this time, black women's longer history of an often forced and exhausting independence began to look different, like an honorable group survival strategy, yet another source of black pride.

But by the late 1970s, the utopian, yearning, highly visible public phase of this extraordinary explosion of new ideas, the Women's Liberation Movement, was over. Around 1974, the media, irritated that feminism was in earnest and no longer new and charming, packed up their lights and departed. Feminist projects continued to develop and take hold, new people were getting involved all the time; but in the conservative turn of public life, organizers were increasingly on the defensive. Their startling demands had frightened everyone—even, sometimes, themselves. By the time Ronald Reagan was elected in 1980, feminists in the US faced a powerfully organized opposition, which aggressively attacked their every demand as morally corrupt, unnatural, selfish, or murderous—a threat to all that is sweet and natural in life. This backlash strategy worked well; people were reminded of the loneliness or the cultural thinness of modern American life, and a mass of women were persuaded to fear unisex bathrooms, the draft, and a freedom they felt they might not enjoy and could little afford while it was still men who had most of the power and money.

Feminist activists began to go to law school, trying to hold on to whatever movement gains could be codified; they went into the universities and did stunning feminist theoretical work; they went into institutions like hospitals, welfare rights and gay rights centers. But, even as it continued to proliferate, feminism was forced to contract in meaning. As in all ambitious, transformative movements, the glamorous aura of big wishes dissipated in the exhaustion of fighting for every inch. The passion and hunger that create mass movements also undermine them, since no movement can fully satisfy. Even the allure of productive new thinking was unsettling, since in spite of theory's promise to take gender apart, it often, also, explored the inconvenient thought that gender difference permeates the world and ourselves; in seeking to change gender systems we would meet with a mighty resistance—and our own ambivalence.

Feminism had escaped from the genie's bottle and could not be stuffed back in, but by 1979 it was losing its wild, free, sexy reputation and began to change in tone to fearsome outrage; some feminists were beginning to wonder if men's violence against women was unchanging. The powerful outburst of feminist rage against pornography in those years struck me as an overheated reaction to the obvious news that sexism would be around for a very long time. Male violence hadn't significantly changed, but now we had brought it out into the open for all to see. Anti-pornography feminists were expressing their shock at male resistance to Women's Liberation: Men are violent! Their sexual fantasies are disgusting! Sex is violence! These constructions of male sexuality struck me as the outcries of deeply disappointed people, who had hoped for so much more from feminist revolution.

The anti-pornography movement that grew from this new mood precipitated what have come to be called the sex wars in feminism, in which I was an active but irritable participant. To me, the idea that women could be protected from sexual violence through ordinances restricting pornographic speech was ludicrous. This new work was passionate and brought many young women into a feminism that was otherwise increasingly on the defensive. Here was anger; here was fresh ground. But many feminists felt as I did that this new excitement was being won at a high cost. Lawsuits against images were to us like battling shadows. Men were to be sued for dirty pictures. Their fantasies were vile, the seedbed of rape. They were to be shamed and punished. To me, shame was the opposite of liberation. We knew so little about men's sexuality—and our own. Why would we begin a campaign against violence with this false certainty that we understood the causes?

It felt particularly thankless to have to criticize other feminists as committed as myself for taking the feminist movement in what I saw as a moralistic and self-defeating direction. But for better and worse, the sex wars seemed to have been unavoidable. They clarified some of the limitations of feminist ideas about sexuality and pointed to the need for greater freedom of inquiry in what Freud called the most ragged aspect of human personality.

On my side of the fight, we were spending our precious energy on this disagreement because we didn't want a feminism of punishment. We were sure it was a mistake to turn to an increasingly conservative state to protect us from male sexual culture. These were the very politicians who were attacking abortion and all other progressive goals. They liked the anti-pornography movement for the "respect" it showed to women who were "degraded" by sexual images. Respect versus degradation! No rhetoric could have been further from my feminist sensibility. And did women's liberation really want to dissolve its ambivalent ties with the sexual revolution, which had given women so much?

So, we fought. Important as I think the quest was for less repression in those increasingly repressive times, the internal rift had its costs. I, for one, was exhausted. Change came to the US feminist movement, and the fact that feminists had always been at odds about what they thought and what they wanted became obvious, debilitating, and sometimes, rather embarrassing.

The slowdown in feminist work in the US by the end of the 1980s had frightened me. I had to maintain energy and hope because I had committed myself, burned boats, tied my heart to the fortunes of feminism. Continuing feminist work was necessary, but how and where?

INTERNATIONALISM

In the early 1980s a relatively small but interesting subgroup of American feminist organizers turned their attention away from the loss of movement momentum and left home. Each journey had its own reasons, of course: imperialist US wars in El Salvador and Nicaragua; new attention to women at the United Nations, inspired by relentless feminist work; the growing recognition of the gendering of crises all over the world; vigorous women-only antinuclear movements spreading over Europe from England. For example, without thinking of it as much of a break from my central commitments in the US Women's Movement, I went to Nicaragua to talk to feminist lawyers working on the new constitution, and to England to join the women and children in the illegal "peace camp" around a US cruise missile base on Greenham Common.

Different as feminist work was in such varied circumstances, these were encouraging episodes, full of adventure and suffused by the atmosphere of hope for imminent change. If for critical Americans before 1989 the ruling idea was always resistance to US imperialism, now these travels were a quest for contact, informed by postcolonial thought, trying to live out the implications of cross-border politics without guilt and alienation. For US feminist internationalism, this was a new maturity. For these critical Americans, the rest of the world was becoming more and more real. The US was being decentered in their imaginations, and, as a corollary, America was no longer the single source of geopolitical meaning. Hating American capitalism and foreign policy was the easy part; these travels laid some groundwork for the more difficult discussions about globalization that were to follow.

THE DREAM OF HAVING AN EFFECT

The declining political impact of US feminism at home was no doubt one catalyst for these particular travels. Those who went were used to having an effect. They sought a frontier where, once again, what they did would be visible and would matter. Nor should one underestimate the pleasure of departure itself, kicking the door shut and leaving behind that bitter mess that was US movement life by 1989.

No doubt, too, there was sometimes the dream of starting over—and doing it better this time. "New beginnings" is a favorite American redundancy. Beyond our fantasies of a world elsewhere lay a hope that feminism, which had not dated at all as a set of insights and urgent demands, might be refreshed in the old world—an irony initially lost on most of us Americans, for whom, later, Eastern Europe was to become a lesson on irony.

FRIENDS

My trips built upon each other; they piled up. Finally, whatever my original reasons for going, I had come to care deeply for some people in East Central Europe. After a while, no simple coming home was possible. I used to tell my horrified father, "I plan to keep working there as long as I can keep taking those endless trips on airplanes." Over all these years, my long, exhausting trips have dramatized distance and, once on the other side, the excitement and new intimacies of arrival.

The writer Jon Anderson once remarked that most Americans have some other country as part of themselves. Loving people who are far away alters the map of the world one carries around in one's head. During the American bombardment of Belgrade, Sonja and Milan phoned us frantically: "They are bombing us." One bomb exploded near Sonja's car. It's primitive, simple: I knew people under those bombs. I could imagine them. Although I was in no danger whatsoever myself, I was shaken, frightened. There is an ever-thickening rope of connection. Love lays down more and more roads.

LONELINESS

My friends Evie and Vivian are flooded with loneliness when they travel. They feel, *Who am I here? I'm invisible, anonymous.* For them, the air in foreign places is thin. Not being known turns into not knowing, not being oneself.

For me, it has always been exactly the opposite. My main fantasy as a child was to be not me. Not being known in adulthood approximates this earlier desire. Invisibility and anonymity erase shame, embarrassment, regret. And even more, they give a rare freedom. The anxiety that keeps me on track when I'm at home disappears. There's no reason not to walk in the park, read at a café, hide in my hotel room and eat peanut butter and crackers I've imported from my over-surveilled life in New York.

As college was drawing to a close, everyone assumed this excellent English major would go off to Columbia, Harvard, or Yale. The track was laid, though it's worth remembering that since this was before the Women's Movement, there were no jobs for women at these institutions. Did I notice this? Not consciously. I simply slept a lot. I felt not oppressed but blank.

So I escaped to do my graduate degree at the University of London, which became my first foreign place of refuge. I had no idea what I was doing, but in those times few women could possibly know this. Self-doubt and aimlessness ruled, but distance and solitude gave me ease.

Hours and hours were my own. I was never lonely. Now I see how many mind-forged manacles I wore during those hours. I often failed to act like a free person, not overlooked, compared, judged by others. But that this free state was what I was seeking is sure. And over the years, as basic confusions and self-dislike have abated, I have gotten better and better at the open emptiness that is the state I still crave. As a visitor, I am a stranger, encountering the exotic but also getting to be exotic myself so far from home, like the eighteenth-century English Lady Mary Wortley Montague, who loved Venice because she could go out freely, masked and incognita in the streets.

Hardly a month goes by without someone asking me why I have involved myself for twenty-five years in foreign quarrels. Aren't things bad enough right here? Obviously, given my secret escape motif, these questions can be painful to answer. One friend says I like being a big fish in a small pond. (Feminism was certainly a small pond in Eastern Europe in 1989.) There's something to that. Another thinks a Jewish angst paints these ravaged cities with romantic melancholy and an alluring intensity. There's something to that, too.

I added something more after a talk I gave to some international lawyers at Harvard. We were hanging out at dinner afterward, talking about why, to me, the women's movements of Eastern Europe are so moving, so riveting. David Kennedy, theorist of international law, was always worried—I thought justifiably—about the opportunities for slumming, projecting, false *bonhomie,* Lady Bountiful pleasures, et cetera, et cetera. I was with him every step of the way. But ultimately, I insisted to the group that contact and exchange can be real, mutually useful, even in the midst of those other compromising possibilities. I argued, "There is no reason not to try because of critique. Critique is not enough. One must take the critique on board, then try anyway."

But then it occurred to me that I should add something more, should admit that self-expression, risk, the adventure of travel, the presentation of a persona needed to pull off the whole exchange are fundamentally exciting in themselves, a pleasure that produces a necessary energy. All these international lawyers seemed amused at this unexpected turn. I explained that this pleasure in performance carries me to far countries where I am lost, but also found, where I meet not only others, but also myself.

THE FEMINIST PICARESQUE

I want to embrace a somewhat absurd oxymoron: the feminist picaresque. I'll drop common associations that don't serve my purpose, but some of those naughty, rejected meanings of the picaresque—the phallic image of the picaro, the sexual miscreant, traveling from place to place with a lance—may linger on as irony. In my travels with feminism, I have been neither a rogue nor a maker of mischief—at least not by design. But sometimes I have been bumbling, wandering, disconnected, with no expectation—or intention—of being accepted. I'm not a criminal, but I did smuggle US dollars into Eastern Europe under my dress. I'm not a carefree rambler, but my trips have been roundabout, segmented, and my writings about these experiences have been anecdotal, incomplete by design. Traveling with feminism has indeed been a quest for adventure; I have been restless, willing to live for a time without any settled context, a sojourner who's always leaving.

My feminist work has deep thematic through-lines, but no single plot. New discoveries on my travels have changed my direction, which, in any case, was never straightforward. Some have found me a sympathetic outsider; others have seen me as an uninvited visitor, whose story is disjointed and whose contact with those she visits is marginal, distorted, or beside the point. The rogue visitor is sometimes disturbing or disruptive. But, luckily, she is never the first to arrive, never able to offer a whole new story. Now everyone moves around.

WHY NOT

eFKa is trying to support a local entrepreneurial project. A collective is helping women to make small crafts they can work on at home. Sławka loves the project, invites me to a show-and-tell at the new women's center on Krakowska Street.

A small audience is offered a presentation as low key as is imaginable. Shy women hold up smallish canvas bags with minimal embroidery. Afterward I explain my lack of enthusiasm by blabbing on about current, numerous critiques of microlending, though this project is hardly that. It is so humble that it seems not to be seeking any support at all. Sławka likes their independence, which arises from this same lack of ambition.

I am on most days a great fan of initiatives at the grass roots, and action taken without assuming all activists need sponsors and grants. But the listlessness here gets under my skin. How much smallness can a movement sustain before it reaches a vanishing point?

And how much failure? In the early days, a small group, inspired by the skilled organizer Hanna Lipowska-Teutsch, daringly established a fragile battered women's shelter in Krakow. They had no money for food but the Hare Krishnas helped, doing the cooking. This resourceful dodge caught the attention of the greatest power in the land, the Church. The priests disapproved of the idea of women loose in the world, free to escape from the duty of returning to their batterers.

On New Year's Eve of the first year, the police raided the small building: Health violations! Food from the Hare Krishnas! Everybody out. Into the cold. On New Year's Eve. Go home to your families. Soon, a new institution was put in the shelter's place, supported by the Catholic charity Caritas. The new message: Your marriage can be saved. You must forgive. The original groups of grateful women who had heard the earlier, feminist message, scattered; no one I asked knew where.

Contemplating the cumulative trauma of failure, I remember a story Sławka once told me about a friend of hers who was active in the movement for several years. Then she disappeared from view. Worried, Sławka sought her out. Was something wrong? Yes, her friend said. Feminism is too hard. We'll never see significant changes in a patriarchal world in our lifetimes. All our effort to make a perceivable, concrete difference seems to be for naught. Her new work was rescuing stray cats. Krakow is full of these homeless cats, and she saves them, one by one. The homelessness of feminism isn't susceptible to repair at this level. Even though I believe with fervor in the possibilities feminism can open up in individual lives, there's a limit to how much frustration some activists can take. When Sławka told me this story about the cats, I laughed and laughed. For her and me, feminism seems to sustain a lifetime of work, and discouragement be damned. But it is entirely easy to see that others might want to move on to something else.

13

AGAINST THE SENSE
OF AN ENDING: 2015–2016

It would be easy to write about the summer of 2015 in Poland as an ending. Feminism was everywhere then, much argued about in newspapers and magazines. The idea that women were too powerful in this up-and-coming world was being noisily debated—for example, on a magazine cover showing a woman holding a fully dressed, grown man in her arms like a baby.

The first post-communist generation of Polish feminists had all written their books—about sex, about sexism, about film, about literature. Thousands attended the openly feminist yearly Kongres Kobiet. And, amazingly, my friend Małgorzata Fuszara had become the head of Plenipotentiary for Equal Treatment; the fine Network-trained feminist lawyer Sylwia Spurek worked in Poland's Office of the Ombudsman, the deputy in charge of gender complaints; Wanda Nowicka, once head of the group she cofounded, the Federation for Women and Family Planning, had become assistant secretary of the Seym, Poland's Parliament, with some power to steer legislation.

But this isn't to say that all these splendid activists were satisfied with the party in power, the Civic Platform, which had not fulfilled its promises to alleviate a wide range of post-communist suffering. Feminists had built a small and fragile niche here, but general feelings of disillusionment and anger were obviously gathering. Everyone knew this weak and scandal-ridden government was going to be replaced by Law and Justice, a right-wing, populist party with a nationalist anti–European Union agenda. (This shift had just happened in Hungary in 2010.) Law and Justice was promising to rectify the neglect of the many left behind in the twenty-five-year neoliberal march to a market economy. They were going to win; the only question was by how much. And would an array of weak opposition parties from the left and center make any mark? Would this scattered and fractious opposition pull itself together? The feminists were expecting the worst. There was a collective, anxious holding of the breath when I traveled to Krakow in the summer of 2015.

2015

SUMMER 2015: I DECIDED to take a break from teaching to explore the swiftly changing political terrain in Poland. How could we Network travelers know at that moment that the virulent nationalist atmosphere was so predictive of what we were soon to see at home? Very simply: We did not know.

Beata Kowalska, founder of gender studies at the Jagiellonian, had invited me to give several talks to her lively gender studies students. On the strength of this invitation, I planned to go to Krakow and disport myself with friends in the beloved city. Other local talks got piled on: one at my friend Masza Potocka's Museum of Modern Art, Mocak, which had a gender exposition; one at an avant-garde art group; and one—amazing to say!—at a big Transfestival, with speakers coming from all over the world. But the sixth talk was to be in Warsaw: Małgorzata had invited me to speak at the Equal Treatment ministry.

As I made my rounds in Krakow, I expressed my anxiety about my talk at the ministry. Everyone knew we were all about to lose—and big. What might be useful to say to people in the government, standing, as they were, on this precipice?

When I got to Warsaw, Wanda Nowicka took charge of me. She put me up in the hotel where Seym representatives sometimes stay, so that each bouquet of flowers I received had to pass through a metal detector. Here someone suspected I might really be a picaro with a sword hidden among the sunflowers!

VIP treatment is fun, but I did wonder why Wanda was giving me this unexpected and lovely experience. We toured the Seym buildings, and I was photographed under various heraldic representations of eagles with crowns. In the evening she took me to a gorgeous opera ballet at the National Theater. Ah, Polish theater. And because of Wanda's high position in the Seym, we sat front and center in the dress circle; they brought us champagne. I was thrilled.

Afterward, we ate a delicious meal outside on the theater plaza. The air was chilly but heaters warmed us; waiters wrapped lovely blankets around our shoulders. Now, this was not the usual life at the dirty grass roots of activism. I was so enjoying myself!

But duty calls. I described to Wanda my frustration with all my friends. I had asked each one with urgency: What shall I say at the ministry? Their answers were maddening. No one seemed revved up about the bad times that were coming. They suggested I talk about the history of American feminism or talk about what it is like to be an organizer. On the eve of cataclysm, these ideas were boring. Here was a rare chance to speak to the government! I told her I knew it didn't really matter what I said, but what, dear Wanda, should I say? Like all the others, Wanda waxed vague: "Tell them about your early life. How did you become a feminist?"

With this, I gave up. Luckily, always obsessive about giving talks with real content, I had been trying to write the dreaded Warsaw talk for days; I had several drafts. Nervous, and with more flowers to put through the metal detector, I thanked Wanda for such a magic night. I was to appear at the ministry in the morning.

I arrived in a cab and was whisked to Małgorzata's office. It gave me joy to see her ensconced in this elegant suite of rooms, more eagles, more crowns. I was proud to know her. Although she had been underfunded as ministers go, she had managed to make subtle but significant changes in policy. Working quietly—always her style—she had also openly supported strong feminist initiatives.

We exchanged furry stuffed animals, as has been our custom over the years. And now the moment had come for my talk—down a corridor and into a large room, draped with flags.

But something was wrong here. This wasn't a ministry gathering. Instead, here was a rather large collection of the dear activists and students it had been my joy to know and work with for decades. This was a surprise party! Elzbieta and Małgorzata had done this! All those friends I'd nagged were there, and they had all kept the secret. I was moved beyond what I can say.

Elzbieta gave a beautiful speech and then made the mistake of asking me if I wanted to make a few remarks. Aha. All those drafts of talks were clutched in my hands. Yes! I want to say something to these much-loved people: Hard times are coming for us. I snatched up the concluding part of the talk I had meant to give, which I had called "How to Survive Backlash . . ."

How to evoke the mood of that surprising afternoon? So often we have sat like this in smoky rooms, talking about what we are doing. So bring out the hookah pipe; lower the lights here at the ministry. On one side I hear chanting in the distance: "Abortion! Abortion! We want abortion!" But as a catalogue of our desire? Hardly! We must not narrow our real wishes to such endless repetition. Repetition of the obvious wears us down, but we must, as we have long done, rescue ourselves from what is tedious and dreary through community play, irony, and laughter. Let the oracle turn mere repetition into brilliant theater.

We are more free, more able to live in a capacious view of history than our detractors. They want to seal us up into a narrow seam of time, while we see how complex is our long-term global struggle. We don't have to worry that the multiple aspirations of many feminisms will evaporate and disappear.

We survive backlash because being part of all great movements of liberation gives us lives of significance. We are people who believe that human beings can change their situation. To believe that and to act on that belief, even with skepticism, is to have an extremely exciting and kinetic relationship not only to ourselves but to the world. Later, these remarks were set to music by the composer Daniel Goode. I have enjoyed being an oracle. At this point, the psychedelic air lifts.

I had no idea that when I wrote my serious little talk, "How to Survive . . ." I would be here, addressing a big room full of Eastern and Central European activists I've been talking with for more than a quarter of a century. I do hope I thanked everyone for their precious company. I do hope I managed to say, Dear ones, we're in this together—for the long haul. I looked up from my haze of amazement, and there they all were. Sonja was there—and that Adam Michnik who had once laughed at ridiculous feminism. To my astonishment, my dear student and now colleague Iva Šmídová had come all the way from Brno, in the Czech Republic. Delina Fico was there from Albania. Agnieszka Kościańska was there, who has told me that her fine books about sex had their beginning in a class I taught that discussed the movement slogan "Sex for Fun." Sławka Walczewska and Roma Cieśla were right there to hold me up. While I was at the theater the night before, they and many others had sneaked up from Krakow by train.

Elzbieta had made a book, *Our Ann*, with a very funny cover by an artist I admire who was there too, Bogna Burska. Her collage shows me as Queen Elizabeth the First, with an extravagant ruff—behind me two city tableaus, one of Warsaw and one of New York. How perfect a representation of my situation, including my moments of grandiosity.

To my surprise, the social theorist Jacek Kucharczyk was there, carrying an armload of purple peonies. For me? But when he had been at the Krakow school years before, feminism had seemed unnecessary to him. Now, he said, that had been a mistake. Now he saw feminism's critique of the transition as a demand for a more thoroughgoing democracy than what the original dissidents had called for. I took my flowers with that special pleasure when, in the fullness of time, someone one respects changes his mind.

Jeff Goldfarb was there and is in the book, fondly and generously remembering our many years of debate; Irena Grudzińska-Gross was there and is in the book, saying I remind her of the nineteenth-century Russian revolutionaries "trudging cheerfully through the endless country mud to teach peasant children how to read and write." But, Irena, surely not! I've taken this up with her. "Do I really seem like such a do-gooder?" I asked her. Is trying to be part of an international feminist conversation anything like teaching peasants to read? "But, yes." Irena pushed back. "It's because you did it even though you didn't need to do it—that is the analogy I intended." But, my dear, reason not the need. I *did* need to do it—to save my own life; in other words, to make the meaning each activist's life seeks.

Included in this surprising book (surprise!) are many quite intimate essays. The well-known Polish feminist organizer and writer Agnieszka Graff remembers our seminar at the SNS (Graduate School for Social Research):

> I can still see the faces around that table: Kazia, Kasia, Agata, Ewa—women who were central to the Manifa organizing a few years later. I still have all the readings you assigned, as well as my notes from that class. It is hard to describe to someone who was not there what exactly happened in that classroom, the sheer intensity of it.

I too remember that intense seminar in Warsaw in the freezing autumn of 1997. I have the course reader in front of me and can see how, in seven long meetings, we galloped through an amazing amount of material, from "How Feminism Enters" (all sorts of ways, including regressive ones) to "Flexible Bodies." (all kinds, ranging from Susan Bordo's account of "the reproduction of femininity" to the silent bodies of Romanian lesbians, seven of whom had at one time been in jail for this crime. A group of us from the Network had demonstrated in front of the Romanian tourist office in Manhattan.) As rarely as we can see each other, we have kept on talking, conversations as suggestive as anything in our lives.

These are the students I've quoted, who, at the end of the course, signed a postcard showing a naked man with lipstick wearing cool designer glasses: "From your Warsaw students, with expressions of irony and transgression." To live with both irony and transgression is to live in a feminism that can and will survive the hard times that lie ahead.

It was a miraculous day: first the non-talk, then the delicious lunch—with testimonials!—then a drunken party at a bar in the Palace of Culture and Science. I staggered back to the hotel, put my beautiful purple peonies through the metal detector, and slept the sleep of the well satisfied.

To all, thank you.

2016

When the Polish general election came around, October 25, 2015, Daniel and I were in Berlin, visiting Sonja and Milan, who were living there for a time. Sławka and Beata were there, too, each one visiting her own new German love.

Berlin seemed to be a way station for hundreds of wandering Polish radicals. Late on the night of the election, they all fetched up at a bar fondly called the Loser's Club. A big screen was announcing the results as they came in, while a hundred people milled around wringing their hands and drinking a lot of vodka. By the end of the night, Law and Justice had such a large majority that they needed no other party to form a government. One-party rule like this had not existed since 1989. The left-wing Razem party (Together), well represented at the Losers, hadn't even gotten enough votes to enter Parliament. Sławka walked me home through a late-night Berlin. Pacing along as has always been our habit, we asked each other: What now?

I can see that in the months that followed, I made the same mistake that I had after Polish women lost the right to abortion in 1993. Horrified, I cried crisis. I'm afraid I infected my exceptional research assistant, Katie Detwiler, with my panic. Katie, who was a graduate student at The New School in anthropology, had been my helper and often collaborator since 2010 and had become director of the Network's Book and Journal Project. When she entered her program at The New School, they told her she had to decide what her research topic would be. She hadn't yet given this a thought, but they pressed her. "Okay," she had said. "The universe." The beautiful dissertation she is working on has turned out to be about so much more. And it has been my good luck that, in addition to so much else, in these years of giving me invaluable help of all kinds, she has become very wise about NEWW and in general about East Central Europe.

Together we started writing letters. We didn't dream that someone like Donald Trump would win at home. Surely not. So our letters were all about *there,* and the tone was a bit hysterical. Just as they had responded to my alarm in 1993, both Beata and Gosia wrote back: Calm down. Why were we so upset? Didn't we know this was certainly the Poland they knew well, the one they lived in? This nationalism and xenophobia, this misogyny, this authoritarian streak—here was the world they knew, and no one should be surprised. Trauma there well might be, but it was of long standing. Panic was a waste of breath; now was the time to buckle down, carry on.

Actually, this insistence on lowering the emotional temperature had differing origins. For Gosia, the last government had been corrupt and hypocritical. For example, they kept promising to reverse or at least modify the strong anti-abortion law but, toadying to the Church, the so-called liberals had never done a thing. She hated the former government's neoliberal, elitist economics. For her, its fall was fine. "But Gosia, look what has replaced them!" For complex reasons, she simply didn't see the new government as I did, as an attack on democracy itself. "It's good they are giving money to mothers." While still running the Network office, she began working as a politician at the local level.

For Sławka, the new government was dreadful, but so was the old. She hated all governments, and for her, feminism was always the work of outsiders; governments will never have women's interests at heart. Feminist activists should put their energies elsewhere and ignore the always betraying realm of state politics. Another world is possible. One should seek to inhabit it—now, beyond the state.

I'm not sure where Beata Kowalska stands on this question of the state. I know she feared the negative, despairing emotions of many after the elections. "Never give up," was her rallying cry. But I believe that as once a member of the radical Freedom and Peace she was very upset by the profile of the new government, sensitive always to any whiff of totalitarian rule.

Listening to all three of them, I took their point that our tone was counterproductive and that I should have known better. After all, one summer, I had structured my whole Krakow course as a critique of the concept "crisis." *Crisis* is the wrong word for something so expected, so common as, for example, the rape of women, or domestic violence, or the lack of equal pay. One needs a different tone and trajectory for responding to these long-term outrages. Outrage alone can't sustain itself.

After some flailing around and perhaps some more overheated prose from New York, Katie and I suggested a strategy meeting in Poland in June. It was the Network's twenty-fifth birthday, and we could celebrate. What did Gosia and Beata think?

Skipping Warsaw, which always gets everything, we started to plan two meetings, one in the north in Gdansk, home of the NEWW office, and one in Krakow, where Beata taught a stream of magnificent feminist students at the Jagiellonian. We began putting out the word, and, unlike our experience working on the Dubrovnik conference in 1991 fundraising was brisk both East and West, with the East raising by far the most of what we needed for travel and hotels.

But at our call for help with an agenda, it was 1991 all over again. Naming the categories of our distress, devising ways for informing each other about each different current situation, projecting possible future action—either together or wherever we were—all this turned out to be very difficult. I recognized that some of this difficulty was endemic to the Network form. Although we knew each other across long distances of time and space, for many the activist work was local, not international, with specifics not easily communicated. This structural anomaly had always been a problem in making sense of what the Network could and could not do. Just what would these meetings be for? How we could help each other was unclear.

Sitting in New York, Katie and I thought that what we all needed were ideas. But we were wrong. Lack of analysis was not really the problem.

The Gdansk meeting was in the grand new building that is an homage—and also a mausoleum—to the Solidarity movement that famously started right there in the Gdansk shipyards, which I could see from my hotel window, great cranes, now mostly unmoving, against the sky. Gosia, with her longtime connection to Solidarity and to the local politics of Gdansk, got us this perk. We were greeted by a city official and given an etching of the gate to the city.

Some sixty once and future members of the Network showed up. From Prague came Lenka Simerska, once active in the Network, whom I hadn't seen in years; from Brno with nursing baby in arms came Lucie Jarkovská, bringing news of hard times for Brno's gender studies program. The Hungarians Enikö Papp and Borbála Juhász arrived, people whose movement was being crushed by the repressive government there since 2010—the first East Central European country to fall into the new pattern of "illiberal democracies," as Poland was now falling. Saule Vidrinskaite, one of our early legal fellows, came. She now lives in Holland with her husband and daughters and doesn't do anything much about feminism. She traveled all this way for the birthday party out of nostalgia for the Network. For me, this was a fine reason for her to be there. Different afterlives. I had thought Lenka, too, was completely done with feminism, but now, here at the next turn in the road, she's back and doing feminist work. Others from the city and the university came, including a Polish feminist writer I admired but had never met, Izabela Filipiak. And in a flying leap from Warsaw, our one remaining person in the government, Sylwia Spurek, made a brief appearance to mark the Network's birthday.

A number of people resisted filling out our registration forms. This was irritating. How are we going to keep in touch without your coordinates, the name of the groups you're working with, and so on? It felt like the bad old days when you could go to jail or be put on a dangerous list if you signed anything. But no, everyone said. "Please understand: At every meeting funded by the European Union, the bureaucracy requires that we do elaborate paperwork, tell all about ourselves on many forms. We're sick of it."

So the old habit of resistance to surveillance has transmogrified into resistance to bureaucracy (and, of course, surveillance)—with the same old habit of distrust essentially intact. And who can say without reason?

Our idea, to analyze our situation and to strategize together, was dead on arrival. Everyone knew what was happening, and no one knew what to do next. The workshop I attended about outsider forms of resistance was groping and difficult. In the opening plenary, the Gdansk University professor Ewa Graczyk captured the problem at a depth the meeting was otherwise far from reaching. She spoke about the lingering traumas of both World War II and communism, and about the need to address common public feelings such as disappointment, humiliation, and anger. On our one free afternoon, Katie had gone to Wester-platte, the promontory on the North Sea where World War II had begun, and had returned stunned, chastened. On the plane over, she had speed-read Patrice M. Dubrowski's *Poland: The First Thousand Years*, and, working with the Network, she had learned a lot. Now she began to glimpse this trail of humiliation and this pride in martyrdom. Ewa observed that backlash has been the prevailing climate in which Polish feminists have worked since 1989. She was seeing the low morale of feminists at the historical moment we were sharing, which had a long backstory in Poland—and, in various forms, elsewhere in the region.

Although we broke up into thematic workshops—media, education, the new pronatalism (Law and Justice was rewarding each new birth with a generous stipend)—the final plenary of the day revealed a listlessness that Ewa's words at the beginning had well predicted. Withering attacks from all sides were exhausting everyone.

At the closing plenary, Delina Fico, as chair, tried to pull it all together, but she was steadily resisted, even resented for a positive tone of uplift few felt. No pattern could be imposed. No comforting list of "things to do" could assuage feelings of loss.

Finally, and to my great relief, it was at the evening birthday party that the group came alive. Reconnecting with each other without any pretense of solving anything was such a pleasure.

We spoke with gory detail about the difficulties we were fac-ing—from growing insult to defunding. We drank and ate a large chocolate birthday cake. When I collapsed and went to bed, the party was still going, and Katie tells me she and the others made a night of it. Many people behind the projects Book and Journal had funded all these years were there together. Although Katie had followed their work through grant applications and corre-spondence, now she knew them differently. This was her first visit, and being there mattered. It was a grand reunion, and we all indulged in satire and derision. Who could believe without laughing that the churches in several countries were mounting well-organized campaigns called such names as "STOP Gender." (In Poland the new government stipulated that no proposed policy could use the word *gender*. Gender is not to be a part of politics; it is natural.) We were living in the absurd, and having one another's sardonic company was everything.

The next day, people recovered from their hangovers, and we were given a tour of the Solidarity museum. Our docent took us step by step through the heroic story of how Solidarity had precipitated the fall of communism: striking workers murdered in the seventies; martial law in the eighties; then the triumph of the Round Tables in 1989 (life-size replica supplied), where a post-communist political order began to emerge. This was a story of heroes, and rightly so.

But walking from elaborately laid out room to room, you would never know how key women were to the entire struggle. Shana Penn's *Solidarity's Secret*, telling that story, was here still a secret. Where was the workers' sign, to us so shameful, "Women go home. We are saving Poland"? For our group, the silence was deafening. We complained to the docent, who listened politely. No change was coming here.

But to me the most disturbing absence in the museum was the way the narrative stopped cold at the moment of triumph in 1989. No account of Solidarity's afterlife, its turn to the Church and to nationalism. This heroic Solidarity was also a part of the deep rightward, misogynistic turn we were living through now—in the whole region.

A few of the women who had come to Gdansk—sometimes from long distances—planned to come to the second meeting in Krakow, too. We climbed onto the train happy to still be together, but no ongoing plans had emerged. Gdansk had been beautiful in a golden June sunlight, but I had the feeling that this was a sunset for the Network, a caesura at the twenty-five-year mark.

But then: Krakow was completely different. This difference came from the head of one of the great Polish organizers, Beata Kowalska. Thank goodness she had simply ignored the agendas Katie and I had tried to concoct in New York. Instead, she convened a bunch of preparatory meetings with her students and local activists. Together they came up with one of the most ingenious conference designs I've ever encountered.

One of Beata's students, Agnieszka Król, had said dismissively, "What's this Network and why should we organize a big meeting for its twenty-fifth birthday?" (Twenty-five was more years than she had been in the world.) This skepticism was Beata's clue, and Agnieszka was to become one of the chief organizers of the startling Krakow event. No one knew how much feminist work had been done in the decades since 1989. The young didn't know about older women; the Poles had little idea what had been done in other countries.

Here's how Beata and her students designed our day together: First, we met in very small groups. Each participant was given strips of paper—blue, purple, and red. We discussed our memories of our lives as feminists in the intimacy of that first gathering. Then we wrote key moments in these feminist histories on the strips. Blue was for large, public events; purple was for local actions; red was for personal movement experiences. Then all the small groups came together in a big room. Circling the wall here was a five-foot-high mural painted with long wavy lines of blue, purple, and red. Years were indicated on the top going all the way back to 1918, when Polish women got the vote. Each of us attached our strips to the mural by year and by color.

The result was feminist magic. Over a hundred women were walking the walls, discussing where to place themselves. "Do you remember the first Manifa?" (This was the post-1989 celebration of International Women's Day.) Here in 2007 Agata Teutsch's Autonomia foundation was established. (This creative young organizer was another of the event's leaders. The new government had taken away a grant it had given Autonomia for a campaign against gender-based violence when it learned Agata was a lesbian.) Here was the first LGBTQ march—in Krakow, in Serbia, in Budapest. (In some places demonstrators had been stoned.) Here was Sisterhood Street and Queer May; Venus de Milo (disabled women empowered) and Bad Girls for Bad Girls (a large online community); here was Lesbian Lambda and Sex Workers' Alliance; and TIK with its frequent demonstrations in support of immigrants, poor women, and against violence. "1980—August—my first date out for the tram strike (Wroclaw)." By the end of an hour, the wall rippled with colored strips, a collective artwork that was beautiful—and to each of us, fascinating, as we walked around the room, reading.

I stood with Sławka, gazing with amazement. She said, "This isn't about success or failure." Those words—and low spirits—now seemed meaningless. Here was a way to explore history that could help us now. We were rejecting the story of disaster, of rupture, and embracing continuity. Instead of a sharp break between the past and the present, the fluttering wall spoke of how activism keeps moving, imagining a future. And we were so many—awed by our very selves. Sławka said, "It's a feminist river of changes."

David Ost, political scientist and expert on all things Polish, was there and made the important observation that rural women seemed not to be on our collective activist agenda. True. Feminist writer and activist Katha Pollitt was there, and everyone got a free copy of her book about abortion, *PRO: Reclaiming Abortion Rights*, which had recently been published in Polish.

In the plenary that followed lunch, each group described its history and its activities, often to the surprise of others. For the students particularly, this part of the meeting was a revelation. For us older ones, memories came thick. People I hadn't seen in years were describing projects I had long forgotten. Here was Marianna Knothe, who had made one of the useful early catalogues of feminist groups cropping up overnight in the region, then had lived for years abroad. Seeing her again completed an old loop of feeling, because I had liked her so much and then she had disappeared. Like Lenka Simerska, she was back. We were calling to mind hundreds of actions, formations of groups, some active now, others long gone. The cumulative effect was ecstatic.

What Beata's planning group had done was to restore the morale of several hundred overburdened feminist organizers. Of course, the work was continuing. Now *this* was the celebration of twenty-five years—not only of Network organizing but also of the work of eFKa, TIK, and the Federation for Women and Family Planning, all around twenty-five years old, with some of the founders of those groups right there at the party—Sławka, Hanna Lipowska-Teutsch, and Wanda Nowicka. Roma Cieśla's presence brought back the deep origins of lesbian organizing stretching back to the beginning.

At a café in the evening, we had vegan birthday cake. (I confessed: I liked the chocolate one better.) The next day, more food, more talk, followed by a feminist tour of Krakow. I trailed around with Roma, as we found the occasional, welcome chance to sit down. Here in this house, in the nineteenth century, women met clandestinely to educate themselves; here in this unmarked building, women assembled a secret library; here lived Marcelina Kulikowska, who had committed suicide in 1910 at age thirty-eight for not being able to realize her professional aspirations after putting years into the women's rights movement—historical plaque missing. Absence and obscurity were being hauled into presence and recognition.

Twenty-five years after the Dubrovnik meeting, our kind of wall, the feminist river, showed a wild proliferation of movements. From such different locations and impulses, a continuity of resistance now emerged. It was finally an act of imagination that fused the sorrowful meeting in Gdansk with the very different vision in Beata's head, a desire to connect feminisms over time. We asked her our usual question, "What next?" And of course, as always, she had plans for a feminist future. The year 2018 was to be an obstreperous celebration of one hundred years of the independent Polish nation, while Beata and her students were already planning for one hundred years of Polish women's having the vote. They were to have a conference, a counter-moment. Asked her theme for the movement's 2018 events to come, Beata said offhandedly, "Utopia, of course." These two days in Krakow were among the most moving of my activist life.

Afterward, I went straight home to New York. Katie, though, continued on to London to do some research at the Jodrell Bank Centre for Astrophysics for her dissertation on the universe. She left England the day of the Brexit vote, which severed the United Kingdom from the European Union. Arriving home, things fused together in her mind: one thousand years of humiliation, the primal scene of World War II, the victory of the Law and Justice Party, Brexit—and she declared to her welcoming friends, "Donald Trump could win the election." (He was ahead, but hadn't even won the primary yet.) Everyone scoffed, as her English friends had about Brexit. Once home, she suppressed her terrifying insight, putting it out of her mind until Election Day.

Rupture? Crisis? Disaster? Or as our friends in East Central Europe might say, "Why so surprised?" Rather, "Let's work together."

14

OUT OF THIS WOOD
DO NOT DESIRE TO GO

As I write this ending, refugees, asylum seekers, and displaced people, in extremes of desperation, are piling up at the borders of the world, including at the very doors of the countries I have visited the most. In Poland, the Church organized a national demonstration. People were to go to the border and reaffirm this boundary as a bastion of Christianity, casting out the unclean stranger from this, the suffering Christ of nations.

One can feel struck dumb in times like these. Who can enter? Which visitors are welcome?

SOME MONTHS AGO I was having lunch with Nanette Funk, that mainstay of the Network of East-West Women for many years, its philosopher, and the sometime convener of the Network's seminar in New York. From the beginning, Eastern and Western intellectuals have been meeting in this group, teaching each other about feminist thought and action in East Central Europe and the former Soviet Union.

To think back over these twenty-five years, we sank into our chairs over coffee. We reminisced about the rough road of our past, calling to mind many Network projects: putting everyone online; sending books—and publishing them; sometimes quite effective feminist lawyering; gathering and disseminating flows of "information" that people craved. Hundreds had crossed paths with the intent to be part of a feminist conversation. Let's listen in on one:

> A few years ago, a Polish feminist in Parliament said she wouldn't support a law to guarantee long maternity leaves. Such benefits, she said, would only bankrupt the new and aspiring young women entrepreneurs who couldn't afford to hire such expensive employees. At the core of her essentially corporate-friendly argument there was also a real fragment of feminist sensibility: a dislike of the Polish cult of the sacred mother. Another Polish feminist ripped into her: "You neoliberal, you destroyer of the ethic of care, which should be at the core of all feminist demands. Are we to say the race is to the swift and all others get out of the way? Is care for birth and children to be gendered, and not a part of the general public good that we must all support?"

Here, at the lunch table, Nanette and I review such confrontations. We agree as we sit there that feminist sensibility moves around, and we recognize it as it surfaces at many levels and in many guises. From the beginning, we saw that feminism was a polyglot undertaking. Movements for gender justice offered wildly divergent accounts of themselves. But this instability added to the fascination of our work. We admitted to each other that we have loved all of it.

"So, how would you sum up the value of the Network's long life?" I ask her. She casts back her head, as if the hundreds of meetings we have both attended were streaming by behind her eyelids. "In the end, I think the Network was a mixed bag."

I have to laugh. Ha: I accept this epitaph, were it time to write one.

And what do I have to say about this mixed bag? I'll let some-one speak first who also sees the Network as Nanette does, with feet flat on the ground: Vesna Kesić, often on the Network's board, a founder of B.a.B.e. (Hag), and one of the five "witches" of Croatia, accused by the press of betraying the nation for their feminism and anti-nationalism.

It was in Dubrovnik that the roots of the NEWW were planted. Personally, I've had my ups and downs with the Network. Sometimes I was at the center of its activities, but sometimes very much on the sidelines. Sometimes misunderstandings had to be resolved at the level of semantics. I remember one meeting in which the topic was how to achieve change in our societies. Several of us felt uneasy about something, not really knowing what it was. Finally it became clear that the word *change* in Anglo-Saxon political discourse had an automatically positive meaning, while many of us in Eastern Europe, some ten years after the fall of the Berlin Wall, were simply fed up with all the talk about change.

But the full impact of that meeting in Dubrovnik is still felt today: in fact the connections, exchanges, and ongoing communication that have continued on many levels and in many areas are much greater now than the organization itself. One of the meeting spaces was certainly Ann's New York apartment where I met so many interesting people from both East and West. This continuity shaped friendships that I consider deep and lifelong, even if months pass when we do not hear from each other, or many years when we do not meet.

With this I am completely satisfied. As the Hungarian visitor said at the Network's twentieth-anniversary party: "It's the consistency." Since nothing in the Network's praxis can be called "consistent" over time (we changed location from the US to Poland; we changed leadership; we changed structure), consistency must mean something else: talk, meet, repeat, read about each other's actions, talk again. In these years of globalization, we began to see our shared condition. We had thought our fates so different in a number of ways. Instead, the analogies among our various histories are becoming plain. Differences are constant—and poignant—but so are resemblances. We need to seek connection to others with similar desires—desires just now so threatened. We are beleaguered but not alone.

Sometimes, at my best moments, I can feel the net that connects us shake. Knowing so many over so many years has been the making of us.

The dormitory of our school in Krakow backs onto a forest, Las Wolski. This perfect patch, once a nobleman's hunting preserve, is shaped like an upside-down bowl. To get deep into the labyrinth of paths and among the soaring, naked trunks of beech trees, one scrambles up a steep incline, the side of the bowl, and arrives at the plateau at the top, where one finds a small zoo, cords of wood, wild meadows. On early summer evenings, when I take my walks, the golden light, shifting down through the great trees, creates a scene so beautiful that I'm breathless with admiration of the world just as it is.

Early in my travels to Eastern Europe I made the discovery—perhaps not news to anyone except a restless cosmopolitan like myself—that traditional societies offer consolation about death. On November first, the Day of the Dead, Małgorzata Fuszara took me with her to clean her family graves and to place new

flowers. We were part of a throng—every grave with its atten-
dants. She crossed herself, and we joined the thousands of others
walking beneath the tall trees of the cemetery.

"Does it comfort you that your family will visit your grave
like this every year?" I asked wistfully.

The answer was palpable: But of course. She told me how
mystified she was by her Jewish friends who chose to be cre-
mated. "After the crematoria, how can you stand the thought?"

Hmm. I stabbed at an answer. "A grave is too stationary.
Your family is gone. No one visits. There is no November first.
But dust blows around. *Look for me under your boot soles.*" I told
her about the Jewish graveyards, the cliché shock of every Jewish
visitor. And even in Vienna, on November first, the section of
the secular cemetery where the Jews are buried is dark. No de-
scendants, no visitors. My own parents' and grandparents' graves
are mostly abandoned relics wherever they stand, absent of any
family rituals.

Instead, I want my ashes scattered in Las Wolski. Here is
the place where I really understood I will die and that it doesn't
matter, that there is no reason to run away from this so obvious piece of news that Americans are excellent at forgetting. In
Las Wolski, among the families strolling along on weekends, or
during the week on the empty paths irradiated by an unearthly
light, I can feel absolutely satisfied by what life has offered. There
is no reason to grieve for oneself, though I have often grieved
for others here, and shed tears, particularly for my mother and
father. Traditional societies offer more solace.

The irony is not lost on me that feminism is usually seen as
the antithesis of this settled and most lovely sense of one's eternal place in the scheme of things. I'm the baby killer, the home
wrecker, the one always anxious and unsatisfied. There is no
reliable promise that feminism can sweeten the world, either in

the family or beyond. The feminism I've learned in East Central Europe would protect private life vigilantly. But our wish is for that private world to have both male and female inhabitants, who would also be collectively responsible for what goes on outside, a burden that never ends, never offers rest.

In my solitary walks in Las Wolski, I have felt both alone and connected to the people I've visited again and again. The feminism I've brought home from our high spirits and from the woods is, finally, about having a rich life and about seeking happiness—a quest that keeps changing.

I had thought to end this book here, in these woods, in the confidence that comes from believing in continuity. With recent and often cruel changes, both East and West, this more settled faith is tested. Still, I believe in taking the long view that emerges from walking in the forest. With his kind permission I end then with Adam Zagajewski's poem (translated by Clare Cavanagh), his abjuration that in spite of constant shocks to our collective hopes, we still must walk in the forest and love the mutilated world.

Try to Praise the Mutilated World

Try to praise the mutilated world.
Remember June's long days,
and wild strawberries, drops of rosé wine.
The nettles that methodically overgrow
the abandoned homesteads of exiles.
You must praise the mutilated world.
You watched the stylish yachts and ships;
one of them had a long trip ahead of it,
while salty oblivion awaited others.
You've seen the refugees going nowhere,
you've heard the executioners sing joyfully.
You should praise the mutilated world.

Remember the moments when we were together
in a white room and the curtain fluttered.
Return in thought to the concert where music flared.
You gathered acorns in the park in autumn
and leaves eddied over the earth's scars.
Praise the mutilated world
and the gray feather a thrush lost,
and the gentle light that strays and vanishes
and returns.

Spróbuj Opiewać Okaleczony Świat

Spróbuj opiewać okaleczony świat.
Pamiętaj o długich dniach czerwca
i o poziomkach, kroplach wina rosé.
O pokrzywach, które metodycznie zarastały
opuszczone domostwa wygnanych.
Musisz opiewać okaleczony świat.
Patrzyłeś na eleganckie jachty i okręty;
jeden z nich miał przed sobą długą podróż,
na inny czekała tylko słona nicość.
Widziałeś uchodźców, którzy szli donikąd ,
słyszałeś oprawców, którzy radośnie śpiewali.
Powinieneś opiewać okaleczony świat.
Pamiętaj o chwilach, kiedy byliście razem
w białym pokoju i firanka poruszyła się.
Wróć myślą do koncertu, kiedy wybuchła muzyka.
Jesienią zbierałeś żołędzie w parku
a liście wirowały nad bliznami ziemi.
Opiewaj okaleczony świat
i szare piórko, zgubione przez drozda,
i delikatne światło, które błądzi i znika
i powraca.

Photo by Katheryn Detwiler, Wolski Forest, Krakow, September 2018.

ACKNOWLEDGMENTS

FIRST AND FOREMOST, *VISITORS* could not have been written without the daily support and sustained sensibility of Katie Detwiler. There is no way to thank her enough for her brilliant company on this long undertaking. My debts to many others reach to the horizon and, unfortunately, far beyond, where memory fails, but I would like to acknowledge the long years of conversation that have enriched *Visitors*. In particular, I thank those who read and commented on the manuscript: Cindy Carr, Alexa Dvorson, Vivian Gornick, Deborah Kaufman, Judith Levine, Sonja Licht, Elzbieta Matynia, Tracy Marx, Linda Metcalf, Julienne Obadia, Henry Shapiro, Alix Shulman, Alan Snitow, Meredith Tax, and Sławka Walczewska.

Without the summer school in Poland that Elzbieta Matynia created and directed, Democracy and Diversity, supported by The New School, I could not have had the sustained experiences that form the backbone of this book. Thank you, too, to my colleagues at The New School's Public Seminar for their warm response to the manuscript.

From 1990 onward, the members of the Network of East-West Women, from both West and East, have played their parts in the unfolding of the far-flung international project that the Network was to become. Our organizing took many forms, and our successes and failures mingled as this book occasionally—but not consistently—chronicles. I thank all who gave so much heart to the Network and its directors who—at key moments—helped it survive: Shana Penn, Melissa Stone, Erin Barclay, and Małgorzata Tarasiewicz. I thank Julie Mertus and Isabel Marcus, who—at different points in the story—created legal projects that survived and flourished, signs of how real the Network could be at its best. Nanette Funk was active in the Network from the beginning onward. She and Sonia Jaffe Robbins were the original conveners of the Network's seminar about gender politics in the region, supported by the Center for European and Mediterranean Studies at New York University. Sonia was the Network's recording angel, and what records we have on which I have relied are largely thanks to her.

Visitors tells about only a few of the many friends in East Central Europe with whom I have with delight and gratitude carried on thirty years of conversation. Each of these friends, particularly Sonja Licht, Sławka Walczewska, Beata Kozak, Beata Kowalska, Roma Cieśla, Gosia Tarasiewicz, Wanda Nowicka, and Małgorzata Fuszara, made a world in which I lived with great happiness for many years.

Daniel Goode accompanied me, particularly in the first ten years of my wanderings, and he knows how much that meant.

I thank my agent, Charlotte Sheedy, and Lynne Elizabeth and New Village Press for their sensitive work getting this book out into the world.

July 30, 2019

AFTERWORD

DURING THE WRITING OF this book, Ann Snitow was undergoing treatment for cancer. She died at home on August 10, 2019, eleven days after completing the manuscript, and together, the two of us saw *Visitors* through publication and beyond. In accordance with the wishes described in the conclusion of the book, Ann's ashes have been placed in a stand of beech trees in her beloved forest Las Wolski, outside of Krakow.

Judith Levine and Katie Detwiler
August 28, 2019

INDEX